DEFIANT

INSIDE THE MAR-A-LAGO RAID AND THE LEFT'S ONGOING LAWFARE

CHRISTINA BOBB

FOREWORD BY DONALD J. TRUMP

Skyhorse Publishing

Skyhorse Publishing books may be purchased in bulk at special discounts for sales promotion, corporate gifts, fund-raising, or educational purposes. Special editions can also be created to specifications. For details, contact the Special Sales Department, Skyhorse Publishing, 307 West 36th Street, 11th Floor, New York, NY 10018 or info@skyhorsepublishing.com.

Skyhorse® and Skyhorse Publishing® are registered trademarks of Skyhorse Publishing, Inc.®, a Delaware corporation.

Visit our website at www.skyhorsepublishing.com.

Please follow our publisher Tony Lyons on Instagram @tonylyonsisuncertain.

10 9 8 7 6 5 4 3 2 1

Library of Congress Control Number: 2025941010

Cover design by David Ter-Avanesyan

Print ISBN: 978-1-5107-8491-8
Ebook ISBN: 978-1-5107-8492-5

Printed in the United States of America

To my best friend and big sister, Carrie. The reader won't know, but you're on every page of this story. You carried my burdens when they were too heavy for me. God knew I didn't have the grace, patience, or skill to navigate this, so He made you first. I'm blessed to have never known life without you.

Contents

Foreword by Donald J. Trump, President of the United States　　　*vii*

Note to Reader　　　*xi*

Chapter 1:　Into the Oval Office　　　1

Chapter 2:　Meet Me at Mar-a-Lago　　　7

Chapter 3:　The FBI's First Visit to Mar-a-Lago　　　17

Chapter 4:　The Raid　　　29

Chapter 5:　Probable Cause　　　39

Chapter 6:　You Shall Not Pass　　　45

Chapter 7:　Classified or Not?　　　51

Chapter 8:　The Bogus Inventory List　　　63

Chapter 9:　In the FBI's Crosshairs　　　71

Chapter 10:　Time to Get a Lawyer　　　81

Chapter 11:　Not Quite Queen for the Day　　　91

Chapter 12:　What We Know to Be True　　　103

Chapter 13:　The Backlash　　　113

Chapter 14:　Presidents and Their Documents　　　121

Chapter 15:　Testifying Before the Grand Jury　　　129

Chapter 16:　Squeezing Team Trump　　　143

Chapter 17:　Surprises and Betrayals　　　149

Chapter 18:　More Harassment　　　157

Chapter 19:　America's Mayor Under Attack　　　165

Chapter 20: Unleashing the Hounds   173

Chapter 21: January 6th—The Federal Government
Targets Americans   181

Chapter 22: Keeping Donald Trump off the Ballot   189

Chapter 23: Amateur Hour   197

Chapter 24: The Indictment   209

Chapter 25: Nine Felony Counts Against Me   219

Chapter 26: Judicial Corruption Run Amok   229

Chapter 27: The Cancer Spreads   241

Chapter 28: The Attorney General Doubles Down   251

Chapter 29: Sued for $1.6 Billion   259

Conclusion: The Final Warning   267

Endnote   *281*
Acknowledgments   *283*
Notes   *285*
Index   *297*

Foreword

by Donald J. Trump
President of the United States

The United States of America is the greatest country on the face of the earth. Our people, our productivity, our success, our wealth, our generosity is tremendous, and our Constitution is tremendous.

But over the last four years, the American people have witnessed their own government engage in a program of persecution and harassment like nothing we've ever seen before. The previous administration obliterated the trust and goodwill of its citizens by weaponizing the vast powers of our intelligence and law enforcement agencies. There could be no more heinous betrayal of American values than to use the law to terrorize the innocent and reward the wicked. But that's exactly what they did.

Radical-left, pro-crime attorneys at the state and local level—together with corrupt operatives—transformed the Department of Justice into the Department of Injustice. Their egregious crimes and severe misconduct rose to levels that were unbelievable.

I went through it personally. I was attacked probably more than anyone in the history of our country. They launched one hoax and disinformation operation after another, they broke the law on a colossal scale, they persecuted my family, staff, and supporters, they raided my home, Mar-a-Lago, and they did everything in their power to prevent me from becoming President again.

Marxist prosecutors went after police officers rather than criminals. The Biden Administration dropped charges against Antifa and violent thugs, and instead they put elderly Christians and pro-life activists on trial for singing hymns and saying prayers. They went to jail for that! While rapists and murderers roamed free.

They tried to scare the hell out of judges, trying to sway them to play along, telling them, in effect, all you have to do is convict Trump, and we'll leave you alone. Judges who didn't cooperate took tremendous abuse from places like the *New York Times*, the *Washington Post*, MSDNC, CNN, and others. You would think that influencing judges has to be illegal, but all of this went on and nobody complained.

Nobody except a handful of brave patriots. Patriots like Christina Bobb. Christina is an incredible fighter and an incredible person. She had a front row seat to the horrible raid on Mar-a-Lago, the crooked Jack Smith investigations, the shameful attacks on Rudy Giuliani, and so much more. She went toe-to-toe with the terrible people who are abusing their power to punish their political enemies—and she got caught up in the crossfire. Before she knew it, she became the victim of insane, unfounded charges, government harassment, and media attacks. But she never gave up—because she believes, like I do, that we can restore America's greatness and return the power of government back to the American people.

Christina is a great American. Her story is one every American needs to read. We cannot ignore the lies and abuses waged on our citizens, and we cannot rest until we root out the corruption and repair the damage of the last four years.

On the walls of the Department of Justice, you will find the words of the great British philosopher John Locke etched in marble: "Where law ends, tyranny begins." As President, I am dedicated to ensuring a return to the rule of law, so that every citizen feels safe, respected, and secure in their God-given rights. But it's not just up to me. As Christina says, "We all have a role to play in restoring justice."

Note to Reader

When I first started putting this manuscript together, I went back to all the notes I compiled as memoranda to my attorneys. Within days of the events described in this book, I had drafted detailed notes about the sequence of events and discussions to inform my attorneys of the facts. The quotes in this manuscript come from those notes. The quotes are my best recollection of the dialogue memorialized within days of those conversations, but they are not verbatim. I do not have transcripts of any of the discussions.

I did testify under oath multiple times about the events detailed in this book. I do not have those transcripts. I have done my best to properly convey the events in the same manner as I did on the record under oath. There should not be any inconsistencies between my testimonies and this book. However, if there are, my testimonies are true and prevail.

Based on public pleadings, court proceedings, and my own interaction with the FBI, DOJ, and defense counsel, I am under the belief that security cameras recorded at least some of the events prior to and during the June 3, 2022 meeting with the FBI at Mar-a-Lago, as well as the August 8, 2022 raid. I am also under the belief that those recordings corroborate my story. I have not seen the footage myself. My exchanges with DOJ strengthen my belief that whatever videos they had corroborate my story, which may be part of the reason I was never charged in the documents case. Between my emails, text messages, phone records, and the video footage, my role in this saga is securely recorded and unalterable. Judicial Watch has filed a lawsuit on my behalf to obtain access to the DOJ and FBI files pertaining to me. What you are about to read is the true story of the consequential events surrounding the explosion of lawfare that ensnared me, along with many other patriots, and of course, our President.

CHAPTER 1

Into the Oval Office

"The President will see you now," the receptionist said to me as I waited in the West Wing lobby of the White House. She smiled and motioned for me to follow her down the hall. President Trump had just finished a meeting with Secretary of Defense Pete Hegseth and members of the media, broadcasting the meeting publicly for the world to see the latest developments in the Department of Defense.

Reporters and camera crew filed past me. Secretary of Defense Hegseth filed out last with his team. I made eye contact with him and smiled to acknowledge him. He doesn't know me, but he politely smiled back.

As I followed the receptionist to the Oval Office, the last four years flashed through my mind and I wondered how President Trump would receive me. We'd been through hell together, but I had gotten buried in litigation, criminal charges, and accusations, unable to connect with him for almost a year. The lawyers told me I needed to distance myself because I faced my own criminal charges. Talking to President Trump could put him in jeopardy—so I was told.

Every deposition, subpoena, grand jury testimony, indictment, and lawsuit I'd endured had all been part of the Establishment's war on

Donald Trump. The fact that my life had been burned to the ground in the process was just collateral damage. Media outlets had written all kinds of terrible reports about me. Did he believe them? I didn't know what he believed.

"Right through that door," the receptionist said, smiling and pointing to the door leading to the outer Oval Office. As I entered, I saw friends and former colleagues I had worked with not that long ago. They greeted me kindly and said, "He's waiting for you," directing me through the door into the Oval Office.

A Warm Welcome

Before I even got into the Oval Office, I heard President Trump's familiar welcoming voice say "Christina! What do you think of our Vice President?" President Trump stood from his desk to greet me, gesturing toward Vice President J. D. Vance, seated across the desk from him.

"Hello, sir!" I smiled at the President. "Sir, he's a Marine!" I smiled at the Vice President. I had never met J. D. Vance before and didn't know he was going to be in this meeting. I extended my hand to the Vice President and said, "Nice to meet you, sir. Christina Bobb. I'm also a Marine."

"Nice to meet you!" The Vice President was very gracious and said, "I know. He told me."

I walked over to President Trump, and he shook my hand warmly, giving me a sort of handshake hug, and directed me to the chairs opposite his desk, next to the Vice President. "Christina, it's so good to see you! How are you?" he asked. Before I could answer, he turned to Vice President Vance and said, "This girl's been through hell. Just terrible what they did to her." He repeated his question. "How are you? Is your case in Arizona over yet?"

"No sir. It's still going on, but I'm hopeful it will be over soon."

"That's just unbelievable." He expressed a knowing sympathy for the injustice I (and many others) have suffered.

We spent several minutes reconnecting and swapping stories. That was the first time it occurred to me that President Trump had never heard my version of events. The conversation felt like old times. All I'd lost seemed to be restored in a moment. The fact that he was the President again brought me so much relief after years of torment, and our friendly banter helped put to rest my doubt that my life could ever recover from the damage done by the lawfare. The President's kindness healed something in me—the fear of being forgotten.

Speaking with Vice President Vance was a bonus. I was already buried in criminal charges and lawsuits by the time J. D. Vance was named as the VP pick, so I had never met him and had no idea what he was like. He was exceptionally kind and easy to get along with.

My Request

At a pause in the conversation, President Trump asked, "What can I do for you?"

"Well, sir, I've written a book." I paused for a second to gauge his reaction.

"Good. About what?" he asked.

"About the lawfare and abuse of the justice system over the last several years." He nodded at me indicating he understood but that I should keep explaining. "I include my experience on your team, and specifically my role in the Jack Smith investigations, and at the raid on Mar-a-Lago. I'd like to publish my story surrounding those events."

He nodded and turned to Vice President Vance. "Christina was at the raid of Mar-a-Lago. Can you believe that?! Christina and Lindsey Halligan, two nice girls, and they were made to stand outside in the Florida heat in the summer for hours." He recounted the story to the Vice President and then turned back to me. "What's the title of the book?"

"*Defiant*," I said.

He thought about it for a beat and said, "Who's defiant? Me? You?" He shrugged as if to ask, *What point are you making with that title?*

"Both," I said, a bit nervously. I took a minute to look around me. How many decisions affecting countless lives have been made in this office? Every single American president has made decisions affecting the course of events for the entire planet. For more than a hundred years, those decisions have been coming out of this room. Many of the decisions that influenced the events in this book likely came from this office—from President Trump's predecessor.

Now, here I am, sitting in the Oval Office of the White House with the President and Vice President of the United States, asking for their permission and support to tell an ugly story. It's the story of how the American government overstepped its authority to the point of oppression. How the institutions that are supposed to protect us from corruption and persecution have been weaponized against ordinary citizens. As a result, the American people need to be *Defiant*. This is the story of what it looks like when political elitists use their positions of authority to steal the power that rightfully belongs to the American people. *Defiant* is my story, but if we don't correct course, it will be yours.

A president who wanted unobstructed power and unopposed authority would *never* let me tell this story, let alone support it.

But President Trump has been exposing the Establishment's abuse of power for years now. His words are different from mine, but the message is the same. As he puts it, "They're not after me, they're after you. I'm just in the way." He knows better than anyone what happens when the political Establishment uses the venerable institutions and the formidable power of the United States government to go after its political enemies.

The Establishment media lies and says that Donald Trump wants power. The truth is that he spends most of his efforts on *reducing* the size and reach of the federal government, on lightening the burden of regulation and taxation. Most importantly, Donald Trump has endured hell for the sole purpose of dismantling the Establishment's stranglehold on power and returning that power to the American people.

I held my breath and waited for President Trump's reaction. He nodded approvingly and said, "Good." I breathed a sigh of relief. "What's in it?" he asked, pointing to the manuscript that I held in my hands.

"Here you go, sir." I had three copies with me and gave him one, Vice President Vance one, and I held one. "Can I walk you through it?"

"I just want to know what you say. How's the story go?" he said, cutting to the chase.

"Okay. The story goes like this . . ."

CHAPTER 2

Meet Me at Mar-a-Lago

When I picked up the phone on June 2, 2022, I had no idea what I was about to walk into.

"Hey, Christina. You got a sec?" asked Boris Epshteyn on the other end of the line. Boris was a close advisor to President Trump, and someone I had worked with since November 2020 when I volunteered to investigate the 2020 election with Rudy Giuliani. Now, eighteen months later, we were colleagues working for President Trump.

"Sure! What's up?" I said as I sat at my desk at my home office in Florida. It was almost 5:00 p.m., and I secretly hoped this call wouldn't take too long.

"So, there's a case in Washington, DC. Local counsel there is handling it," he started.

"Okay," I confirmed I was listening.

"They need someone down in Mar-a-Lago tomorrow for a meeting with the FBI," Boris said. That made sense. I figured Boris was up in New Jersey, where he lived at the time. And I knew President Trump had already left or was getting ready to leave Florida for the summer and move to Bedminster, New Jersey. Most of President Trump's advisors lived outside of Florida at that time. I was in the area, and available, so that's probably why Boris called me.

"Okay. Sure. I'll help however I can," I said, curious where this was going.

"The Washington, DC, lawyer is handling everything. He's down in Florida now. He's been working on a document production the last few days. He spent the day at Mar-a-Lago today dealing with it. So, you won't have to do anything. He just needs someone on site who can be present with the attorney. Are you available tomorrow?" Boris asked.

"Uh, sure," I said. "I can make myself available. Who is this meeting with? The FBI?"

"Yeah. The attorney would like to meet with DOJ and the FBI tomorrow at Mar-a-Lago to turn over some documents. But don't worry about it. He told me everything has been taken care of already. You literally don't have to do anything other than be present. The DC lawyer is handling everything and will take care of it all tomorrow." Boris was clear I would have no formal role other than to assist the attorney. The attorney just needed me to help with this one little thing.

It struck me as odd that I wouldn't need to do anything. There is no legal necessity to have a "potted plant" at a meeting with the FBI. Besides, why was the FBI coming to Mar-a-Lago? What was this meeting for? Why were we giving them documents? What documents were we giving them? If the FBI was involved, it meant this was a criminal matter, so my guard was up. But I didn't have enough information to form an opinion about anything yet.

Apparently reading my thoughts, Boris said, "Don't worry, the DC counsel will explain everything to you. Can I connect you with him and have you work directly with him?" Boris asked.

"That would be great. Please do," I responded.

"Thanks. His name is Evan. I'll connect you via text now."

At 4:58 p.m. on June 2, 2022, Boris texted me and Evan Corcoran, the local counsel in Washington handling the case, to connect us. The text said: "Christina Bobb and Evan Corcoran—connecting you as discussed with both of you." I responded at 5:00 and said, "Thanks Boris! Evan nice to meet you. I'm happy to chat whenever you are free."

Evan didn't respond to the text right away. Although I wasn't worried, I was eager to talk to him and find out what this meeting with the FBI was all about. We connected via a phone call around 7:00 that evening.

"Hi Evan, very nice to meet you," I said as I answered the phone.

"Nice to meet you as well!" Evan sounded happy and kind, which made me feel comfortable with him. "Thanks for your willingness to help me out tomorrow."

"Sure! I'm always happy to help. Can you tell me what's going on?" I asked.

"Of course," said Evan. "The Department of Justice has issued a grand jury subpoena to President Trump wanting all classified documents in his possession."

A grand jury subpoena? Classified documents? He had my full attention. "How long ago did this happen? Is this new?" I was trying to understand the timeline.

"It was a few weeks ago," Evan seemed to understand where I was going and explained, "We've been negotiating this process. This is not something that just happened today."

"Oh, okay, thanks. Go ahead." I felt better hearing that they had been handling this issue and I was the only one new to the party.

"Yeah, so we've been negotiating this, and we finally came to an agreement where we're going to turn over what we've got," said Evan. *We*, I assumed, meant Evan and the Department of Justice.

"Okay. Has there already been a thorough search conducted?" I asked.

"Yes. We've done a very thorough search, and the scope of the location is very limited. There really isn't much there. It's really limited to this one storage area at Mar-a-Lago. The FBI is looking for any classified documents that President Trump may have taken from the White House. I've narrowed the location of relevant documents to this one storage area at Mar-a-Lago. There's no reason to believe that there could potentially be any classified documents anywhere on-site other than the storage room," Evan explained. "The Department of Justice understands that the search is limited to this storage room at Mar-a-Lago, and they are in agreement with the limited scope."

"Okay," I said, still on alert due to the fact that the FBI was involved.

"So, I've done a very thorough search, personally examining every single piece of paper in the room. There really weren't many documents with classified markings, but I collected the few that were there. I collected all of the responsive documents from the storage room and have prepared them to be turned over to the FBI."

"How'd you retrieve them?" I asked, needing clarification. "Who conducted the search?"

"I conducted the search. The storage room is a limited area, so I personally handled this," said Evan.

That struck me as odd, but at that time I had never responded to a grand jury subpoena before. I had no idea how something like this would work.

"Do you have a security clearance?" I asked. I have had a security clearance, a TS/SCI (Top Secret/Sensitive Compartmented Information), and am very familiar with the procedures for handling classified documents. Rule #1: Anyone handling classified documents must have the required clearance.

Evan was quiet for a brief second before he answered, "No. No, I don't have a security clearance."

I had trouble reconciling the situation. How could he be responsible for handling classified documents when he didn't have a security clearance? DOJ's okay with this? He said he'd been negotiating with DOJ, so were they aware he'd done the search?

Before I could formulate my thoughts into my next question, Evan continued, "But I followed all the necessary procedures for handling classified documents. I compartmentalized any documents with markings on them and then hermetically sealed them to prevent anyone from seeing them. The search was conducted very thoroughly and there were not that many responsive documents. There's not much to this."

Hmmm. "Okay," I said. "So, what do you need from me?"

"We need a custodian of records," he said, "Someone from President Trump's staff who can attest to the documents searched and produced."

Oh, here it was. The kicker. This is why they needed me. As a custodian of records, I'd need to sign for the documents. "As the custodian of records, what do you need from me?" I asked, expecting him to tell me he needed my signature.

"We just need you to sign the certification saying that a thorough search has been conducted and that all responsive documents have been produced," Evan continued.

"Okay. But I don't have personal knowledge of that. I wasn't part of the search or review. So, I can't attest to that," I said.

"Right," said Evan. He didn't seem surprised by my pushback and explained, "This is all really just a formality. No one is ever going to question your role in this. But just to make sure you're comfortable, let's meet at Mar-a-Lago a little early and then I can show you everything. Once you see it all and what happened, you'll have a better understanding. But, just to be clear, your signature really is just a formality and isn't going to matter. These things are signed all the time, and you don't have to be the one who conducted the search," said Evan.

"Why don't *you* sign the certification?" I asked. "*You* conducted the search and have the personal knowledge of what was done."

"I'm the lawyer," Evan said, sounding a bit surprised by my question. "I can't make myself a witness in this case, so I can't sign the certification."

I didn't want to be rude, but I thought to myself, *You made yourself a witness when you conducted the search. If you didn't want to be a witness, you shouldn't have handled the search alone.*

Instead, I said, "Well, I won't sign anything that says I have knowledge that I don't have."

Evan jumped in to reassure me. "We'll put language in there that says this is based on information provided to you. Custodians often are not the ones doing the search, but report based on what people have advised them. We can do that in this situation," said Evan. He was clearly trying to be helpful and accommodate my concerns. Never once did he pressure me to sign anything I didn't want to sign. He even said, "You don't need to sign anything you're uncomfortable with. You'll have a chance to review it and can make any changes you want to make it work for you. In fact, you can draft it if you want. Do you want to draft the certification?"

"I can't draft it! I have no idea what took place, the location searched, or anything. I can't draft this," I said a bit defensively.

"It's okay," Evan said jovially. "I'll take care of everything. Don't worry."

"Okay," I said. "I appreciate your understanding. It's very important to me that there is specific language that says I did not personally do the search or review. I won't sign it otherwise."

"No problem at all." Evan seemed perfectly content to include the qualifying language. "Just send me your email address, and I'll send you the document to review. Let's plan on meeting tomorrow morning at 9:45 before the FBI arrives to go over everything."

"Sounds good. Thanks. See you tomorrow," I said.

Immediately following the call, at 7:23 p.m., I texted Evan my email address so that he could send me the certification to review. I was a little nervous about the language and wanted to make sure that it was accurate. But by 8:55 p.m., I still had not received the document. So I texted him again and asked him to send me the certification for review, saying, "When you have a sec, please send me the doc." No further communication came from Evan that night.

At 7:49 the next morning—the day of the meeting—I received a text from Evan saying, "Christina—sent via email. Let me know if you would like to discuss any aspect or make changes. Thank you. Evan."

I responded at 7:56 a.m. saying, "It hasn't come in yet. You sent it to [my email address]?" Evan responded a minute later simply providing the Word document of the certification. At this point, I was getting nervous. It was only about an hour before I would have to leave to meet Evan. There needed to be enough time to make any corrections or changes.

Carefully reading through the entire one-page document, I couldn't find any qualifying language. I printed it out and read it again. The document clearly implied that I had personal knowledge of the search and review, which I did not. I could not sign it.

The Department of Justice had been after President Trump, and anyone close to him, for six or seven years at this point. Any document signed to swear to any fact would be turned into a weapon. The document needed to be factually accurate or someone would get charged with a crime. I needed the document to be true from my perspective, not just Evan's. I needed the document to be true based on my experience at the time I signed it. I had no way of knowing whether anyone would challenge the legitimacy of the search, but I wanted to make sure that I could stand by my decision.

Should I refuse to sign the document? If I did, they likely couldn't get anyone else to do it on this short notice, which would scuttle the meeting and make the FBI suspicious. I was trying to facilitate turning over documents, not impede it. On the other hand, if they did find someone else to sign the document, it would likely be a junior staffer who wouldn't know how to handle the situation and could potentially end up in jail. I couldn't do that to any of my younger colleagues. This was a very precarious situation.

I texted Evan at 7:58 and said, "Can we add a phrase that says 'I have been informed . . .'? I don't want it to look like I'm attesting that I was part of the search or review." Based on our previous conversation, I was confident Evan understood my concerns, so I did not elaborate. At 7:59, Evan responded with, "Yes, I will add." I responded immediately and said, "Thanks!"

At 8:08 a.m. Evan texted me again and said, "Just sent via email a revised version. Let me know if you would like any other changes."

I reviewed the revised version and saw that he had added the phrase "Based on information provided to me." I would have preferred the disclaimer be a bit more robust, but I guess it was fine. I responded to Evan at 8:12: "This is perfect. Thanks!"

I expected to get a full brief from Evan upon arriving at Mar-a-Lago, so I wasn't too concerned at this point that I didn't really have much information. I assumed the lead criminal defense attorney for the President had the information, had conducted a proper search, and that I would get the information at the meeting.

At 8:13, Evan texted me and said, "Great. Will you have the ability to print out and sign and bring this am? (And scan a signed copy?)" I knew I wouldn't be able to print or scan anything at Mar-a-Lago. The club was already closed for the season and the office was not open. I would not have access to a printer or computer, and neither would Evan. My only option was to print, sign, and scan it back to him before getting down there.

At 8:16 a.m., I texted Evan and said, "Sure!" I printed the certification and signed it, believing a thorough search had been conducted, all responsive documents were gathered and sealed, and that I would be briefed when I arrived at Mar-a-Lago.

Evan responded immediately and said, "Let's plan to meet at 11:30 a.m. at Mar-a-Lago. The FBI/DOJ guys just let me know their flight has been delayed, so they will get to MAL at around 11:45." I responded to Evan at 8:17 a.m. and said, "Ok. Sounds good." I wondered if fifteen minutes would be enough time to go over everything before the FBI arrived, but figured Evan knew best.

At 8:22 a.m., I emailed Evan the signed copy of the updated version of the certification. My email said to Evan, "Here's a scanned copy, I'll bring the original."

At 8:29 a.m., I was cc'd on an email from Evan to President Trump's scheduler saying:

"[Scheduler,]

Christina Bobb and I will be at Mar-a-Lago at 11:30 a.m. for a short period to complete work I started yesterday.

If the President has 3 minutes to do a meet and greet at 11:45 a.m., that would be great.

I will call him this morning to explain the purpose.

Best regards,

Evan"

I didn't think much of the email at the time, but it became relevant later—when lots of lawyers were asking me about what President Trump knew and when he knew it. Apparently, he had less notice than I did.

Evan later explained that President Trump, against Evan's recommendation, felt it was important that he personally let the FBI know that they are welcome to see whatever they wanted. Evan didn't want President Trump talking to the FBI about the documents at all, because anything he said could be used against him. President Trump felt he had nothing to hide. He wanted to make sure the FBI knew, straight from his own mouth, that he was fully cooperating and that they could have access to whatever they needed.

CHAPTER 3

The FBI's First Visit to Mar-a-Lago

I arrived at Mar-a-Lago at 11:30 a.m. and Evan was already in the living room, a large room right off the main entrance where guests arrive. The club was already closed for the season, so it was empty and looked as though it was packed up. Evan was sitting on one of the chairs in the living room and waved to identify himself as I walked in. He was friendly as he introduced himself.

"Hey, Christina. Thanks for coming!" Evan said as he stood to shake my hand.

"Hi. It's very nice to meet you," I responded. I sat down on the couch next to his chair and asked, "So, how long have you known Boris?" I figured they'd known each other a long time. I thought I was the new kid in town and figured Evan was a long-established member of the legal team.

"Oh, just a couple weeks. I actually just got connected with him," Evan said.

"What do you mean 'you just got connected with him'? How did this all come together?" I was confused. Hadn't this been going on for a while?

"I actually just met Boris. It was just a couple weeks ago," Evan said.

"Oh! Okay." I said a bit surprised. I couldn't quite wrap my mind around the situation. Why were we meeting with the FBI so soon, if the case was that new? Maybe Evan was just new to the case? I was sure it would all make sense eventually. "You're out of DC, right? Do you primarily practice criminal defense in DC?" I asked, wanting to get to know him better.

Evan was extremely kind and gracious. He told me about his career, working as a prosecutor at the Department of Justice, and eventually now as a criminal defense attorney. He had nearly thirty years of experience as an attorney working criminal law, on one side or the other, which reassured me that he knew what he was doing. At that time, I'd been an attorney for fourteen years, and the last two I had worked as a journalist. I was confident Evan was the expert and I felt comfortable that he was in charge.

"I spoke with the President this morning, and mentioned you," said Evan. "He said very nice things about you and was very laudatory about your Marine Corps service. He says you're a fighter." Evan and I quickly built a good rapport. I respected him and still do. Despite all that's happened, I still think Evan meant well.

"That's so nice to hear. Thank you," I said. "So, want to get started? Where are the documents and the search materials?" We didn't have much time before the FBI would arrive, I was thinking, so we should probably get to work.

"Well, everything has already been done and taken care of," Evan said matter-of-factly. "I've already compiled the responsive documents and hermetically sealed them here." Evan pulled out a makeshift container made of cardboard and packing tape. It was taped up every which way and would need some serious box cutters to get it open. "If you want to see the documents, I'll open it for you," Evan offered.

"No. Thank you." I didn't have enough time to meaningfully examine any of the documents and my security clearance was not currently active, so I declined the offer. I also wasn't sure if he'd even be able to get that thing open quickly. Either way, I didn't want to see the documents. "So, what am I supposed to review?" At that point, I wasn't even sure what I was asking for. My brain was working to make sense of the situation. I expected everything to be laid out waiting for me, so I had never formulated in my own mind what I needed to see.

"Like I said, the search and everything has already been finalized and cleaned up, but I can show you the storage room if you like." Evan was confident and eager to answer any questions I had.

"Yes. That'd be great. Let's do that," I said, hoping the storage room would help me get my bearings on what was happening. There wasn't much information available, and the FBI would arrive shortly, so we didn't have much time.

Evan led me outside and downstairs to the lower level. As we walked, he explained that "the Department of Justice has subpoenaed President Trump for classified documents. It's a nonstarter of a case. There's not really much to it, but of course we're cooperating. I'd like to be a bit more measured, but President Trump wants to open everything up to them and let them see whatever they want." Evan sounded surprised that the President would be so accommodating.

"Wow," I responded. "That's a bit bold to give the FBI free access to whatever they want," I acknowledged, sympathizing with Evan's position.

"I know! Right?" Evan responded. "But that's what the client wants. He even wants to meet with them!" Evan was in a slight state of disbelief at how open President Trump wanted to be. "I told him I didn't think that was a good idea, since they were investigating him criminally, but he really wants to. So, I need to make sure that when he meets with them today, the FBI understands they can't ask him any questions, and this isn't a formal DOJ interview."

It was at this point that Evan explained his conundrum. President Trump wanted to fully cooperate and give DOJ and the FBI unfettered access to whatever they wanted, *including him*. To be clear, President Trump was willing to answer their questions. Evan emphatically (and prudently) said no. President Trump insisted that he personally meet with the FBI, and not simply relay the message through his lawyers. Evan rightly didn't want the President to meet with the FBI or make any statements in front of them.

Evan was in a bit of a tight spot, because anything President Trump said to DOJ or the FBI can and will be used against him in any criminal proceeding. So I understood Evan's concern about not allowing that opportunity. The President wanted to be transparent, but Evan wanted to protect him from a rogue FBI out to get him. They'd twist his own words and use them against him. Evan was doing his best to accommodate his client but also prevent him from stepping into a trap. It was a delicate situation, and I was along for the ride.

"The FBI wants to go through the boxes, but I don't think we should allow that right now," Evan said, getting me up to speed on his negotiations with DOJ. "The President wants to give them full transparency, but at this stage, I just don't want to have FBI agents hanging out at Mar-a-Lago all day rummaging through whatever they want. I'd like to give them what they asked for, let them see the room, and then we can figure out any further questions later," Evan said, running his thought process past me.

"Okay. Sounds good to me," I said, not really having much to add.

We wound our way underneath the main level to the storage room, which was tucked away, in sort of a basement area. The door, buried behind unused folded tables, chairs, flags, and ceremonial items, was locked. Evan pulled out the key and opened it, then stepped inside to make room for me to enter.

I stepped into the storage room, which was small and only noticeable to those in the lower level if you knew it was there. It was about ten feet by fifteen feet and held two to three dozen boxes. There was a clothing rack with full garment bags hanging, shoeboxes, and other household items inside. Most of the boxes were closed, so I couldn't see what was inside. I crouched down to one of the boxes at my feet, which had a flap that was flipped open, and I looked inside.

"You can go through the boxes if you want to," Evan offered, eager to make me as comfortable as possible with the process. "You're welcome to check my work."

"I don't have time to go through the boxes," I said as I continued to look into the one box with the open lid. I saw newspaper articles, what looked like a magazine, and notes on articles that had been printed out. That was about all I could see.

"If you want more time, I can tell the FBI they'll need to wait," Evan offered again.

I didn't think that I could actually do an adequate search in any reasonable amount of time, especially without a security clearance. Without a clearance, I could end up getting myself indicted. I also preferred not to have any actual knowledge of what was in the boxes, given the statement I'd signed. It needed to remain "based on information provided to me," and not anything I had personal knowledge of. The last thing I wanted was to somehow have responsibility for a search I didn't do. Since I didn't have any involvement in the process, my perspective was to simply be honest with DOJ and the FBI about what I knew, and more importantly, what I didn't know. Again, I declined to go through the boxes.

Evan and I spent no more than five minutes down in the storage room and then returned to the living room. Within minutes, DOJ and the FBI arrived.

DOJ and the FBI Arrive at Mar-a-Lago

Evan and I picked a table in the front dining room for the meeting. It was a rainy Florida day, and we sat and watched as the DOJ representative and FBI agents walked through the pouring rain to get to the front door. I remember the agents struggling with umbrellas that were failing under the Florida downpour. As a Marine, that stood out to me. Marine Corps brainwashing made me critical of umbrellas. Ask a Marine, they'll tell you.

The Secret Service agents greeted the DOJ attorney and FBI agents and led them from the reception area, through the living room, and back up to the front of the dining room to meet with me and Evan.

Jay Bratt, the lead attorney on the case and DOJ representative, had three female FBI agents with him. Everyone was polite. Evan seemed to know everyone at the table already and introduced me to the group. "This is Christina Bobb. She's joining me today as the custodian of records."

Mr. Bratt said, "Nice to meet you." Looking intently as if trying to be kind, but direct, he asked, "Who are you?"

"I work for President Trump," I said. He asked me a few more identifying questions, which I answered.

Evan handed over the container of documents that he had thoroughly taped up and sealed with cardboard and packing tape. "Here's everything that's responsive to the subpoena. We've done a very thorough search. There wasn't much, but we've compiled it here," he said.

He then slid the certification that I had signed across the table. I was a bit annoyed he handed it over, because the FBI hadn't asked for it. Why give them something they can use as leverage if they haven't asked for it? But, whatever. They likely would have asked for it anyway.

Bratt looked at the certification, then looked at me and said, "So you did the search?"

"No. I did not do the search," I quickly responded. "I was briefed on the search, and was informed of all of this information. I was not personally involved."

I made sure to thoroughly explain to him—and the agents present—that I was relying on representations made to me. I had been briefed and the information provided to me was all the information I had to make the representation.

"Who did do the search, then?" Bratt asked

I looked at Evan to respond.

Evan shuffled in his seat briefly before he said, "We're not prepared to discuss the details at this point, but it was a member of the legal team." It seemed pretty clear to me that Bratt believed it was Evan.

After an awkward silence, Bratt asked Evan, "Do you have a security clearance?"

Evan responded, "No."

Bratt then turned to me and asked, "Do you have a security clearance?"

"Yes," I said. "I have a TS/SCI, but it is not currently active as I am not currently employed by the federal government." I wanted to make sure there was no confusion as to whether I had a clearance or not. Mr. Bratt shrugged, nodded, and indicated he understood.

President Trump Makes an Appearance

Secret Service came over and indicated to Evan that President Trump was coming. A few seconds later, President Trump walked into the room and all six of us at the table stood. The President greeted everyone warmly.

"Hello, everybody." President Trump shook hands with the three agents and Jay Bratt as he welcomed them to his home. "I hope you all are enjoying your visit and getting everything you need." He recognized Evan and shook his hand and thanked him for setting up the meeting.

The President directed his attention at our DOJ and FBI guests. "I'm glad you're here, and it's important to me that you know you have access to whatever you need," he said. He then turned to Evan and said, "Please make sure you get them whatever they need." Evan nodded, indicating he understood his orders.

Turning back to DOJ and the FBI, President Trump said, "We have nothing to hide and want to make sure you know we'll show you anything. Whatever you need, please ask Evan."

The DOJ and FBI officials were polite and nodded in agreement with President Trump. President Trump talked to the group for no more than two minutes but made it clear that he wanted to personally welcome them to his home and give them access to whatever they needed.

The DOJ and FBI agents thanked him for his willing cooperation. At no time, with or without President Trump, did DOJ or the FBI object or raise concerns that they had been denied access.

DOJ and the FBI Visit the Storage Room

After President Trump departed the room, Evan and Jay chatted briefly as the six of us sat around the table. I don't remember anything significant about that conversation. Mr. Bratt then said, "I think I know the answer to this, but can we see the storage room?" It seemed like he expected Evan to say no.

Evan responded, "If it were up to me, I'd say no, but President Trump gave clear instructions that you can see whatever you want. So, if you want to see the storage room, I'll take you to the storage room."

Jay Bratt, the three agents, and I all followed Evan downstairs to the storage room. The agents were shown the door, the lock, and were allowed inside to take a closer look. Evan and I stepped out of the way and allowed them to look through the room as closely as they wanted.

One agent said, "That door does not look secure."

Frustrated that the FBI was nitpicking, I responded. "I'd like to remind you that Mar-a-Lago itself is extremely secure. There's private security. You wouldn't have been able to access the facility today without a pre-arranged meeting. Then, you've also got Secret Service. This area is closed to guests, so very few staff members even have access down here. And then, this storage room is locked and there's only one key. This storage area is not easily accessible and is very secure."

The agent nodded in acknowledgment.

At one point, one of the agents started to open the boxes and look through the contents. Evan said something to the effect of, "Just wait on that please," indicating he did not want them going through the boxes. "I'm not prepared to have you going through the boxes today. Let's just leave it at examining the room for now."

The agents did not push back. Never once did they object. Never once did they say, "But President Trump said we could see whatever we wanted." Never once did they ask for clarification about whether they would have an opportunity to see what was in the boxes. When Evan asked them to stop, they stopped. That was the end of it.

Evan gave the government officials as much time as they wanted to look around. When it appeared they had concluded, he asked, "Is there anything else you need to see here?"

Mr. Bratt responded, "No. This was very helpful. Thank you for letting us see the room."

Before we could head for the stairs, the Secret Service informed Evan that the President was moving, and we needed to stay put. This is standard operating procedure for the Secret Service. Any time they transport the President on or off the property, everyone on site must stay in their same location until the President has, in this case, departed. It happens all the time. I've never worked for another US president, but I imagine this is the same protocol for every president.

Anyone who has come to an event at Mar-a-Lago when the President arrives knows that no one can move when the President arrives, or in this case, departs. If you have to go to the bathroom—you hold it. It'll only last a few minutes. In this situation, the President was leaving Mar-a-Lago to head to the airport. So, we waited about five minutes until the Secret Service cleared us to move again. We just stood down by the storage room awkwardly staring at one another until we were released.

Once released, we all went back up to the dining room table where we had previously met. At no point did any of the FBI agents or DOJ representative gave any indication that they had been denied access to anything. They made no objections about their visit.

Mr. Bratt said to Evan, "Thank you for arranging the visit." He seemed genuinely grateful for the cooperation.

"Absolutely," said Evan. "Do you need anything else while you're here?"

"Uh no, I don't think so." Mr. Bratt looked at the three FBI agents who shook their heads no. "I think we've got everything we need." To be clear, they made no objections. Never once did they push back on not being allowed to go through the boxes.

"Great!" said Evan. "If you need anything, or if anything else comes up, please just contact me. You heard the President say that we want to be extremely cooperative. So, whatever you need, I'm happy to help." Evan was clear with them that if they needed anything else, or had any specific requests, they should reach out to him and he would accommodate them.

Everyone was very friendly and professional. We all shook hands, said good-bye, and Evan showed DOJ and the FBI to the door. I watched them depart, but stood back at a distance. After escorting them out, Evan turned to me and said, "What do you think?"

I shrugged and said, "I think it went well. You gave them what they came for. So . . ." I shrugged again. "How do you feel about it?"

"I think it went as well as it could have gone. They understand we're being cooperative, which is the most important thing. I'm relieved the interaction with the President went well. That could have gone off the rails but didn't. So, yeah. I'm happy with it." Evan also shrugged. "What are you doing now?"

"I was just going to go home. What are you doing?"

"My flight is not until tonight, but I may head to the airport now and see if I can get an earlier flight. Would you mind giving me a ride?" Evan asked.

"Not at all! The airport is just a few miles from here and an easy stop for me. Let's go," I said. Evan grabbed his briefcase and we headed for the door.

Once we got in the car, Evan said, "We should call the President and let him know it's over and the FBI has left."

"Definitely. Give him a call," I said.

He pulled out his cell phone and dialed President Trump on speaker so that I could be a part of the conversation as well.

"Evan. Hi," President Trump said, "Is it over? How'd it go?"

"Yes, Mr. President. It's over. The agents are all gone. I think it went well. They seemed to be satisfied with everything we gave them. After you left, we took them down to see the storage room. I reiterated that they had our full cooperation, and that was pretty much it."

"Great. I think it was important that I showed up to tell them personally that they could see whatever they wanted. That needs to be very clear that we are fully cooperating. Just so you know, we're taking off now, so I'm about to lose connection," the President said, indicating he was on his plane heading to New Jersey for the summer.

"Absolutely. I'm in complete agreement. I thought it was great. Christina Bobb is here with me. Christina, what did you think?"

Before I could answer, the President said, "Oh, Christina! Were you there?!" He paused slightly before the dots connected, "Oh! Was that you sitting to the left of Evan? You were sitting in front of the window, and the light was shining in my eyes, so I couldn't see you. Was that you?"

"Yes, sir," I said. "That was me."

"Oh good! I'm glad you were there! What did you think of everything?" he asked. "How did it go?"

"I thought it went well. Evan did a great job. He handled the meeting well. He promised full cooperation. So, it seems pretty straightforward."

"Did you think that it was a good idea that I met with them personally?" he asked.

"Yes. You did a great job. I was a little nervous when Evan said you wanted to meet with them, but the way it played out was very good." I wanted to continue to explain, but he interrupted me.

"Oh no! I had to be there. I had to tell them personally that I was cooperating. Otherwise, they'll say that 'it's just his lawyers trying to cooperate,' or whatever. They'll make up some lie about how I'm not cooperating. I had to be there and personally tell them that they have my full cooperation. All right. I'm going to lose connection. Great job, guys. Bye." He hung up.

Evan and I chatted the rest of the way to the airport. I dropped him off and headed home. Boris called me either that day, or a day or two after, and thanked me for taking the meeting. I had no other contact or discussion with anyone about it.

I assumed the matter was closed. Until I got a call from Evan on August 8, 2022, asking me to get to Mar-a-Lago immediately. The FBI was raiding the place.

CHAPTER 4

The Raid

August 8, 2022

It was 9:50 a.m., and I had just pulled into the Palm Beach County DMV for a 10:00 a.m. appointment. I sat in my car flipping through my documents to make sure I had everything I needed to complete my license and registration.

My phone rang, but I missed it. At 9:53 a.m., Evan texted me, "Christina—Evan—please call me asap. I need you to go to Mar-a-Lago ASAP."

Dang it, I thought. *I have to get my car registered. It can probably wait a few minutes.* I responded to Evan, "Ok. Give me ten minutes to wrap this up." That nagging feeling hit me. I should at least find out what's going on. I called Evan. "Hey! What's going on?"

"Are you in the Palm Beach area?" Evan asked in a polite but serious tone. "Can you get to Mar-a-Lago quickly?"

"Yes. Why? What's going on?" I asked.

"The FBI is at Mar-a-Lago and they're raiding the place. We don't have any lawyers there. Can you please go and be my point of contact with the FBI? I'll work with you on everything once you're down there, but I need someone on site for me." Evan waited for my response.

"What?!" I asked. That didn't make any sense. "What do you meaning *raiding* the place?"

"They got a warrant and are executing it as we speak. I'm in DC and can't get there quickly. Can you please go down there and talk with them and tell me what's going on?"

"They're executing a warrant?! Like smashing through doors? Or are they waiting for me to get down there to talk with them?" Certainly, after how cooperative President Trump had been just weeks earlier, they didn't go straight to a raid?!

Evan was patient with me but stated the obvious, "I don't know. I don't know anything right now. I need you to get there quickly so that we can get all of these questions answered."

The whole situation didn't seem right. They couldn't possibly be raiding Mar-a-Lago. At the last meeting, we had fully cooperated and Evan told them to ask him if they needed anything else. They knew they had full access to whatever they wanted. A raid was totally unnecessary and wrong. "Did they tell you they were going to do this? Did you know this was coming?" I asked, confused.

"No." Evan was as confused as I was. "They didn't tell me anything. I have no idea why they're raiding the place. We don't have any lawyers there right now. Can you please get down there and figure out what's going on?"

My brain was still trying to make sense of the situation. "Have they already started the search, or are they waiting for us to talk to them?"

Evan insisted, "Christina, I have all the same questions you do. Can you please go there right now and call me when you get there?"

"Yes. I can be there in twenty minutes." I said. "Ummm . . ." I debated whether I should even ask, but it would take me three weeks to get another appointment for my car and I was already driving on expired tags. "I'm at the DMV and *really* need to get my car registered. Do you think I can complete my appointment first and then go?"

Evan was silent long enough to make me regret asking the question. "I really don't think that's a good idea. You should get down there as quickly as possible."

Right. "Yeah. I figured. Just checking. Okay. I'm on my way and will call you when I get there." I headed south to Palm Beach, confused and still not thoroughly convinced it was an actual raid.

Maybe the agents were waiting for one of us to let them into the storage room so they could go through the boxes now? Maybe they were simply following up on our last meeting and just didn't tell Evan? Maybe this didn't have anything to do with our meeting? It didn't make any sense to me. As I drove, I figured I'd be greeted by a couple polite agents, similar to June 3, asking permission to have access to certain areas. Even though Evan said they were raiding the property, that probably wasn't right. Surely, it would make sense once I got there.

Arriving on Site

During the offseason, the gates to Mar-a-Lago are all closed and locked, with no access whatsoever. The north gate is the only one that has a guard there for access to the property. Secret Service had their SUV, like always, blocking the driveway so they could check IDs before anyone entered the property.

A Secret Service agent stepped out of the vehicle and approached my car. That's when I realized I'd forgotten to call ahead to request access to the property. I did not have unlimited access to Mar-a-Lago but am placed on an access list when I have a meeting with the President. The property is extremely secure, and I hoped Susie Wiles, Evan, or someone, had notified Secret Service that I'd be coming. Susie is President Trump's "right-hand man" and would eventually become his Chief of Staff at the White House for his second term. Everything happened so fast that I just forgot to call.

The agent, in a Kevlar vest and mirrored aviator sunglasses, approached my vehicle and said, "Can I help you?"

"Yes. I'm Christina Bobb, I'm on President Trump's staff. I'm here to meet the FBI, but I may not be on the access list," I said as I handed him my ID. "Can you please check and let me know if I need to make a phone call?"

He took my ID and grabbed his radio, saying to another agent on the other end, "I've got Christina Bobb at the gate. Is she clear?"

Someone responded, "Yeah. She's clear."

I started to apologize that I hadn't called, but the agent kindly cut me off. "He said you're cleared. You're good to go." The agent handed back my ID and went back to his vehicle to move it aside so I could pass.

As I approached the side entrance, the entrance to the living room where we met with the agents on June 3, I noticed the whole thing was boarded up and closed. It was inaccessible. I called Evan.

"Hey, Evan. Where are the agents expecting me to meet them?" I was looking for a couple agents in a car, similar to the June 3 meeting, but they weren't where we met them last time.

"They told me they're at the circle drive," Evan said.

"Okay. Let me go over there and I'll call you back." *That's weird,* I thought. *What are they doing over there?* I drove around to the other side of the estate to check out the circle drive and see if I could find any FBI agents.

Meeting the FBI

"Oh my gosh! They're *raiding* the place!" I said to myself as I pulled into the circle drive. "This can't be real."

Mar-a-Lago has a gorgeously manicured circle drive with tropical Florida foliage, palm trees, and flowers in the center. The circle drive is located outside the main ballroom where most of the large formal events are held, with a canopy covering the sidewalk to the smaller dining room and poolside cabana. Although, this time of year, the club is closed, so the canopy had been removed, likely for maintenance.

I expected to find a couple of agents waiting for me to talk about searching the boxes in the storage room. I was off—by a lot.

Parked in the circle drive, the government had about a dozen black SUVs, at least one fifteen-passenger van, a few smaller vehicles, and a large Ryder moving van ready to load up the President's personal belongings. Why on earth were there so many people here? What are they looking for?

I could see agents walking back and forth from their vehicles to the inside of the ballroom, or heading over toward the storage room, which was on the other side of the property. Those conducting the raid were in plain clothes, all wearing COVID masks and sunglasses, a great way to hide their identity from any cameras. The agents standing by the vehicles were in business suits. Some had their service pistols in their side holsters and other were unarmed. At that time, I did not see any agents with rifles. They came later.

As I got out of my car, the lead Secret Service agent on site, whom I knew, greeted me. "Hi, Christina. So, you're aware of what's happening?" This agent is extremely professional and considerate of President Trump as well as his staff. He's tall, fit, and everything you'd expect from Secret Service. I've always been grateful when he's on site and helped me navigate various locations when I've accompanied President Trump. Today, he was dressed in a golf shirt and khaki pants.

"I know the FBI is raiding the place. Other than that, I have no idea." I didn't even know where to begin. My mind hadn't comprehended what I was seeing.

"Okay. The FBI is here, with a warrant, and executing that warrant now. I'll take you over to the lead agents and they can explain the rest to you."

"Okay. Thank you," I said, but I stalled for a moment. As I stood by my car at the end of the circle drive, behind the Ryder truck, I got angry.

Watching the agents walk around like they owned the place disgusted me. This is the home of an American President. We are the United States of America!

By this point, I'd already experienced US Marshals coming to my home and subpoenaing me to testify before Congress about January 6th. I'd complied and testified for six hours. They buried my testimony. I'd watched as friends and colleagues were arrested and tried on make-believe charges. Americans were in jail in deplorable conditions for their political views, and the January 6th Committee made a mockery of our justice system. The FBI had lied to courts, spied on Americans, invaded privacy rights, abused their power, and spread lies in the media. Now this?

I felt grief and anger well up.

I called Susie Wiles as I lingered behind the Secret Service agent. She was in frequent contact with President Trump in Bedminster, New Jersey, and I needed a sanity check for what I was witnessing.

When she answered, she got right to the point. "What's going on?"

"I honestly don't understand this. I just got here and there's dozens of agents, a Ryder truck. This is crazy! Do you have any information? Am I missing something?" I was grasping for something that would make this all make sense.

"No." Susie answered abruptly. "Where are you? What do you see?"

"I just parked in the circle drive." I described the scene to her as I followed the Secret Service looking for the FBI agent in charge. I had the phone to my ear as a Secret Service agent pointed two FBI agents in my direction and waved me over.

"Make sure they know you're the President's point of contact," Susie added. "They need to give you more information than we've got."

"Okay. I think I found the guys in charge." We didn't hang up, but I left her on the phone, with it pressed to my ear, as I talked to the agents.

Show Me the Warrant

Two FBI agents approached me from behind a vehicle. The first agent (Agent #1) was a bit robotic and arrogant, so I pushed back on his condescending stance as I said a tad aggressively, "What is going on here?! What are you doing?!" I still had the phone to my ear with Susie on the line.

He motioned with his hands downward as if that would calm me, and said, "Calm down. We have a warrant and we're executing it. Who are you?"

"I'm President Trump's representative. Show me the warrant," I demanded.

"No. I don't have to show it to you." He stood there defiantly with his hands on his hips. My mind exploded.

"What the hell is wrong with you?! Yes, you do! You absolutely have to show me the warrant!" I started to argue with him about the Fourth Amendment and constitutional rights. He seemed a bit surprised at my reaction and again tried to "shush" me, telling me to calm down and be reasonable. He also insisted that he had no legal obligation to show me the warrant.

"You're invading the personal residence of the President of the United States and you want *me* to be reasonable?! You have an obligation to follow the law. You can't roll up here, raid the place, and expect me to just take your word for it that you actually have a warrant. Show me the fucking warrant!!" At this point I realized Susie was still on the phone that I had pressed to my ear and could hear everything. So I turned my attention back to her.

"I found the agents."

"Sounds like it. Call me later." She hung up.

Before I could finish the deep breath I was taking to continue my argument about why they had to show me the warrant, the second agent stepped in and indicated he understood my points. He clearly wanted to lower the temperature.

The second agent (Agent #2) also looked like a typical FBI agent but was a bit more human and relatable. He took his sunglasses off when he talked to me, which I appreciated. He was dressed in a suit and carried himself in a compassionate manner.

He stepped closer and said, "Look, I need to verify who you are before we show you anything. Can you please show me your ID?" I gave him my ID and pulled out my cell and called Evan on speaker phone. The second agent jumped in and said, "Hi, Evan. I just need you to verify that Christina is your representative here on site and you want us working with her."

"Yes. I'm in DC and obviously can't get to Florida before you finish. I'll be in touch with Christina all day, so please work with her as my representative," Evan said. The agent agreed and I told Evan I'd call him in a little bit.

Satisfied with my identity, the second agent said, "Here. I'll show you the warrant, but I can't give you a copy until the search is complete." He motioned for me to follow him to the other side of the car, where he opened the trunk and pulled the warrant out of a stack of papers he had in the back.

He showed it to me but held on to it as if to suggest that I should just look at it without touching it. I grabbed it, but he didn't let go. I tugged a little harder, looking at him as if to say, "I'm not going to run away with it." He let go.

The first thing I looked for was which court had issued the warrant. US District Court for the Southern District of Florida. Okay. That makes sense. Who is the judge? Bruce Reinhart, a Magistrate Judge.

Interesting. A magistrate? Since I was new to Florida, I didn't know Florida judges, but I made a mental note of the name, because someone would know who he was. Then I noticed the application to have the warrant and accompanying documents sealed.

"It's fucking sealed!!" I said, outraged. The agent's face indicated he regretting letting me see the documents, but he didn't say anything. He just nodded and let me rant. It's not uncommon to have warrants sealed, so this wasn't necessarily unexpected. That didn't change my opinion that sealing this warrant was only to obscure the truth from the American people. DOJ and the FBI have been on a consistent descent into tyrannical political oppression, and they didn't want to be held accountable by anyone, in my opinion.

"Absolute chicken shit! Chicken shit!" I was so angry I couldn't even think of what to say. "You're a coward. You're all a bunch of cowards! The Department of Justice is so corrupt. You know what you're doing is wrong and you're trying to hide it from the American people. Chicken shit! Absolute chicken shit. You all should be embarrassed to be here." Even at the time I wished I could think of something worse than *chicken shit*, but it was all that would come to mind. So, I said it—a lot.

Thinking It Through

Part of me knew Agent #2 was nice, and maybe I shouldn't be expressing my frustrations to him. Wasn't he just doing his job? Should I simply be polite to him, play along, and professionally mind my own business while they raided the President's home? Should I wait patiently for them to finish and give me the information I was looking for? No.

This was a raid on every single American, and I could not sit idly by. As a Marine Corps Judge Advocate, I conducted legal training for service members on their roles and responsibilities as US military members. Every service member receives a large amount of legal training, and will tell you that as a service member, you have a legal obligation to disobey an unlawful order. Raiding the President's home was illegal, and they all should have refused to do it.

The agents would likely argue that the warrant was signed by a judge, making their actions lawful and necessary. At the very least, the raid was not "*patently* criminal conduct." The agents *couldn't* disobey the order to raid President Trump's personal residence. That's what they'd say.

Maybe. But at what point will Americans stand up and push back, saying, "Enough!" From my perspective, the agents should have refused to execute the warrant—even if it cost them their jobs.

Authorized Use of Force

It wasn't until two years later, in 2024, that we'd all learn the FBI had authorized deadly force for the raid.[1] That's an absolutely preposterous and dangerous authorization. The FBI knows that the only people at Mar-a-Lago with weapons are Secret Service members—federal law enforcement charged with protecting the President with their lives. What's the FBI going to do? Get in a shootout with the Secret Service?! Were they prepared to shoot me?

Attorney General Merrick Garland would later claim that the language was just "standard operating procedure."[2] *Standard* operating procedure? When have they ever raided a president's home before with Secret Service present? There was nothing *standard* about this operation. Garland's "ho-hum" attitude, waiving off the outrage that DOJ could have killed people at Mar-a-Lago, demonstrates the type of "copy and paste" job that this operation was from the beginning. It was never a real criminal investigation.

CHAPTER 5

Probable Cause

It didn't occur to me at the time, but when the FBI agent gave me the chance to review the warrant, he handed me the entire package of documents, including the affidavit. The affidavit is the probable cause DOJ relied on when petitioning the court for the warrant. That's likely why he didn't want me to handle it initially.

We, President Trump and his team, had no idea what DOJ relied upon to believe any crime had been committed, and we wanted to know. Affidavits are typically sealed and remain sealed unless DOJ decides to indict. What direction were they taking this? Who was their affiant? Where did they get their probable cause from? We didn't know, and I had the affidavit in my hands. I could have read it.

Once I ran out of words to express how corrupt the FBI's actions were, I turned my attention back to the warrant and began reading every single word. The second agent realized I was actually reading the documents carefully when he saw me take my time on every single page. Even on the warrant, which is a template document filled in by hand, I read every single word. He watched me closely. When I had freaked out about it being sealed, he knew I would eventually get to the affidavit, which I wasn't supposed to see.

At this point, the nice agent calmly grabbed the warrant.

As I tried to pull it away from him, he calmly looked at me and said, "I'm pointing you to the part you're looking for." There were a few dozen pages in my hands, and he was turning to Attachments A and B—what they were searching for and where. I let go and let him flip the pages. I didn't notice at the time that he caused me to skip the affidavit and only see the parts I was authorized to see. Very smooth move. Well played. I kicked myself later for not catching it.

The Attachments

Attachment A was one page and recorded the property to be searched. In one paragraph, it basically described the entire property of Mar-a-Lago and gave DOJ and the FBI carte blanche access to whatever they wanted.

I was more interested in what they were searching for. Why were they here? And why were they raiding the property? Attachment B was one page and recorded the property to be seized. It said in its entirety:

> All physical documents and records constituting evidence, contraband, fruits of crime, or other items illegally possessed in violation of 18 U.S.C. §§ 793, 2071, or 1519, including the following.
>
> a. Any physical documents with classification markings, along with any containers/boxes (including any other contents) in which such documents are located, as well as any other containers/boxes that are collectively stored or found together with the aforementioned documents and containers/boxes;
>
> b. Information, including communications in any form, regarding the retrieval, storage, or transmission of national defense information or classified material;

c. Any government and/or Presidential Records created between January 20, 2017, and January 20, 2021; or

d. Any evidence of the knowing alteration, destruction, or concealment of any government and/or Presidential Records, or of any documents with classification markings.

When I finished reading the attachments, I pulled out my phone to take a picture of Attachment B. I held my phone over Attachment B and looked at the agent to make sure he knew I was taking the photo. I waited for his approval. He nodded and I snapped the picture.

The Department of Justifying the Means

Standing on the sidewalk between the main ballroom and the poolside clubhouse, I looked around at the cars and agents, trying to make sense of it all. My brain wasn't processing the information fast enough, so I pulled out my phone and started taking pictures to document the raid. I took a video of the circle drive to document all the cars the FBI had brought to the scene to conduct the raid, then proceeded to take still photos of the cars, agents, or anything else I could find.

Agent #1 didn't like that I was taking photos. "Hey, put your camera away," he said.

"No," I said over my shoulder to him as I continued to slowly walk the circle drive and film the vehicles.

Agent #1 didn't give up. "You can't take photos! You need to put your camera away."

"Says who?" I said. "I'm not stopping you from executing your warrant. You do what you came here to do, and I'll do what I came here to do." The FBI was there to raid the property, and I was there to observe the raid for President Trump. Speaking of which—where were the agents?

I put my phone down and turned back to the two agents. "Have you already started the search? Where are all the agents?" At that point,

I'd seen a handful of agents enter the main ballroom, but not much else.

"We have started the search," said Agent #1. "We have authority to search this entire property and can search any area where we believe we'll find the evidence we're looking for."

"I know. I read the warrant," I said dryly. "*Where* are they actually searching?"

"Right now, they're in the storage room."

I started to walk toward the storage room when the agents stopped me immediately. "You can't go past this location."

"What do you mean? I can't leave the parking lot?!" I was confused. They were actually preventing me from observing the raid?

"That's right. You need to stay out here," said Agent #1. "You have no right to observe the agents."

"I do have a right to observe the raid! I'm President Trump's representative. This is his property, and he asked me to come observe." I pushed back as they insisted that I was not allowed to observe the raid. "It's better *for you* if you let me observe," I said. "It makes it look like you're doing sketchy things if you won't let me watch you."

Agent #1 shook his head no.

Agent #2 then told me he had called the local Assistant US Attorney and let her know that I was on site. He kindly explained that she would be able to answer all my questions and explain any legal challenges I had. Until she got here, I wasn't allowed to observe anything.

"Great," I managed to say.

"Can you please tell me your name?" I asked Agent #2. He gave it to me, although I figured it didn't really matter. He had been working with Evan, so Evan probably already had any info I could collect anyway.

"What's your name?" I asked Agent #1. He refused to give it to me, turned his back and started to walk away. "That's okay," I said. "I'd be embarrassed to be here too if I were you. Can I please get the badge number of the agents on the property? Or, at the very least, the number of agents here on the property?"

"No. You don't have the right to any information," Agent #1 said as he continued to walk away from me. Agent #2 didn't blow me off; he just reiterated that when the Assistant US Attorney arrived, she'd be able to answer all my questions.

Fantastic.

Turn the Cameras Back On

While I was waiting for the Assistant US Attorney to arrive, I continued to take pictures and try to record whatever I could. The Secret Service agent in charge on site came over to me and said, "Here's the thing. The FBI agents really don't want you taking pictures."

"I'm allowed to, though," I said as nicely as possible.

"I know. And I told them that," he said. "Before you got here, they told the staff that they needed to turn the security cameras off."

"Turn them back on!" I interrupted.

He smiled patiently at me. "They did. Don't worry. They called Evan, and Evan told them to turn the cameras back on." He was trying to be kind, but clearly didn't want to play referee between me and the FBI.

Another attorney working for the Trump Organization arrived at the circle drive, walking from the other side of the property. We spoke about what had transpired since I arrived. He was there to check in on the Trump Organization employees, answer any questions they might have, and make sure they knew what they *had* to do, and more importantly what they *didn't* have to do. As a local Florida trial lawyer, he was familiar with the local courts and asked me if I knew who signed the warrant.

"Do you know Judge Reinhart?" I asked.

"Oh yeah. I know who he is. He's a magistrate," the attorney said.

"Yeah. What do you think of him?" I asked.

"Well, he used to be a criminal defense attorney, so I would hope that he would maintain a true standard for probable cause requirements and the rule of law," he said. We both looked at each other like we weren't sure that had happened in this instance. "Did they give you a copy of the warrant?" he asked.

"No. They let me see it, but they didn't give me a copy," I said.

"That's not surprising," he said. "Frustrating, but not surprising. They'll hopefully give it to you once the raid is over." We both shrugged. "I'm going to go finish talking to the employees and will come back soon." He walked back in the direction he'd come from.

CHAPTER 6

You Shall Not Pass

By now, it was roughly 11:30 a.m. I had been on-site for about an hour, a very full hour. My emotions were drained, and the FBI had backed off, basically leaving me alone to make my phone calls and take my pictures. They still wouldn't let me go anywhere other than the circle drive, but both sides had largely calmed down and agreed to disagree. I saw a car pull up with the Assistant US Attorney inside. Someone explained to me that she was the attorney who had processed the request for the warrant in the Southern District of Florida. Nobody told me, but it seemed someone had briefed her that I was difficult, because she was aggressive as soon as she got out of the car.

She approached me authoritatively, with a stern expression, as I stood on the sidewalk at the top of the circle drive. "Are you President Trump's representative?" She wore a navy blue pinstriped pantsuit with oxford loafers. By contrast, I was in a blue cotton button-down with the sleeves rolled up, white shorts, and flip-flops. Remember, I came from the DMV.

"Yes." I said. *Great*, I thought. She's either a radical democrat or she does a great job playing one. Her attitude matched the liberal activists who believe they are better than the rest of us. Lucky for her, she also had the Department of Justice behind her to reinforce that idea.

"Okay. I'm going to be very clear with you. I'm in charge here. I have authority to search the entire property and can go anywhere I want, searching anything I want. You have to stay right here and can't observe anything," she said.

"Right. That's been made very clear. As President Trump's representative, I should have the right to observe what you're doing. I would like to accompany your agents as you search the property," I said.

"No. That's not going to happen," she said curtly.

"Why? Why wouldn't you let me observe what you're doing?" I asked, surprised that DOJ would be so fishy.

"You don't have a right to," the DOJ attorney answered shortly.

"I do have a right to watch you. This is President Trump's property and I'm here as his representative."

She scoffed as if to indicate I was no better than an intern. "You're going to stand right here. That's how we're going to do this." She made an overly dramatic circle motion with both her arms and then pointed to the ground showing me where I had to stand.

"It's ninety-five degrees outside." The obvious implication being it was too hot to make me stand outside all day.

"Yep," she said as she cut me off and walked into the air-conditioned ballroom where all of the agents had stationed themselves to escape the heat.

Updating Susie

Standing outside the main ballroom, feeling the burst of cool air from inside waft over me as the DOJ attorney opened and closed the door, I figured it was a good time to call Susie back.

"What's going on there?" she asked.

"Well, they still won't let me observe the search. So, I'm basically stuck outside waiting for them to give me an update, whenever they feel like doing that," I said.

"Do you have any idea what they're looking for, or think they'll find? Have they said anything to you about the search?" Susie asked. Like the rest of the team, she had no idea what they were after or what crime the FBI wanted to believe occurred. What evidence could possibly be stored at Mar-a-Lago?

"No," I answered. "The only indication I have is the Attachment B." I had texted it to Susie earlier so she could read it herself. "I do get the impression, at least for now, that they actually are looking for classified documents. They may stretch their authority and look for more than that though."

"That's what I'm worried about. I'm worried this is all a charade and that they're actually doing something else," she wondered.

"Like what? What could they possibly find at Mar-a-Lago?" I questioned.

"Who knows." Susie thought for a second. Like the rest of us, she was grasping to make the situation make sense. It didn't. "I have no idea what they think they'll find there."

"Are we going to make this public?" I asked. I had been there for about two hours at this point and hadn't seen any word of the raid come up on my news feed. I wanted to shout it from the rooftops and tell the entire world how ugly and awful the FBI was by raiding the President's home for no reason! We had been completely cordial in our previous meeting, and the President himself had told them they could have access to whatever they wanted. This raid was nothing more than harassment—an abuse of government power to do whatever they wanted to a political opponent. It was disgusting and un-American.

"I think we'll have to. I don't know how something like this stays a secret," Susie answered. "DOJ leaks like a sieve. There's no way they'll keep it a secret."

"Mmmm. I don't know. I actually think they're trying to keep it a secret," I responded. "Call me crazy, but I don't think they're going to leak this."

"You really think DOJ would keep this quiet?"

"I do. They're acting like they don't want anyone to know. And they sealed the warrant so there is no public record. Also, the grand jury subpoena didn't leak. I think they think they can do whatever they want and President Trump won't say anything about it."

"Interesting. Well, it could look bad for President Trump to have his personal residence raided. They may be banking on the fact that he would be embarrassed and not want people to know." Susie was thinking out loud. "I just don't see how we could possibly keep something this egregious quiet," she said, almost to herself.

"I'll keep it quiet if you ask me to, but I support him making a statement." Earlier, when I arrived at Mar-a-Lago and saw the raid, I wanted the whole world to see how terrible this was. But it wasn't my story to tell. I really hoped President Trump would make it public.

"Well, we need to keep it quiet for now. But I'm sure he'll make a statement when he decides he's ready to," Susie concluded. We agreed to talk again soon.

Cameras Are On—Who's Watching?

Hiding from the heat as best I could, I sat at the base of the pillars outside the main ballroom. One of the Mar-a-Lago maintenance staff who works on the security cameras walked by. I stopped him to confirm if the cameras were actually on and capturing everything that was happening.

"Hey! Can you confirm that the security cameras have actually been turned back on and are recording?" I asked.

"Oh yeah. They're on. Corporate is in control of that now, not me," he said.

"Okay. But they're on, right?" I asked.

"Yeah. They're on," he confirmed.

"Okay. Good," I said. I didn't know who was watching, what they could see, or where cameras were located. Hopefully someone had a better view of the events than I did sitting outside the door.

CHAPTER 7

Classified or Not?

After my call with Susie, I sat down against the column outside the main ballroom. The Assistant US Attorney from DOJ walked back toward the circle drive from the direction of the storage facility and stopped to talk to the Trump Organization lawyer. Someone told me I should go join that conversation.

As I walked up, the DOJ lawyer turned to update me. "We've reached the point in the search where we need access to the locked area of the storage room," she said. The storage area had a smaller closet that had an extra lock on it. This was the location that Evan showed me and DOJ and the FBI back on June 3. Evan told me later that after the June 3 visit, the FBI had asked him to put an additional lock on the door, which he did within a few days.

"Okay. Is there a problem?" I asked.

"The only employee with a key won't open the door without someone from President Trump's staff telling him he's allowed to unlock the door for us," she said, looking annoyed that the employee had the audacity to question her authority.

"Okay. Well, I'll go down there and tell him to open it," I said. Easy, right?

"You're not allowed down there. I've already told you that. You can't go down there!" she said emphatically.

"Ooookay." What did she want from me? "Well, then why don't you have the employee come up to me and I'll tell him to open the door for you?" Also an easy solution, right?

"No. I'm not willing to wait that long," she said emphatically, acting as if the extra five minutes would ruin her day.

"Okay. So if I can't go down there, and you don't want him to come up here, how would you like us to open the door?" I asked.

"We have our own way of doing things." She smiled, arrogantly implying that they would just bust the lock.

"So you're going to just bust the lock?" I asked.

"Yeah," she said, very proud of herself.

"Why would you do that when we're willing to open the door for you?" I asked her, shocked at her complete disregard for the personal home of President Trump. Was I actually having this conversation? Why did she even bother to come talk to us? If she was intent on busting the lock, she didn't need to talk to me about it. And if we were willing to cooperate and open the door without doing damage, why wouldn't they let us do that? She just wanted to bust the lock. So stupid.

"It's how we do things. There's nothing you can do about it," she said, with a level of arrogance not frequently displayed by someone in the President's personal residence.

"Okay," I said as I shrugged and walked back to sit in front of the column outside the main ballroom. Those columns were one of the few shaded areas out front, so I camped out there for the day.

As I walked back to the shaded area, Agent #1 stopped me as he exited his black SUV. We both had calmed down by this point, and it seemed to me that he recognized that I was not trying to interfere with their investigation.

"How are you doing?" he asked me, recognizing that I'd been outside in the heat for a while.

"I'm okay. Thank you." I didn't really want to talk to him, but he was being kind.

"Do you need any water?" he offered. "You're welcome to join us in the car. We've got the air on and it's cool in here." Agent #1 was clearly trying to extend an olive branch.

"That's very nice of you. Thank you, but I'd rather not." We had worked our way to a civil relationship, but I still would rather suffer in the heat than pretend that this raid was business as usual. It was wrong, a massive overreach on the part of the Biden Administration, and an affront to our Constitutional rights.

I'll just wait until I pass out.

Agent #1 and I gradually tried to set aside our differences. At one point, he said, "You know, we didn't come in here with lights and sirens and make a big spectacle of this. We're not trying to make a big show of this."

I simply nodded in response, understanding that he was trying to cooperate with me. But I wasn't sure how to take that statement. Did the FBI really believe they could raid the personal residence of President Trump and no one would know? How could they not make a big deal of this? This was a *huge* deal. Our government was using its power to target their political opposition. This is the kind of corruption we'd expect in Venezuela or North Korea—not the United States of America.

The Employees Go Home

I sat down again on the base of one of the columns to try to figure out what I should do next, when the Trump Organization attorney came back from talking with the employees and asked for an update.

"Well, DOJ's here now, and she also won't let me observe the raid," I said, interested to see his response.

He scrunched his eyebrows as if that wasn't the answer he expected. "DOJ *also* said you can't watch the raid?" He wanted to be sure he understood me correctly.

"Correct. The Assistant US Attorney also won't let me go anywhere inside and is making me stand in the heat," I said.

He rolled his eyes a bit, acknowledging the ridiculousness of the situation. I wondered if he thought I was exaggerating.

As we stood there, chit-chatting about the situation, the DOJ lawyer walked out of the ballroom, heading toward the storage facility. She didn't even acknowledge us standing there. So the Trump Organization lawyer very politely called to her and said, "Excuse me!"

She stopped and looked at him. "Yes?"

"Christina here is President Trump's representative, and I think it's appropriate for her to observe the raid," he said very politely.

"She's not allowed," said the DOJ lawyer and just kept walking toward the storage room.

"Oh! She does *not* like you," he said to me surprised by how rude and aggressive the DOJ lawyer was.

I laughed and said, "I know. I didn't even do anything to her." Even the FBI and I seemed to have settled into a cordial-enough relationship.

"How are the employees? Are there many here?" I asked him. The club was closed, so Mar-a-Lago was largely vacant. There were some groundskeepers there, but I hadn't seen many of the club staff.

"Yeah. There are a few here. They're okay," he said. "A little shaken up by the surprise visit by the FBI. But I told them all to go home so they didn't need to worry about interacting with the agents. The employees should all be gone soon." The FBI had indicated that they didn't intend to question anyone, and did not object to allowing the employees to go home. Sending the employees home was the best way to minimize the stress they experienced from an FBI raid.

While we talked, the facilities manager on-site came by to let the Trump Organization attorney know he was leaving. The facilities manager has worked for the Trump Organization for many years in various capacities and was now responsible for Mar-a-Lago. He was very polite and accommodating. He said he was going home but gave me his phone number in case I needed him to come back for any reason.

At this point, Lindsey Halligan, another Trump attorney, arrived at Mar-a-Lago from Fort Lauderdale. Lindsey had responded to a request from Boris to get to Mar-a-Lago to figure out what was happening. She arrived in true South Florida style, wearing black skinny jeans with high heels, a white top, and a very nice long blazer, which she ended up putting back in her car, because it was too hot to wear. Her long blond hair and makeup looked great. She's gorgeous.

As she approached us, the Trump Organization attorney chuckled. "*That* attorney," he said, pointing toward the storage room to indicate the DOJ lawyer, "is not going to like her either." I agreed and suggested he talk to the DOJ lawyer without us. Maybe he could make more progress than I had. He said he'd try and walked away to find her.

Lindsey and I sat on the base of the columns outside the main ballroom discussing what we knew. A few minutes later, the Trump Organization attorney returned and said, "Well, that didn't go well. I don't think there's anything else here for me to do." He stayed for a few minutes to wrap up with us, and we exchanged contact information in case he needed to come back. Then he left.

Lindsey and I stayed in our little spot waiting for information. I filmed every agent, box, and piece of information going in and out of the main ballroom. Most of the agents had COVID masks on with sunglasses, likely to conceal their identity, but I filmed the process anyway.

The Secret Service agent approached us and explained that the FBI had narrowed their search to three specific locations. They would search the storage area, President Trump's personal home office, and the residence. The Secret Service agent accompanied the FBI during the entire search and stayed with them throughout the whole process.

Based on my interactions with Evan back on June 3, I was under the impression that the subpoena only included the storage room. If true, the FBI was way out on a limb searching areas they'd never requested to search. I needed to figure out the scope of the subpoena.

The Search Continues

Lindsey and I talked while we waited to get another update from DOJ or the FBI. As the agents filed in and out of the air-conditioned ballroom, Lindsey and I complained about how hot it was outside.

"I wish we could have had maintenance turn the air conditioning off in the ballroom, residence, and storage area," Lindsey suggested.

"I love that idea!" If they were going to make us suffer in the heat, they should too. "The maintenance supervisor already left, but I could call him and ask," I thought out loud trying to figure out how to turn the air off.

"We can't," Lindsey said. "They already looked into it and said the system was too complex. It would take too much effort to turn it off and then on again." We continued to sit outside and just wait for something to happen.

On at least one occasion, I called Evan to see if he had heard anything new or if he had information I did not. He didn't.

"Evan, what do you think they're going to find?" I asked.

"I don't know. There aren't any classified documents there," Evan said dryly.

"Right," I acknowledged, "but certainly we don't expect the FBI to raid President Trump's personal home and walk away empty-handed. They would look so foolish," I said. "They have to claim they found *something*." I wondered aloud what would happen next.

After I finished my call with Evan and rejoined Lindsey at our spot, I realized I needed to use the bathroom. The women's restroom was just inside the ballroom doors, so I approached the ballroom to ask for permission to use the restroom. The DOJ lawyer rushed out as if I were trying to sneak into their investigation.

"You can't come in here!" she insisted.

"I understand," I said calmly. "I just need to use the bathroom. I won't interfere with your work. Can I just slip in and slip out of the bathroom, please?" I said, pointing to the bathroom door inside the ballroom.

"No. You need to find somewhere else to use the bathroom. You can't come in here," she insisted. The Secret Service agent was with her and pointed out two maintenance workers who had stuck around to facilitate the search. He told me to have them let me into one of the guest bathrooms over by the spa.

While I was with the maintenance workers, I asked if they could get me some water. I had started to feel a tad dizzy, most likely from dehydration. The maintenance workers gave me a bottle of water, and I headed back to the spot with Lindsey.

Lindsey and I spent the next few hours sitting outside the ballroom, getting periodic updates on the progress. Most of the updates were simply, "We're still in the storage room." The DOJ lawyer stopped by again to let us know that some of the agents had moved on to the office.

By now, it was about 3:30 or 4:00 p.m., and Lindsey mentioned that she had a filing due by 5:00 p.m. She needed to get back to Fort Lauderdale. The DOJ lawyer came by to let us know that the search was almost over, and she hoped to have something to us in an hour.

"Will you be okay waiting here by yourself?" Lindsey asked.

"Of course," I said, encouraging her to get on the road so she could make it back to Fort Lauderdale in time. I knew she might hit traffic. I was alone, again, outside the ballroom waiting for an update.

What's in Those Boxes?

At this point, agents started walking from the storage area back across my pathway into the ballroom with boxes in hand. I took out my phone and started filming. I couldn't tell what was in the boxes or whether the agents had brought them to the search, or if they were boxes from the storage room. All I knew was that agents were carrying boxes from the storage area into the ballroom. I needed to call Evan.

"Hey. What's the latest?" Evan asked, calmly looking for an update.

"Well, I know we're nearing the end of the search, because DOJ let me know that she expected to be done soon. I'm outside the ballroom and agents are carrying boxes into the ballroom," I said.

"What kind of boxes? Did they come from the storage room?" Evan asked.

"I don't know. I think so. They are brown moving boxes. It looks like they could be original boxes from the storage room, but I really can't tell. I don't know why they are taking them into the ballroom."

"Are they putting them in the Ryder truck?" Evan asked.

Dang it! The Ryder truck was missing. I hadn't noticed that they'd moved it. They must have done it when I went to the bathroom. "Ugh! The truck has been moved! They must have moved it around back to load boxes," I said, annoyed that I hadn't noticed the missing truck. I wasn't sure if I should try to run around to the back of the property and watch them load the truck or stay where I was to watch the agents carrying the boxes.

"Can you tell what's in the boxes?" Evan asked.

"No, but I did see one agent with a clear Rubbermaid tub. I could see inside and it had classified cover sheets in it. It looked like they brought those materials with them to use in case they came across classified documents and they needed to transport them," I said.

"Classified cover sheets?" Evan sounded confused. "Why would they have those?" Evan asked, almost to himself, clearly believing there were no classified documents on the property.

"Well, they would need them if they found classified documents. It doesn't mean that they did. I'm pretty confident those were just cover sheets they brought in, because if they had classified documents, they couldn't transport them in a clear Rubbermaid container," I said referencing the proper way to transport classified documents. "So, I think those are just their materials they brought with them."

It could have been these same classified cover sheets that the FBI used to stage the photos that they leaked to the press. The famous classified docs photo from the raid—was it nothing more than a picture of the materials the FBI brought with them to the raid? Court documents later claimed those file folders were found on-site—if you believe DOJ.

"You haven't seen them moving classified documents, have you?" Evan asked. It was the first time he sounded concerned that day.

"No," I responded. "But I wouldn't see classified documents if they were moving them. They wouldn't carry them openly, so I don't know."

"Hmmm." Evan was thinking. "Keep me posted."

I called Susie and gave her the same information I gave Evan. "That doesn't sound good," she said.

"I don't know. It doesn't mean they found classified documents, but it sure looks like they were working with classified docs," I said.

"Have you talked to Evan?" she asked.

"Yes, but he didn't really have much to say about it. He's waiting until I learn for certain whether there were classified docs or not," I explained.

"Okay. Keep me posted." Susie seemed more concerned than Evan.

A short time later, the DOJ attorney on-site stopped by and quickly said, "Well, we found classified documents."

"That's not possible. There was a thorough search and everything was turned over," I said.

"Apparently not," she said, and went back into the ballroom.

I immediately called Evan back. "Evan," I was direct, "they're saying they found classified documents."

He was quiet for a moment, then said, "That's not good." He paused for another moment, then continued, "Did they say *where* they found the documents? Was it the storage room, or the office, or residence?"

"I don't know. She's coming back right now," I said as I saw the DOJ lawyer approaching me again. "Let me ask her and I'll call you back." We hung up.

"Where did you find the classified documents?" I asked her.

"Everywhere. There were dozens. We found *a lot*," she said, calmly and professionally.

"That can't be right. A very thorough search was done and all the documents were turned over," I pushed back, questioning myself more than her.

Another attorney from the Department of Justice in Washington, DC, was walking by and she stopped him. "Hey, where did you find most of the classified documents?" she asked him.

"All over," he said. "Most were in the office, but we found a lot in the storage room too," he said plainly and then continued to walk into the ballroom.

She turned to me and said, "Yeah. We found a lot of classified documents in multiple places. Weren't you the custodian of records?" she asked me professionally.

"Yes. I was," I acknowledged. "That's why I'm having a hard time believing this. I am aware that a thorough search turned everything over."

She shrugged and said, "Nope," as she continued inside the ballroom.

I called Evan back. "Evan, they say they found classified documents in the storage room and the office," I said with a bit of urgency, expecting an explanation from him.

"Okay," Evan said, as he thought about the situation before he meekly added, "Well, I didn't search the office."

"You didn't search the office?" I asked calmly. I wanted to strangle him through the phone, but I tried to keep my composure. "Why didn't you search the office?" I asked, wondering if the office was part of the original subpoena. I'd never seen the subpoena, but was under the impression it only covered the storage area. Now I wondered if the subpoena was broader. Everything happened so fast, I never asked Evan about it during the raid. It came up later.

"I didn't think there were any classified documents there and I didn't think it was part of the area to be searched." Evan was a bit more nervous now than when I had spoken with him earlier.

"Evan, you had me sign a document swearing that you had done a *thorough* search, and that everything had been turned over."

He cut me off before I could finish. "Christina, don't worry. The statement you signed is true. *Based on the information provided to you—* the statement is true. I will clear it all up if anyone even asks about it. I will acknowledge that I told you I did a thorough search. Don't worry about that." He seemed genuinely willing to clear up any questions, which made me feel a little better. I really didn't like being in that position.

"Okay. They need someone to sign for the warrant and the inventory list," I said. The inventory list is the list of items that the FBI seized in the raid. "I'm the only one here, so I'll get the warrant and the inventory list to you right away. I'll send you pics from my phone and then scan and email everything once I get home."

"Okay," said Evan. "Let me check with the President and make sure he's okay with you signing for it."

Oh, now *you're being careful?* Still, he was right—I did need express consent to sign for the warrant. He called me back a few minutes later saying I had permission to sign for it.

The DOJ lawyer came back outside for a moment and told me that the search had almost wrapped up. It was now about 6:00 p.m., and I still didn't have the warrant or the inventory list. She said the agents were finalizing the inventory list now and she would be back out shortly to review it with me. She asked me if I was authorized to sign for the warrant.

"That's why I'm here," I said dryly. I could have been a little nicer, but after eight hours in the Florida sun, no food, and limited water, I was annoyed at everyone and short on charm. I'd been outnumbered by a few dozen FBI agents all day, and I'd just learned that my colleague possibly had me sign an inaccurate statement which he gave to DOJ. Everyone was on my shit list. I just wanted the warrant, the inventory list, and dinner.

CHAPTER 8

The Bogus Inventory List

At around 6:15 p.m., the DOJ lawyer re-emerged from the ballroom, a burst of cool air wafting over me as she opened the door to join me in the heat. She had a supervisory special agent and a special agent with her, as well as another DOJ lawyer. I was soaked with sweat and hoped they couldn't see it on my clothes. Any hair that wasn't plastered to my face had been pulled up in a ponytail earlier to keep it from sticking to my neck. My flip-flops stuck to my feet, and my shorts stuck to my legs. After eight hours of standing in the humid Florida summer heat, without food, I was physically and emotionally exhausted.

The DOJ and FBI agents stood around me as I sat at the base of the pillars outside the ballroom. I was too tired to stand up, and they didn't make me. One of them handed me the first inventory list, which had the longer list of items seized in the raid. The DOJ lawyer explained to me that this was the inventory of everything they seized. Scanning the list, I realized it was mostly useless.

The first item on the list was "1- Executive Grant of Clemency re: Roger Jason Stone, Jr." *Really?* I thought. *Roger Stone's grant of clemency? That is what you wanted? You raided President Trump's personal residence, setting an unconscionable precedent of political opposition—for*

Roger Stone's clemency grant! Unbelievable. The list continued: Info re: President of France. Wow.

Box labeled A-1, Box labeled A-12, Box labeled A-15 . . . How was I supposed to know what was in the boxes?

"This doesn't tell me anything," I said dryly. "How am I supposed to know what you actually took?"

The DOJ lawyer was polite but not willing to give me any information. "This is how we've labeled the boxes," she said.

"I understand that, but it's not how *we* know the boxes. So I have no way of knowing what's in each box you took. Did you take entire boxes of documents, or did you remove the items that you wanted and put them in a new box? In other words, are these boxes original to this property? Or did you create them when you were taking items?" I asked.

The DOJ attorney just looked at me and waited for me to ask all my questions, both of us knowing she wasn't going to answer any of them.

I continued. "But I also see here that it says 'Miscellaneous confidential documents.' Those appear to be loose documents that you took, not in a specific box," I looked to the DOJ lawyer to explain why some were loose documents, some were complete boxes, and there didn't appear to be a rhyme or reason for either.

"Correct, we also took separate documents. The agents had the ability to do both, take boxes or documents. It's their discretion," she said.

"This list doesn't really tell me anything," I said, pointing out the obvious.

The DOJ lawyer shook her head and said, "I can't say what it does or doesn't tell you." She asked me to sign the bottom of the inventory list and write my title under my name. I did.

A few seconds of silence passed before she continued. "Okay, here's the second inventory list," she said as she handed me a much shorter list with only six items on it. "This is the list of potentially privileged information that we've seized."

"Wait," I stopped her. "You seized privileged information?!"

"*Potentially* privileged. That means when we saw something that looked like it could be attorney-client privileged or executive privilege, we noted it." She seemed to believe that would make me feel better.

"You're actually taking attorney-client privileged information out of President Trump's office? That's so wrong!" I said.

"*Potentially*," she stressed again. "We'll have a separate team look at it, isolated from the team investigating this case." Again, she seemed to think that would make me feel better. It didn't. "When the agents were going through the boxes, if they saw something responsive to the subpoena, they took the entire box," said the DOJ lawyer. "Some of those boxes contained *potentially* privileged information."

"You could have just removed the responsive pieces and respected the privilege," I said. "You *could* have respected privilege," I pointed out, knowing it wasn't going to change anything.

She tilted her head as if to say, *That's not how we do things.*

There was no way the Department of Justice could appropriately compartmentalize this information. They'd proven repeatedly to leak like a sieve. Worse, they clearly believed Donald Trump was a criminal; they just needed to find the crime he committed. They'd been looking for seven years and found nothing. But that hadn't stopped them from looking.

There was no way they could objectively evaluate his attorney-client privileged documents. I didn't care which team within DOJ did it. The entire department was suspect when it came to Donald Trump. But I knew there was nothing I could do about it right then and there. The lawyers handling this case would have to fight it in court. I just needed to sign for the inventory and the warrant, and get the information to Evan.

The DOJ attorney handed me the privileged inventory log and asked me to sign it. She had me sign two copies, one for me and one for her. She then had the agent and supervisory agent sign as well. I handed my copies back to the DOJ lawyer and asked her to have the agents sign my copies too, so that I had complete copies. They did and gave them back to me, time stamped at 6:19 p.m. I had what I needed.

After the DOJ lawyers and FBI agents went back into the ballroom, the lead Secret Service agent that had accompanied them all day came out to speak with me.

"Hey, Christina. They are done and have vacated all three areas that they searched. Did you want to go into the storage room, residence, and office to see the areas now that they're out?" he asked.

"Have you seen those areas?" I asked.

"Yes. I did. I watched them all day, and I was the last one out to make sure everything was in order," he said.

"Did they toss the place, or were they at least decent?" I asked.

"They did not toss the place," he assured me. "Everything was done orderly, and they left it in order. You can have the maintenance manager let you back into those areas if you want to check it for yourself before you go," he offered.

"You're positive the areas are in good condition?"

"Yes. Absolutely, but you're welcome to go check," he said as he went back into the ballroom to make sure the FBI made it out and off the property.

I thought about it for a minute, and decided not to. The Trumps just had their personal belongings and space violated by dozens of people. They didn't need one more person rummaging through their private lives.

Follow-Up with POTUS

Throughout this long, hot, frustrating day, I had called Evan, Susie, and President Trump himself with updates. Now I called the President one last time to inform him I had received the warrant and inventory list. The raid was over.

I closed the call screen on my phone and took a minute to walk back to my car. I still needed to close out with Evan, but I needed a second and preferred to talk to him from my car anyway, where I could use the air conditioning.

Evan picked up right away and got straight to the point. "Did you get it?"

"Yes. I have a copy of it in my hand. I'm taking pictures of it and sending them to you. Let me know once you get them and I'll explain to you what DOJ explained to me."

"Okay," he said as he waited for the pictures to go through.

"Once I get home, I'll scan and send you the document in a PDF," I explained.

"Okay. All right, I've got the pictures. What am I looking at?"

Evan and I spent the next five to ten minutes going through the inventory list. I explained the difference in the two lists, and that DOJ had taken attorney-client privileged information, and likely executive-privileged documents as well. The conversation was straightforward, both of us acknowledging that the inventory list didn't really tell us anything. I promised to get him a PDF copy as soon as I got home.

Once I hung up the phone with Evan, I noticed a Save America email notification of a statement by Donald J. Trump. The President issued his public statement at 6:51 p.m., notifying the world that his "beautiful home, Mar-A-Lago in Palm Beach, Florida, is currently under siege, raided, and occupied by a large group of FBI agents." Word was out, thank God. I was grateful that the statement published as I was leaving. Who knows what would happen, now that word was out. I was eager to leave.

The Drive Home

I pulled out of Mar-a-Lago like I had many times before, but this time it felt different. It felt dirty. I made the rest of the thirty-minute drive home in silence, without the radio, just trying to process what had happened. As I neared my home, I debated whether to stop for food or go straight home to shower. Uncertain of what I needed most in that moment, I pulled into a nearby parking lot and just sat in the car, finally letting my brain process the day. Susie would know what to say.

"Hi. How are you?" Susie was kind and gentle.

"I'm okay. I think. I don't know what I think. Today was a really terrible day. Not just terrible for me. Terrible for our nation. What are they doing? Why are they doing it?" I said almost to myself.

"It was a very ugly day," she agreed. "It was a really tough day for all of us. I can't imagine what it was like for you. How are you doing? Are you feeling okay?" She seemed genuinely concerned for me.

Susie was the first person to sincerely ask me how I was feeling, and I didn't know. Violated, overpowered, humiliated, powerless, exhausted. What else did I feel? How could I explain what I was feeling?

I quietly responded, "I feel like someone I care deeply about was raped today and I had to stand there and watch for eight hours." Certainly, I care about President Trump and hated to see his home violated, but my grief wasn't for him personally. The raid was a violation of all of us. It was a raid on America and the freedoms we proudly boast to the world. Some may criticize me for the analogy, but that was honestly what most closely matched my emotions. It's what I told Susie. It's how I truly felt.

Susie gently responded, "Oh. Take care of yourself. Do what you need to do tonight to feel better and call me tomorrow when you're up for it. You did a great job today. I really believe you were the perfect person to be there. I couldn't have picked anyone better."

"Thank you," I answered weakly. She did make me feel better, and I was truly grateful for her. "I'll call you tomorrow."

I grabbed some food, drove home, and emailed a scanned PDF of the warrant and inventory list to Evan. Now that President Trump had put a statement out, I was free to speak about what happened—and I had a lot to say.

CHAPTER 9

In the FBI's Crosshairs

Not long after arriving home and getting cleaned up, my phone started blowing up from reporters. The *Washington Post*, the *New York Times*, *Bloomberg News*, CNN, NBC, the *Wall Street Journal*, and any other publication you've ever heard of. I was eager to recount my experience and share it with the public, but I wanted to make sure it wasn't through an outlet that would twist my words or mislead the public. I knew from bitter experience that most of them do.

I anticipated that the Department of Justice would come out with a strong—likely misleading—statement about why they raided, what they expected to find, and all the dirty crimes they believed they could pin on the President. The truth is there were no crimes committed, by anyone. But that wouldn't look good for the Department of Justice—who had just scuttled our Fourth Amendment freedoms in one of the most shocking, corrupt moves in the history of our nation.

I would not sit silently by as DOJ crafted their own narrative, disregarding the truth and painting a radically different picture of what transpired. The public needed to know the truth and I was ready to tell it.

Ed Henry reached out to me from Real America's Voice (he's now with Newsmax) and asked me to join their live morning show. Real America's Voice is a conservative network and I've gotten to know many of their reporters and videographers from my time at One America News. I agreed to join Ed Henry and Karyn Turk on their live morning show the next day.

Both hosts were warm and gracious and allowed me to tell about my experience without cutting me off. Karyn asked a few questions, which resonated with me as questions the audience probably had as well. She asked me if I was concerned that the FBI had planted evidence. At the time, I had no information suggesting that the FBI had planted evidence, and said so. But I added that we know the FBI has a history of falsifying evidence and lying to the court, so I'd reserve judgment until the conclusion of the case. The fact that the FBI refused to allow me to observe them certainly fueled my suspicion, but by itself was not proof of anything.

Karyn then asked the appropriate follow-up questions: What happens in a situation like that? How would President Trump be able to combat falsified evidence if the FBI planted anything? We had a brief exchange over the fact that the case would then become a he-said-she-said type case, and that the government had the burden to prove their case beyond a reasonable doubt, which they likely couldn't do. Then the interview ended.

Liberal media outlets, bloggers, and typical trolls got to work trying to discredit me, writing stories about how I accused the FBI of planting evidence. I didn't. But facts don't seem to matter to radicals trying to push an altered version of reality. DOJ and the FBI looked terrible, and their flunkies needed to help take the heat off them and put pressure on Team Trump.

From my perspective, this would now be a media war to shape the perception of the American people. I never believed the Department of Justice had any actionable evidence against Donald Trump. I don't believe there were any top-secret documents that threatened our national security at Mar-a-Lago. I don't believe Donald Trump mishandled any documents. I don't believe Donald Trump did anything to warrant a raid on his home. What do they have to show for themselves? Not much.

Fifteen Days to Execute the Warrant

One key point that I pushed during my media interviews was that the warrant was signed three days prior to the raid and gave DOJ fifteen days to execute it. That surprised me. Typically, a warrant needed for national security purposes would need to be executed "forthwith," which means the agents leave the judge's chambers and immediately execute the warrant. After all, wasn't this a matter of utmost national security? Wasn't our entire republic at stake?

There was no urgency, because they knew there was no real threat. It was a sham. The agents had three days between when they got the warrant signed on Friday and when they actually executed it on Monday. Did they play a round of golf in West Palm Beach over the weekend? Or indulge in an afternoon on the beach? If they were really concerned about our national security, what took them so long to execute the warrant, and why did the judge give them fifteen days?

The Media Covers for DOJ

Over the next few days, I spent most of my time doing interviews. Between interviews, I'd check the news to see what the Left was saying. Had DOJ issued their statement yet? Nope. That's odd, I thought. Surely, they'll make a statement soon. DOJ hadn't come out directly, but had clearly been leaking pieces of information, true or not, to their trusted media outlets at the *New York Times* and *Washington Post*.

One ridiculous speculation that the Left pushed, when they had nothing else to say, was that the raid recovered nuclear secrets that put our national security at risk.[1] Any proof? Nope—it's classified.

Was the FBI actually accusing Donald Trump of selling nuclear secrets to our adversaries? Were they accusing Donald Trump of trying to make money from our nuclear secrets in some bizarre way? Of course not. I'm confident the FBI and DOJ had no information to prove or even suggest he did. But Leftist media outlets ignored the obvious questions. They never even bothered to ask what the secrets were or how anything at Mar-a-Lago put our nation in danger. They just speculated and stirred up doubt. They couldn't tell us because it was classified. Good grief.

The Left also tried to push the lie that the Biden Administration didn't know about the raid and that no one in the Biden Administration approved it. We're supposed to believe that some rogue FBI agents raided the President's home all by themselves, unbeknownst to the Attorney General or the Director of the FBI? You've got to be kidding me. They have so little respect for the American people they actually thought we'd believe that garbage.

During my tenure as the Executive Secretary at the Department of Homeland Security, I worked very closely with the Secretary and the rest of the front office of the Department. No one would *ever* dare to do something so brazen without express *written* Secretary approval. Said another way, Merrick Garland likely had to expressly sign for this operation before the agents would have acted. It also would have had to go through the FBI Director, Christopher Wray.

Any agents acting without the express written consent of at least the Director of the FBI and the Attorney General would have lost their jobs immediately, if not worse. It's truly inconceivable that raiding a former (and potentially future) President's home without approval would ever occur. Just another cowardly lie that the Left tried to hide behind.

As the White House and DOJ leadership tried to distance themselves from the raid, saying that they didn't know about it ahead of time[2], I became fully convinced that they never intended to inform the public about the raid. Biden's Press Secretary, Karine Jean-Pierre, told the American public at a press briefing: "The president and the White House learned about this FBI search from public reports. We learned just like the American public did yesterday and we did not have advanced notice of this activity."[3] Lies. Lies. Lies.

They were completely unprepared for the public backlash. They didn't have a statement ready. They didn't have a communication strategy prepared. They had no response for the anger of the American people, because they never planned on the American people finding out. Days went by without a peep from Merrick Garland, and rumors surfaced that he refused to claim responsibility.

It became glaringly apparent to me that DOJ only planned to disclose the raid to the public if and when they found a way to use it for some case in the future. The grand jury subpoena never leaked, so they likely figured President Trump would keep the raid quiet too. If the public didn't know that the FBI had raided Mar-a-Lago, DOJ was free to use or not use whatever information they wanted, with no accountability.

If the search was fruitless, or didn't provide anything noteworthy, which is likely the reality, they would never have to explain themselves. But once President Trump made it public, they were trapped in the corner they painted themselves in. They needed to explain why they were there and tell the public what crimes they believed were committed.

Think about it. If President Trump had not put out a statement to inform the public, but kept it secret, DOJ could have sat on the information for months, or even a year before announcing they had raided the President's home. President Trump would look as if he had tried to cover up something by not announcing the raid himself. The public might even have believed President Trump was guilty simply because he didn't disclose the raid. Perfect for DOJ. They wouldn't need to prove anything; the public would just assume it.

It's shocking to realize that DOJ never thought through the scenario of *what if President Trump discloses the raid?* They were caught completely unprepared. I continued doing as much media as I could over the next two days to try to take advantage of the fact that DOJ wasn't saying anything.

The public was outraged and demanded an explanation from DOJ, which they refused to give. Even Democrat journalists from far-left outlets like CNN published statements saying the raid was wrong and they expected an explanation from DOJ.

Never to be deterred, radical leftist activists in the media tried to tell the story that President Trump was obviously guilty of something. To make that point, they used the fact that the warrant had been sealed, and that *President Trump* wasn't releasing it. Somehow, leftists argued that President Trump, not DOJ, owed the nation an explanation.

War for the Narrative

A few days later, I went on Steve Bannon's podcast, *War Room*. Bannon brought up two crucial points. First, he questioned the evidence that DOJ used to actually get the warrant. That, from my perspective, was the biggest question. Did DOJ tell the magistrate *the whole truth* when requesting the warrant? I find it hard to believe that if they had informed the magistrate that President Trump himself offered DOJ and the FBI free access to whatever they wanted, that the judge still would have approved the warrant. The FBI has a history of lying to courts when it comes to President Trump, and I still wonder if they lied in this case too.

The second crucial point Bannon raised in my interview was the fact that DOJ was silent on the raid. It had been three days since the raid, and they had not issued a statement or metaphorically done a victory lap. Why not? "Normally when you do a raid like this," I said, "you hold a press conference. This was historic. And we have heard nothing from the Department of Justice or the FBI, both of which have their own briefing rooms. Just as the White House holds press briefings, they can hold their own. The briefing room is for such a time as this. Tell us what you did, why you did it. What's your probable cause? Explain yourself to the American people. Now they've gone radio silent, and they're trying to distance themselves."

In his closing remarks with me, Bannon responded, "Let's see the affidavit, and let's see it today."

Hours after Steve Bannon made the case on his show, the Department of Justice announced that Attorney General Merrick Garland would hold a press conference that afternoon.

Judicial Watch Steps Up

Two days earlier, on August 9, 2022, and less than twenty-four hours after the raid on Mar-a-Lago, Judicial Watch had filed a motion with the court asking the Southern District of Florida to unseal the search warrant and accompanying materials. Judicial Watch relentlessly investigates apparent government overreach and abuse of power. Their timely motion to unseal the documents, along with pressure from media heavyweights like Bannon, likely played a pivotal role in Attorney General Merrick Garland's decision to hold a briefing and announce his position, especially considering the court had not yet held a hearing or made a ruling on Judicial Watch's motion.

DOJ Makes an Appearance

On the afternoon of August 11, 2022, Merrick Garland took the podium in the briefing room at the Department of Justice in Washington, DC, to address the raid on Mar-a-Lago. For three days, the Department had been completely silent on the shocking invasion of Biden's political rival, and likely the most popular President in American history, Donald Trump. Now, Garland would finally address the questions himself, publicly.

I braced myself for baseless accusations against President Trump as Biden's Attorney General paraded on national television some great victory he'd accomplished. Would he claim he saved the nation from some grave catastrophe that's so top secret no one can ever know about it? Who knew what he was going to say? Whatever he did, I expected it to be big. He needed to quell the outrage and give the liberal media outlets something to work with. He did neither.

Merrick Garland addressed the reporters from a prepared statement that took approximately three and a half minutes to read. He opened with, "Since I became Attorney General, I have made clear that the Department of Justice will speak through its court filings, and its work." *Wow*, I thought, *he's on defense!* It was a terrible way to start, which told me he didn't have an answer for the public's outrage.

Garland then said that DOJ had filed a request to unseal the search warrant and inventory list so that the public could view them. He then spent the next three minutes reiterating what the public already knew: DOJ had a court-approved warrant for the raid; they raided the approved property, which was the residence of the former President; the matter was still under investigation. Blah, blah, blah.

The only fact of any significance revealed in his speech was that Merrick Garland himself had ordered the raid. He personally approved it. Rather than taking pride in that fact, he appeared to be taking responsibility for something the Biden Administration had already lied about.[4]

Garland's performance confirmed, in my mind, that DOJ never intended to make the raid public. Garland was completely unprepared and on defense. Based on his weak scripted statement, I was sure that

DOJ would have kept the raid a secret until they found a way to use it against President Trump. They never anticipated he would expose it first.

Garland's entire speech, including his walkout, departure, and attempted press questions, totaled three minutes and fifty-six seconds.[5] I was shocked that the Attorney General's statement was so pathetic, especially after the White House Press Secretary had said from the White House podium that no one in the White House was aware of the raid. They were sacrificing their Attorney General. If it wasn't so tragic, it would be a joke.

FBI Stole Passports and Personal Effects

Shortly after the raid, President Trump announced that the FBI had seized three of his passports. He had a diplomatic passport, a personal passport, and one expired passport. Clearly, the FBI had gone *way* outside their authority and seized whatever they wanted, without regard to the limits of the warrant.

Liberal media outlets salivated over the idea that the FBI stole President Trump's passports to prevent him from leaving the country. They wrote fantasy "news," telling the public this was a sure sign President Trump was about to get indicted. Fake news. It had exactly zero basis in reality. If DOJ wants to prevent someone from leaving the country, they don't break into his house and steal passports. They get a court order.

Not only did DOJ not have a court order to prevent President Trump from leaving the country, but they also didn't have any authority to take his passports, and were forced to acknowledge that. A few days later, DOJ returned the illegally seized items back to President Trump, acknowledging they should never have been taken in the first place.

Seizing personal items, including President Trump's passports and other personal objects, shows a complete disregard for the rule of law.

Taking something that belongs to another person that you do not have authority to take is typically called theft. Unless you're the FBI, I guess. The FBI has an obligation to honor the authority they've been given by not abusing it. If they are this cavalier while ransacking the President's home, imagine how they treat ordinary Americans.

Court Cases and Criminal Lawyers

For a week, Team Trump and liberal pundits duked it out in the press over what should be released and why. On August 18, 2022, Magistrate Judge Bruce Reinhart, the judge who had approved the warrant in the first place, heard the dispute brought by Judicial Watch over whether the government needed to release the warrant and accompanying documents. Judicial Watch, now joined by most major media outlets, sought the release of all the documents, to include the affidavit. The government opposed releasing the affidavit but did not object to the others.

By the end of the hearing, Judge Reinhart ruled that DOJ would need to release a redacted version of the affidavit, and that DOJ would get the first crack at the redactions. If the judge didn't like their redactions, he would un-redact them and order it released. They had a week to complete the redactions. End of hearing.

A week later, after DOJ and the court agreed on the redacted version, I quickly read the entire thing to determine whether the FBI had informed the judge that President Trump had fully cooperated. They hadn't. There was nothing in the affidavit about President Trump's cooperation. The FBI had misled the court, again.

The raid was completely unnecessary, because President Trump had personally told the FBI and DOJ that he was fully cooperating and willing to show them whatever they wanted. "Anything you need, just ask," he had said. They didn't ask. They lied to the court, forced their way into his home, and took whatever they wanted.

CHAPTER 10

Time to Get a Lawyer

A day after the hearing, I finally headed to Tennessee to visit my family. What was supposed to be a trip for the month of August turned into five days. It was a nice respite from the craziness surrounding the raid.

I was not watching the news, checking my social media, or following the headlines at all, trying to take a break from the horrible attacks and things people were saying about me. But when my phone started ringing I thought, *Huh, I wonder what's prompting the new flurry of requests.*

Then, I started getting text messages from friends: "How are you? Are you okay? Do you need anything."

What on earth is going on? I wondered.

Then the questions started getting more specific. "Are you going to cut a deal with DOJ to avoid prison? Are you going to turn on President Trump? Would you testify against President Trump?"

What the hell is happening? I thought.

Finally, Chris Kise, President Trump's new attorney, called. "I'm just checking in on you. How are you holding up?" he said.

"What the hell is going on?" I said, sounding terribly sick from a bad cold I'd developed. "Why is everyone now texting me again?"

"Oh boy. You sound terrible," he said. "Well, have you seen the latest court filing?"

"No." I hadn't seen anything, dreading what he'd say next.

"Here. I'm texting it to you now," he said. "You're getting blown up because DOJ raised it in their latest pleading."

I checked my texts and opened the attachment, skimming to the part where DOJ raised my certification. Page 8, subsection F is titled:

> In Response to the Subpoena, Counsel for the Former President Provided a Limited Number of Documents Accompanied by a Certification that All Responsive Documents Were Produced Following a Diligent Search.

Hmmm. I wondered if DOJ would try to paint me as someone who intentionally deceived DOJ and was a co-conspirator in some nonexistent conspiracy theory. I held my breath and braced for the worst as I read that section. The body of the argument states:

> On June 3, 2022, three FBI agents and a DOJ attorney arrived at the Premises to accept receipt of the materials. In addition to counsel for the former President, another individual was also present as the custodian of records for the former President's post-presidential office. . . . The individual present as the custodian of records produced and provided a signed certification letter, which state in part the following:
>
> Based upon the information that has been provided to me, I am authorized to certify, on behalf of the Office of Donald J. Trump, the following: a. A diligent search was conducted of the boxes that were moved from the White House to Florida; b. This search was conducted after receipt of the subpoena, in order to locate any and all documents

that are responsive to the subpoena; c. Any and all responsive documents accompany this certification; and d. No copy, written notation, or reproduction of any kind was retained as to any responsive document.

I swear or affirm that the above statements are true and correct to the best of my knowledge.

That was it. There was nothing else in the thirty-six-page document referencing me. Okay, I thought. That's not so bad. It also doesn't accuse me of a crime.

I said to Chris, "Okay. I mean, it sucks that I'm in this position, but they don't accuse me of a crime. Why should I be concerned about this?"

"Well, it's not great. You're right that they don't accuse you of a crime, but the fact that they raised it at all isn't good." He waited for my reaction.

"Okay," I said somewhat plainly. I wasn't thrilled, but I also knew I hadn't committed any crimes. Surely this would all get cleared up through a simple discussion.

"So, remember how I told you I would tell you if I ever thought you needed to retain an attorney?" he asked.

"Yeeeeesss?" I said, not liking where this was going.

"Now would be that time," Chris said.

Getting a Lawyer

On September 7, 2022, I met with my new lawyer, John Lauro, and Chris Kise in Tampa for a day of questioning and preparation.

I was sick over the whole situation. I hadn't done anything wrong but was sure that DOJ wanted a Trump ally to hang in the press and put pressure on the President. Would DOJ hang me just to hurt Donald Trump?

"Okay, let's play worst case scenario," I said. "If they try to prosecute me, it would have to be in Florida, right? I live in Florida, I signed the certification in Florida, and the June third meeting was in Florida. Every single event that took place took place in Florida. Jurisdiction is in Florida, right?"

John and Chris looked at each other and winced. Chris said, "The case should be brought in Florida for all the reasons you stated, but they would most likely try to bring it in DC, because the grand jury is currently in Washington."

That felt so corrupt to me. The grand jury for these facts *should have been in Florida!* As it related to this incident, I had nothing to do with DC. I hadn't even been there since I moved to Florida. DOJ would want to bring the case in DC simply because it would be easier for them to get a conviction. I knew I hadn't committed any crime, but I was nervous that DOJ just wanted a prosecution and would do whatever they could to frame me. They'd already done that with the January 6th protesters. Was I next?

"Okay, so if I *did* get charged, and if I *did* go to trial, I'm supposed to expect to get a fair trial in Washington, DC? There's no way! DC is so liberal and the entire jury would convict me of anything DOJ brings just because I work for President Trump!" I pushed back, hoping they would somehow convince me I wouldn't be a political prisoner.

"Christina, I think it's very unlikely that you're going to get charged," said John, "and if you do get charged, I'm very comfortable taking this to trial right away. It's clear you did nothing wrong. Honestly, DOJ would look so stupid if they actually tried to prosecute you."

"Do you think you could win this case in Washington, DC, with a staunchly liberal jury?" I asked John, curious what he'd say.

He thought about my question for no more than two seconds and said, "Yes. I could win this case in Washington, DC. I could win it tomorrow," he said emphasizing his confidence in the facts of my case.

"With a liberal jury?" I added a condition he forgot to mention.

"With a liberal jury. Yes," John said.

I looked over at Chris to see his reaction to my exchange with John. He looked at me and nodded confidently saying, "This would be a very difficult case for DOJ to prosecute, and they would look really bad doing it. I don't think they'll prosecute you. I do think they'll force you to testify before the grand jury, but that will likely be it."

Rumors of a Target Letter

"Hang on. I just got a text from CNN asking me to confirm that I've received a target letter from the FBI? What's that all about? Do you know what they're talking about?" I asked the two experienced criminal defense attorneys, hoping they'd tell me everything was fine.

Chris blew it off. "That's stupid. They're just fishing. Don't let it bother you. They really *want* you to be a target, so they hope if they write it, it will come true. There's no way you're a target."

My only experience as a criminal attorney was as a defense counsel in the Marine Corps. Military justice is substantially different from federal criminal defense. I wanted to make sure I understood exactly what we were talking about. "Okay. This may be obvious, but please explain to me what a target letter is, just so I fully understand what we're talking about." I asked the obvious question to make sure I wasn't taking anything for granted.

Chris jumped in: "A target letter is official correspondence from the FBI advising you that they are targeting you in an investigation. That's it. It gives you a chance to obtain counsel, review your rights, but other than that, that's it."

John added, "A target letter is a formality, and usually the first step before an indictment. It gives the defendant an opportunity to prepare for a legal battle." He could see that I was concerned.

"How do I know if the press is right?" I asked.

"We wait and see how the FBI contacts you," John said. "Christina, the government is required to notify you if you are a target of their investigation. They cannot subpoena you to testify without telling you that you are a target of the grand jury. If you *are* a target, the best they can do is *invite* you to testify before the grand jury that may end up indicting you," my attorney said, trying to calm me down from the unfair and awful accusations. "This entire situation as it relates to you will be cleared up by a conversation. We'll have to have a discussion with the FBI, but that will likely be the end of any threats of indictment as it relates to you."

I went back and forth with John on the specifics of a target letter, a grand jury subpoena, testimony, interviews, anything and everything that could possibly happen. We talked for hours until I felt like an expert on the topic. The significance of a target letter didn't hit me at the time, but this experience became invaluable to me two years later when the Arizona Attorney General was a bit too zealous in her political crusade to jail Trump supporters.

The FBI and Reading My Rights

After meeting with John and Chris all day, I immediately drove three hours home from Tampa. I was exhausted. So the next day, I sat in my home office in my sweatshirt and running shorts, working through emails and responding to various issues. My home office window faces the street, and I noticed a black car in front of my house that I hadn't seen in the neighborhood before. Was the FBI stalking me? *No way, that's ridiculous.* A few minutes later, the doorbell rang.

As I opened the door, two agents held out their badges and announced themselves as FBI. *Ha!* I thought to myself. *I'm not so crazy after all.*

The female agent had a manila envelope in her hand. This was not my first visit from federal agents, so I knew the drill. Without saying anything, I just held out my hand to receive whatever they were there to deliver.

One of the agents said, "We're looking for Christina Bobb."

I nodded and again put out my hand. They didn't look like they were there to arrest me, but it's quite unsettling for federal law enforcement to show up at your personal home, uninvited. I wanted them to leave as quickly as possible. "We're here to formally serve you on behalf of the FBI." She hesitated before giving me the folder, apparently not done with her explanation, but she handed it to me anyway.

I started to close the door when she said, "Oh wait—all of your rights are written down for you and you can read them inside the envelope. Please make sure you understand your rights."

My rights are written down for me. Great. "Okay, what is this?" I asked.

"A subpoena. It's a grand jury subpoena," she said.

I instantly felt relieved that I wasn't being targeted, at least not yet.

"Have a nice day," they said.

"Thanks. You too," I said, and closed the door.

I walked over to my kitchen counter and took a deep breath before opening the envelope. There were four pages loosely stacked inside. As the document slid out from the envelope, the front page said "United States District Court for the District of Columbia." The next line said in all caps "SUBPOENA TO TESTIFY BEFORE A GRAND JURY." It was dated September 6, 2022, and signed by the clerk of the court.

September 6 was the day *before* I met with Chris and John. That means the whole "target letter" rumor was completely fake news and had no basis in reality. The subpoena for my testimony had already been signed. I shouldn't be surprised that the press was pushing fake news, but the level of animosity they show for people who oppose their views still shocks me. They are callous and cruel.

Flipping through the documents, the first two pages were the subpoena and then the declaration of the process server, in this case the FBI. Page three was Attachment A, a "list of documents, information, and objects subpoenaed by grand jury." They wanted any documents that related to my selection as the custodian of records or any communications with President Trump and Evan Corcoran, as it related to my role as custodian of records.

The fourth, and final, page was the "Advice of Rights," which basically was a document that spelled out my Fifth Amendment rights against self-incrimination. Legal counsel was not offered, but the document said I could retain my own counsel. This was the second time in my life I'd been advised of my rights.

Read Me My Rights—Again

The first time I had my rights read to me was at Officer Candidate School (OCS) (the officer equivalent of boot camp) for the United States Marine Corps, in Quantico, Virginia. My suspected crime? While cleaning up gear after an exercise, I had left my rifle farther than arms' distance, without a guard. A cardinal sin in the Marine Corps. You *never* leave your weapon.

One of the drill instructors, a staff sergeant, snagged my rifle and lined up the entire platoon in the squad bay to berate me. She paraded up and down the squad bay with my rifle as I stood at attention. "Don't you know that the enemy could come and steal your rifle and kill you and your entire squad with *your* weapon?" she screamed in my face. "Are you so selfish that you'd sacrifice the lives of your fellow Marines because you're too lazy or too weak to take your rifle with you? Will you visit the families of the Marines that are dead because of your weakness?"

The staff sergeant continued her lashing until the female platoon commander, a captain, came into the room. The captain announced in a loud voice, "Candidate Bobb," referring to my status as an officer candidate, "you are believed to be guilty of the offense under Article 108 of the Uniform Code of Military Justice—wrongful dispossession of military property of the United States." She continued, "You are believed to have willfully or negligently lost, or have been dispossessed, of your service rifle. Do you understand the charge against you?"

"Yes, Ma'am!" I screamed, unsure of the whole situation. Screaming is the only acceptable way to respond at OCS. The rifle clearly wasn't lost. The staff sergeant had it. But it seemed very real, and all the screaming made me nervous.

The platoon commander then proceeded to read me my rights. "You have the right to remain silent. Anything you say can and will be used against you in a court of law. You have the right to an attorney. If you cannot afford an attorney, one will be appointed for you. Do you understand your rights?" she said firmly.

"Yes, Ma'am!" I screamed in response.

"Do you wish to make a statement and explain how you lost your rifle?" she said again, firmly.

"No, Ma'am. This candidate requests counsel," I responded in the third person—there is no "I" permitted at OCS. I didn't know if this was real or not, so I just did what I'd do if it were real.

Her response let me know that I ruined their fun. "Oh. Okay," she said, somewhat surprised. That's when I realized they were going to terrorize me just long enough to teach the lesson that you *never* leave your weapon. The platoon commander then yelled at the entire platoon to sufficiently terrify us all into never leaving weapons or gear behind.

Imagine my surprise when, in August 2021, Joe Biden confirmed the surrender of Afghanistan, where I had served a tour, leaving behind billions of dollars of weapons and gear. The Biden-Harris Administration surrendered "22,171 Humvee vehicles, almost 1,000 armored vehicles, 64,363 machine guns, and 42,000 pick-up trucks and

SUVs."[1] Additionally, under Biden's lack of leadership, the US military left "358,539 assault rifles, 126,295 pistols, and nearly 200 artillery units,"[2] all of which can be used to kill American service members.

Leaving weapons and gear behind is unthinkable, but the truly abhorrent behavior was the fact that the Biden-Harris Administration left American service members to die in a botched withdrawal, while our civilian partners were left to fend for themselves, most likely to die a brutal death at the merciless hands of the Taliban.

I had my rights read to me over a rifle farther than arms' length. Somebody owes this nation, and the grieving families, an explanation.

Turning my attention back to the document in my hand, I finished reading my rights and then texted John Lauro. He coordinated with DOJ and called me to let me know he'd arranged for an interview to clear things up. "Don't worry," he said, "They'll give you a limited immunity—Queen for a Day—so that you can have a candid conversation with them without fear that they'll use it against you."

Ugh. Great. I still didn't understand why I needed to go to DC. How does Washington, DC, have jurisdiction? Didn't this supposed crime occur in Florida?

CHAPTER 11

Not Quite Queen for the Day

Around 3:00 a.m. I woke with my mind racing about what would happen in the next few hours. Unable to get back to sleep, I grabbed my phone and went through my texts. John had texted me the limited immunity agreement, which the government called a "proffer agreement," so I opened it and went through it.

It was terrible. It didn't really protect me from anything. The truth would protect me better than this crappy little agreement. Basically, the agreement said I was not allowed to lie to the FBI or DOJ during the conversation. Got it. I wasn't going to lie anyway.

I was in a position where I knew I wouldn't say anything incriminating, because I hadn't committed any crimes. I can't imagine how people feel who don't know how to document and protect themselves and who are just trying to clear up information. It's a disgusting abuse of authority.

I went through the rest of the document and hated the entire thing. It made me sick. As soon as I signed anything with DOJ, the press would get hold of it and say, "Trump attorney signs immunity agreement to avoid prosecution," even though it's not true. If I actually signed this agreement, it could *only* be used against me.

As badly as the press had treated me over signing the certification, signing an immunity agreement with DOJ would be a thousand times worse. But I knew that if I didn't sign the agreement, I'd be waiving any opportunity for immunity in the future. I needed to talk to John.

To Sign or Not to Sign

I waited until 7:00 a.m. to call John, hoping I wouldn't wake him. "Good morning. How are you?" I said, hoping he wasn't annoyed by my early call.

"Good! How are *you?*" he stressed. "Did you review the agreement?"

"I did. I don't like it and don't want to sign it," I said, and waited for his reaction.

"Okay. Let's just make sure we think this through," John said thoughtfully.

We went round and round for a couple minutes hashing out what my risk would be of talking to the FBI without *any* protection from prosecution. "If DOJ wants to create some BS way to prosecute me when they know I didn't do anything wrong, they're going to. This agreement won't stop them," I said. Ultimately, I decided not to sign it.

John accepted my decision, but I wanted to be sure. "You really think I'm okay to decline immunity?"

"Yes, but let's just be very clear. The FBI hates you. You're about to walk into the Washington Field Office of the FBI, which has spent the last seven years trying to put your boss in prison. They would love nothing more than for you to give them a reason to indict him. If they can't indict him, they could indict you to try to get you to say something incriminating against the President. You do understand that the people you're about to talk with want to see you, your boss, and his supporters in jail, right?"

Ugh. That was a punch to the gut. "Yes. I understand," I said. I hated the idea that I wouldn't get any protection. The FBI or DOJ wouldn't protect me. The only thing that I could use to protect myself, and the President, was *the truth*. Would the truth really set me free? I was about to find out.

Meeting DOJ and the FBI

Our ride pulled up to the Washington Field Office and dropped us off fifteen minutes early. The building is a couple blocks from my old apartment, and I'd walked by it a hundred times, never thinking I'd have a reason to go inside.

We walked into the building, and one of the FBI agents I'd met with at Mar-a-Lago in June was waiting to greet us. She welcomed us, got us checked in through security, and led us to the elevator and up to the corner conference room several floors up.

The conference room was spacious, with windows covering two walls, an extra-large TV on one wall, and a large rectangular table in the middle of the room. John sat next to me at the table; five people sat across from us and introduced themselves.

The prosecutor who signed my subpoena identified himself and said, "We met in Mar-a-Lago outside the ballroom," as he shook my hand.

"Oh yeah!" I recognized him from the raid. He was the attorney who told me they found classified documents in the office and storage room at the end of the raid. He would be leading the questioning today. "Nice to see you again."

The two women to his right, my left, I also recognized as agents I'd met with in June at the meeting with the FBI two months before the raid. I was glad they were there. They reintroduced themselves and gave me their names. The attorney then introduced his other colleagues. There were two more attorneys from DOJ's National Security Division, a man and a woman, both wearing masks, which made me a little nervous. The final introductions came from John. Two attorneys from John's law firm joined the meeting remotely. Their faces appeared on the large TV screen, and they introduced themselves to the group. Then we got started.

"Christina, thank you for coming today. We're happy to talk to you," the attorney leading the questioning said. He opened his binder and said, "So we typically start by going over the limited immunity agreement and making sure you're aware of what it does and doesn't do."

I shook my head no and then looked at John. "We appreciate you doing that, but it's not necessary," John jumped in. "We've reviewed the agreement and don't believe we need it. So, thank you, but we can just get started." The lead attorney looked a bit confused and quickly glanced to his colleagues to gauge their reactions.

I wanted to make sure he knew I was not being difficult by refusing to sign, but wanted to cooperate, so I said, "This is the thing. I understand why you have questions about my involvement in the case and the certification that I signed. So, I'm here to just answer your questions. I'm not trying to make this more than it is, and we don't need a formal agreement. I'm just here to explain what happened."

Everyone on the other side of the table seemed a bit surprised, but didn't say much. The lead attorney said, "Okay! Well, that cuts out the beginning and makes this part easier. That said, you understand that you're talking to the Department of Justice and FBI?" He implied that anything I said could be used to prosecute me.

I nodded.

"So, you can't lie, and anything you say we have the right . . ."

I cut him off before he finished and politely said, "I understand." I didn't want to hear my rights read or the implications of talking to the FBI. I didn't like any of this and just wanted it over with.

"Okay. Great. Let's get started then," he said.

Starting the Interview

The lead DOJ lawyer asked me about my background and work history. They had done a detailed review of my career, and asked me questions about my background, possibly to determine the level of detail and veracity with which I would answer their questions. The questions shifted to my then-current role.

"So, how did you get involved as the custodian of records?" he asked.

I responded, "I had just started working at Save America maybe two months before the June third meeting. When I joined Save America, I moved from Washington, DC, to Florida for the purpose of being in the area in case they needed someone available." I didn't mean for emergencies, I just meant for delivering documents or being physically present for a meeting. Under the circumstances, my response seemed funny.

The DOJ attorney smiled and said, "It didn't take long."

I chuckled. "No. It didn't. I was asked to join a meeting with the FBI on June third. So, I was not familiar with the case at all and had no prior knowledge of any communications with DOJ or the FBI."

The lead DOJ lawyer then slid a stack of papers across the table to me. The document on top was the certification I had signed. "Have you seen this document before?"

"Yes," I acknowledged.

"Is that your signature?" he asked.

"Yes," I said.

"Do you know what this document is?" the attorney asked.

"Yes," I again acknowledged.

He went through a few more questions about the certification to determine if I would challenge the document in any way. Would I try to say it wasn't my signature? Or would I argue the document had been altered after I signed it? Once he was satisfied that I was not challenging the document, or my signature on it, he moved on to the next document, the subpoena.

"Have you seen this document before?" asked the DOJ attorney referencing the grand jury subpoena.

"I have now, yes. I had not seen it until recently though," I said.

"You did not see it prior to signing the certification?" he asked.

"No. I was just told about it."

"When was the first time you saw this subpoena?" he asked.

"My lawyer got a copy of it and showed it to me a couple weeks ago. Maybe a day or two before I was served with this subpoena," I said, pointing down to the table to indicate the grand jury subpoena for the meeting we were having now.

"You hadn't seen this before the meeting on June third either? Or any of the recent events?" he clarified.

"Correct. I had not seen it before I signed the certification, the June third meeting, or the raid," I said. "Actually, I remember wanting to see it during the raid, because I was confused over the scope of the search. I was under the impression that the subpoena only included the storage area. So, when you raided the entire property, I thought you were going way outside the scope of the subpoena. That made me angry."

"Okay," said the lead attorney, leaning back in his chair. "Let's back up. How did you first get involved as the custodian of records?"

"I received a call from Boris Epshteyn the evening prior, June second," I said. Then I looked down at the stack of documents they had handed me, which included my text messages I had disclosed. "Can I use these texts to walk through the story?" I asked. I wanted to make sure I got the order accurate, so using the texts would be helpful.

"Yeah!" the lead DOJ attorney said. "If that helps you remember, go for it."

I pulled out the text messages from my phone that the forensic team had collected. The first one came from Boris Epshteyn connecting me to Evan Corcoran. "Okay, so Boris called me the evening of the second. I'd worked with Boris on and off for almost two years at this point," I said, explaining my relationship to Boris. "He didn't give me a lot of detail but said there would be a meeting at Mar-a-Lago the next day, the third, with the FBI. He told me there was a legal team in Washington, DC, already assigned to the case and handling everything. They just needed someone on site to facilitate the meeting when the legal team turns over the records."

"Did he say anything to you about being a custodian of record?" the lead attorney asked.

"I don't think so. He didn't mention me needing to sign anything," I said. "He just told me there was an attorney from DC who needed a local representative, and asked if he could connect me to him. Boris told me the DC lawyer had already handled everything and that there wasn't much for me to do. He said the DC lawyer would explain everything he needed from me. Boris was just connecting us."

"Then what happened?" asked the lead attorney.

"I told Boris I would help however I could. He said he'd connect me to Evan Corcoran, the DC attorney handling the case, and we could take it from there."

Then, I pointed down to the piece of paper in front of me, which had my text history on it. "You can see this text here, where it's the beginning of a chain with me, Boris, and Evan."

"Had you had any prior communications with Evan?" asked the DOJ attorney.

"No. This was the first time I'd ever communicated with him," I said.

"Did you know him, or know of him, prior to this connection?" asked the lead attorney.

"No. I didn't know of him at all. This was the first time I'd heard his name."

"What happened next?"

"Evan didn't respond right away, but he eventually called me that evening."

"How did the conversation with Evan go?"

"It was cordial. We introduced ourselves. Evan explained that DOJ had subpoenaed the President asking for classified documents and the meeting the next morning was to turn over the documents DOJ had requested. He told me he had done a very thorough search, investigated to determine where responsive documents would be located, and went through everything. He told me he'd 'hermetically sealed' the responsive documents, and he could meet with me in the morning to show me everything that had been done."

The female attorney from DOJ mentioned that Evan had told her something similar.

"What was your reaction to what he told you?" asked the DOJ attorney.

"My initial reaction, talking to him on the phone, was that they had gone overboard on the search and document production. He used the phrase 'hermetically sealed' for how he handled the classified documents. That's not a requirement for how to handle classified documents, so I thought it was overkill. Other than that, I took him at his word, and figured he'd confirm it all for me in the morning when I met him."

"Did he tell you that you were designated as the custodian of records?" asked the lead DOJ lawyer.

"Yes. He told me he needed me to sign a declaration that a thorough search had been done and all responsive documents were being turned over. I told him that I couldn't sign anything about the search or review, because I didn't have personal knowledge of it. Any statement on my part would have to include qualifying language that I was provided the information, and not that I had personal knowledge."

"Did he give you a hard time about that? Was he irritated that you asked for that language?" asked the lead attorney.

"No. Not at all. He was very receptive and said that wouldn't be a problem."

"Then what happened?"

"Nothing, until the next morning. I was anxious to get the document, because I wanted to know exactly what I needed to sign. You can see here from my text messages," I said, pointing down to the paper documenting our conversation, "that I reached out to him again that night and the next morning to try to get a copy."

"Did it upset you that he hadn't sent it to you?" asked one of the FBI agents.

"Yes. I don't take signing something for DOJ lightly. I wanted an opportunity to review and edit it if necessary."

"When did you finally get it?" asked the lead attorney.

"The morning of the meeting. You can see he texted it to me at 7:57 a.m. on June third. But this version didn't have the qualifying language in it," I said, pointing to the original version that I produced to DOJ in response to my subpoena and was in my pile of papers. "See, in the first version he sent me, it doesn't include that language. So," I again pointed to the text message chain, "I texted him again at 7:58 a.m. and said, 'Can we add a phrase that says 'I have been informed . . .'? I don't want it to look like I'm attesting that I was part of the search or review.'"

"That was the second time you had insisted on that language?" asked the lead DOJ attorney.

"Correct." I said.

"Did he make the change?"

"Yes. Right away. You can see he emailed me at 8:08 the updated version. That's the final version that I signed."

"Then what happened?" asked the DOJ lead attorney.

"You can see from the text messages he asked me to print it out and sign it. He also wanted a copy of it. I knew Mar-a-Lago was closed and I wouldn't have access to the office. So, I signed it and emailed it back to him before I went down to Mar-a-Lago. That was the only way we could have an exact copy of what we turned over to you."

Throughout the meeting, I recounted to the best of my recollection the events of the day. They continued to drill down on my thoughts, impressions, and motives for every action. The meeting was nerve-racking, even though both the FBI agents and DOJ attorneys were professional and kind. My stomach was in knots, and I was eager to get through the meeting, but we weren't quite done.

Reviewing Old Ground

"So, when did you get to Mar-a-Lago on June third?" The DOJ attorney continued his questions.

"Based on my text messages," I said, pointing again down to the papers in front of me, "Evan told me to arrive at 11:15 and the meeting would be at 11:30. So, I got there at 11:15," I said.

"Was Evan already there?"

"Yes. He was waiting for me in the living room. The club was closed, so it was very quiet. We were the only ones there. I sat on the sofa across from the chair he was seated in, and we introduced ourselves and discussed our roles and backgrounds briefly," I explained. "Then, I asked him if I could see 'everything.'"

"What did he say?"

"He said there wasn't anything to see. All of the documents had already been culled through. Any responsive documents were sealed, and everything was put away," I said. "I was a bit surprised and didn't know exactly what to say. So Evan offered to show me the storage room. He also offered to open the sealed documents so I could see them. At this point, he showed me what looked like a makeshift folder of cardboard and packing tape."

The FBI agents who had attended the meeting and had received the makeshift folder from Evan smiled and nodded to indicate that's exactly what it was, and none of us knew what to call it, so we called it "the thing."

"I didn't want him to open the thing, because I wouldn't have time to review anything, and I didn't want to be accused of having knowledge of what was inside or accessing classified documents without a clearance. So I told him I didn't want to open it. But I did accept his offer to see the storage room."

I continued to explain the story to DOJ and the FBI. I recounted how Evan showed me the storage room and offered to let me go through the boxes, but I declined. However, I added, at least one of the boxes was open and I could see newspaper articles and media clippings inside. We then went back up and sat at a table in the front dining room, waiting for the FBI to arrive. "And then you guys showed up, and we started the meeting," I said, nodding to the FBI agents in the room who had attended the meeting.

"All right, so even though the agents were there with you, I'd like you to walk us through your recollection of the meeting. Tell me what happened," said the lead DOJ lawyer.

I relayed the sequence of events as I remembered it, but had to be corrected about the timing of President Trump's appearance in the dining room. I was grateful the FBI seemed to believe I had not intentionally misstated the timeline. Once we cleared that up, we moved on to the question of Evan's search.

"There was no one else involved in the search?" she asked.

"No," I said.

"How can you be so certain if you weren't there?" she asked, leaning forward over the table.

"Evan told me that he was the only one who searched the room. No one else at any time has indicated that anyone else was involved in the search. As I sit here, I believe Evan was the only one involved in the search. If you came back to me and said you had video surveillance of someone else, showing a third person was involved, my response would be 'Okay,'" I said as I shrugged my shoulders. "I'm not trying to convince you no one else was involved. I'm simply saying everything that has been presented to me indicates Evan was the only one involved. But you're right. I wasn't there."

"Okay!" she said, satisfied, as she leaned back in her seat again.

My attorney, John, added, "No other names have come up at any point, right?"

"Correct," I said.

The Details

DOJ and the agents went over some of the events again, getting more specific. "So, how much time did you have to evaluate the situation and reconcile it with what Evan told you?" asked the lead attorney.

"A couple minutes," I said. "I arrived fifteen minutes before you did, spoke with Evan for a few minutes, and then realized there wasn't much to see. So, maybe five minutes before you arrived."

The FBI agent on the end smirked and said quietly, "That's more notice than we were given."

"What?!" I asked her. "You didn't know you were going to Florida until the day of?!"

She just smiled and looked like she wasn't going to say any more, but it was clear that the agents were notified at the last minute that they needed to get to Florida immediately. That struck me as odd. Certainly, a meeting like this would take at least a week or two of planning. But based on the reactions from the FBI and DOJ, it appeared that they were in the dark as much as I was. Weird. What happened?

CHAPTER 12

What We Know to Be True

DOJ and the FBI continued to ask me very detailed and nuanced questions, most of which I didn't know the answers to. I told them I was doing my best to answer their questions, but many of my answers were speculation. They dissected my conversations with Evan, and I answered everything as precisely as possible. When they asked what I believed about Evan's intent, I responded "I didn't think anything of it at the time, and I still don't believe that Evan was lying to me. I believe he believed what he was telling me was true."

"How do you reconcile that with what we now know to be true?" asked the lead DOJ lawyer.

"I think Evan didn't properly conduct the search. There appears to be a misunderstanding about what area of the property was to be searched. I didn't know that at the time. I first had this idea at the raid after you told me you found classified documents. I wondered if Evan didn't know what to look for and probably didn't know what different classification markings meant. I also thought, what if he didn't know that 'confidential' is a classification?

"I doubled checked the inventory that you guys put out. The documents that you took from the storage room, most of them were 'confidential.' That's likely because when he searched there, he didn't know he needed to remove documents marked 'confidential,'" I explained.

They all stared back at me blankly as if they didn't agree, which made me a little nervous.

The other male DOJ attorney asked me if I was concerned about the handling of classified documents. "Christina, you've handled classified document throughout your career and even held a TS/SCI clearance. Haven't you been through countless trainings on the proper way to handle classified documents?"

"Yes." I openly acknowledged my training. "By the time I got involved in this matter, there was nothing for me to review or handle. Everything was already done and packed up." He shrugged and nodded as if understanding. "Remember," I continued, "I was under the impression that the subpoena was limited to the storage room. Evan expressly told me the search was limited to the storage room based on discussions he'd had with you, which was why I was confused when you raided the entire property."

I later kicked myself for not adding that when the agents were at Mar-a-Lago, *they* never inquired about anything other than the storage room, which furthered my belief the only area in play was the storage room. The agents' own actions confirmed what Evan told me—they only discussed the storage room.

Because He Said It

"Do you know why the agents weren't allowed to look in the boxes?" asked the lead DOJ attorney.

"I don't think you were denied access to the boxes," I said quizzically. Why would they think they couldn't see in the boxes? "The President himself came and told you that you had access to whatever you wanted."

The agents shifted at my answer, which appeared to be at odds with their perspective. The DOJ attorney continued, "But the agents weren't allowed to look in the boxes, were they?"

"I wouldn't say that. My understanding was that was not the purpose of the visit, but that could have been arranged if you'd asked for it. Like 'not now, but later,'" I said. Remembering back to the June 3 meeting, even DOJ attorney Jay Bratt assumed they wouldn't have access to the storage room. Jay said to Evan "I think I know the answer to this . . ." when he asked for access to the storage room, assuming the answer would be no. I wasn't part of their prior discussions with Evan about the purpose of the meeting, but *they* were. If my belief was wrong, they could correct me if they wanted to. They didn't.

"What makes you believe that the FBI had access to whatever they wanted?" asked the lead DOJ attorney.

"Because the President said it to your face," I responded plainly, thinking the answer was obvious. "He made the effort to personally greet you and let you know that you could have access to whatever you wanted."

"Right," said the lead attorney, "but what was it that made you believe we *actually* had access to look in the boxes if we'd wanted to?"

"Because he said it," I said firmly. "It was important enough to President Trump to personally greet you and let you know you could have access to whatever you wanted." I was starting to get nervous and didn't understand the line of questioning.

One of the agents said, "Okay, but just because the FBI Director comes in and announces something to the room doesn't mean we take it at face value," she said as she pointed to the door, pretending the FBI Director had walked into the room. That struck me as odd. Why wouldn't they take the FBI Director at face value? They *should* obey whatever the Director orders. Don't they?

"I'm not really sure how to answer these questions," I said, sitting very nervous and confused in my seat. President Trump said they could have access. What more did they want?

Fast forward to 2025 when President Trump is back in the White House. It's because of this very attitude that President Trump needed to fire all of the agents that worked this case. They so brazenly defied political leadership that the agents were comfortable arguing to me, a subject of their investigation, that they didn't have to follow the direction of the FBI Director. How could President Trump lead the executive branch, which the FBI is part of, when the agents don't believe they need to follow directions?

Liberal media went to work arguing that President Trump fired "good people" who just "did their jobs."[1] Wrong. These were political activists who burrowed into our nation's top law enforcement agency and believed they were accountable to no one.

A Well-Orchestrated Move

"I'd like to drill down a little bit," said one of the FBI agents. "When we were down in the storage room on June third, everything seemed very coordinated," she said.

"Okay?" I wondered where she was going.

"Did you coordinate beforehand with Evan how that would go?" she asked, seeming to hold something back.

"Um, not really," I said, unsure of where she was going with the question. "I mean, I went down there with Evan before you got there, but that was it."

"Well, what I'm getting at is that it all seemed very orchestrated. There was a moment in time when we weren't allowed to leave the area. Don't you think that was all well-orchestrated?" she asked.

I was so flabbergasted that she thought the meeting was well orchestrated that I accidentally spit as I exhaled sharply through my lips, quickly covering my mouth and apologizing. "Well, I'm glad we gave you that impression," I said smiling, but shaking my head no.

"It wasn't well coordinated and planned out?" she was surprised by my response.

"I mean, no, I don't think so," I said. "If it were well coordinated, I wouldn't be sitting here having this meeting with you." I spread my arms out to the five federal officers questioning me to point out the obvious. Certainly, the meeting could have been better planned than this.

I didn't understand at the time why the FBI would be asking me about the Secret Service standard operating procedures, but it hit me later. The movement was very well orchestrated, but that was the Secret Service, not me or Evan. They interpreted the Secret Service's standard operating procedures as somehow Evan hiding documents.

When the Secret Service moves the President (in this case, when he left Mar-a-Lago after meeting with the FBI), everyone in the area has to stay in place. Because of the Secret Service operation, DOJ believed Evan and I were hiding something, when in fact, it was just normal procedure for another federal law enforcement agency. They could have easily checked with Secret Service to confirm that *they*, not me or Evan, were calling the shots. The FBI was salivating to find evidence of obstruction, so they misconstrued the standard operating procedure of federal law enforcement as "orchestrated" obstruction. How embarrassing.

What Went Wrong

"When you were with Evan, before the FBI showed up, what was your reaction to the situation?" asked the DOJ attorney.

"Once I realized I wasn't going to be able to review anything, I realized the process had not been handled the way that I would handle it, but I didn't think it was wrong at the time," I said.

"So, you think Evan just did sloppy legal work?" asked one of the agents.

"Basically, yeah," I said. John noted that *sloppy* was the FBI's word and was not to be attributed to me.

The room was silent for a few seconds as the attorneys and agents processed my perspective. I wasn't accusing Evan of lying, and I clearly believed the entire ordeal was a mistake and simply handled poorly, but no crime had been committed. After a few seconds of silence, the other male DOJ attorney looked at me and said, "You have very strong convictions. I mean, you're almost visceral in your convictions."

I simply smiled and nodded politely in response, thinking, *So are you*. He wasn't frustrated with my "convictions." He was frustrated I wasn't giving him the answers he wanted.

He continued, "Weren't you concerned at all about the cavalier nature that this was handled? You've had extensive training to handle classified documents. Didn't you have any concern that our national security was at risk?"

This is where it gets political, I thought, so I wanted to be careful. "Honestly, no," I said. "This wasn't my case. I trusted my colleagues to handle the case appropriately. I'm also aware that every administration negotiates with NARA [National Archives and Records Administration] about the documents they take with them. I didn't see this as being any different. The fact that DOJ got involved was abnormal, but President Trump has been treated abnormally for the last seven years. So, the abnormal has become normal in Trumpworld," I said.

He seemed dissatisfied with my response, but didn't push the matter any further.

"Do you know if the documents that were turned over were classified?" asked the other male DOJ lawyer.

"I don't know."

"What about Evan? Did Evan believe the documents were classified?" he asked.

"Yes. Evan believed they were classified," I said.

The female DOJ attorney sat up straight and repeated the question. "Wait, I want to clarify this. The documents in the Redweld that Evan turned over, did Evan believe they were classified?"

"Yes. Evan believed they were classified," I repeated. The DOJ attorneys seemed happy and smiled at each other like I'd just given them a gift.

The lead DOJ attorney clarified further. "You know President Trump has claimed they had all been declassified, right?"

"Yes. I understand." I waited for them to understand my point, but I don't think they saw my distinction. "Can I explain?"

"Yes, please," said the lead attorney.

"I'm just saying that *Evan* believed they were classified. I have no idea if they actually were classified or not. Even if they had classified markings on them, it's quite possible that they had been declassified before. So, I can't tell you one way or another whether they *were* classified or not. All I can say is that Evan believed they were." I doubted that Evan had done the exercise of figuring out what actually was and wasn't classified. He obviously didn't even take every document with markings on it. This was Evan's baby. No one else saw anything or had any input into what was turned over to DOJ.

"Did you talk to Evan at all during the raid?" asked the lead attorney.

"Yes. Several times throughout the day to update him on what was happening," I said.

"Did you tell him that we had found classified documents on site?" asked one of the lawyers.

"Yes. I was nervous about that, so as soon as you told me, I called him."

"What was his response?" asked the lead attorney.

"He asked *where* they found classified documents. I told him in the storage room and the office. He then told me that he hadn't searched the office."

"He what?" The female DOJ attorney asked me to repeat myself.

"He said he didn't search the office," I said, dreading to repeat myself, because I was frustrated with the truth.

The female DOJ lawyer looked intently at her male colleague as if they were communicating. They had masks on, so I couldn't read their facial expressions. But I could understand that they were shocked Evan hadn't searched the office.

Remember, the office was never discussed, at least not in my presence, prior to the raid. DOJ and the FBI did not discuss the office on June 3. They *did* request to see the storage room. I felt bad for Evan that something that seemed so obvious—search the office—likely was a miscommunication between him and DOJ and the FBI, despite the fact that it was included in the searchable area for the subpoena.

My Turn with the Media

The DOJ attorney slid another stack of documents across the table. Looking through them, I realized they were printouts of post-raid media interviews I had done. Direct quotes of mine were printed horizontally on the paper, coupled with a screenshot of the interview. We spent the remainder of the interview dissecting my media interviews. They challenged some of my statements, which I ardently defended as accurate. They tried to get me to say the facts as I knew them at that time had changed, but I refused to agree.

"But, Christina, you know we found classified documents at Mar-a-Lago. Wouldn't you agree that saying 'there were no classified documents on site' is no longer, correct?" asked the lead attorney.

"No. I wouldn't. I don't know what you found at Mar-a-Lago. The inventory is sparse with almost no usable information. I also don't know what had been declassified before you took it. Also, I say this with the most respect possible, I don't necessarily believe DOJ or the FBI. You are known for lying, especially about Donald Trump. So I don't take you at your word," I said, hoping to make my point without angering them. They all seemed to handle it well.

"But you agree that the FBI was not allowed to search through the boxes to find out for themselves on June third?" asked the lead agent.

Ugh. This again. "I would not say that. I'm of the opinion that you could have searched whatever you wanted if you had arranged to do that with Evan. Evan didn't want to take the time to do it that day, but you could have insisted. President Trump was adamant you had the ability to see whatever you wanted. I don't know what more we could have done to let you know you had access to whatever you wanted. I mean, the President of the United States literally came to tell you himself. What more do you need?"

I was starting to get defensive the more they pushed me. They suggested that when Evan said, "Let me know if you need anything else," that was merely a pleasantry, and he didn't mean it. I insisted they were wrong. He meant it. We all meant it. All they had to do was ask, but they never did. They went straight to raiding Mar-a-Lago.

"And why are you so sure that President Trump meant it?" the lead attorney asked again.

"Because I know him, and he said it. He wasn't kidding, bluffing, or whatever. When he said you had access to whatever you wanted, he meant it."

"As you sit here today, are you aware of any classified documents anywhere at Mar-a-Lago?" asked the lead attorney.

I thought about it for a few seconds and then answered, "No." Thankfully, the interview was over. The agents and the DOJ attorneys politely thanked me for my time, and one of the agents escorted John and me out of the building.

CHAPTER 13

The Backlash

We made it back to the hotel and sat at the bar in the lobby. "Christina, you understand that these people hate everything about your boss, and they hate everything that you stand for, right?" John reclined in his high back chair, looking intently at me, trying to measure whether I comprehended what he was saying. He wanted to make sure I understood the playing field.

"Do you think they're going to try to prosecute me?" I was concerned that they would try to do so simply because they wanted to make President Trump look guilty. He wasn't, of course, but if they couldn't get him directly, they'd take out his team. They'd been doing it for years. Was I next?

"No, I don't think so. You didn't do anything wrong. But, don't forget, just a few blocks from here, there are January 6th protestors in jail, pre-trial, under horrible conditions. They are suffering as political prisoners because of this same DOJ and FBI team. It is the same people investigating the January 6th protestors that are investigating President Trump, *and you.*"

That thought was unnerving. The January 6th protesters had been in jail for nearly two years at this point, some held, incredibly, in solitary confinement. Dozens of the political prisoners had recently signed a joint letter asking to be relocated to Guantanamo Bay, where the prisoners are treated more humanely. The letter detailed the malnutrition, medical concerns, and inhumane treatment they suffered at the hands of the guards.

It's hard to comprehend that the United States of America has imprisoned its own citizens simply for having different political views. Our nation is in trouble. President Trump is the largest voice working to save our freedoms, and the Left will not stop trying to take him down. I was grateful John hadn't mentioned that before the meeting.

Breaking It Down

"They seem convinced that the President committed a crime. Do you really believe it's just blind hatred?" I asked John. "I mean, there's got to be some level of objectivity somewhere within these groups, no?"

"I think they see what they want to see in the evidence. Their bias is causing them to draw inaccurate conclusions," John said.

"It's interesting that they thought President Trump was lying when he told them they could have access to whatever they wanted. They completely disregarded that and threw it out. That's a really big deal," I said.

"You're proving my point," John said. "Any objective observer would at least consider the possibility that President Trump was telling the truth," John explained, "especially because they don't have any evidence to the contrary. All the evidence points to cooperation, yet they see obstruction."

Media Leaks

The next morning, back in Florida, I checked my phone to see if any stories had been published about my meeting. Nothing. I was relieved, but it was a Saturday. Monday morning headlines would reveal whether DOJ or the FBI leaked our conversation.

When Monday morning rolled around, I started to get text messages from reporters again. Someone, I assumed DOJ or the FBI, had leaked the story to NBC and they had published a lengthy article on our meeting. There were enough details in the article to make it clear that someone present at the meeting must have shared them, and neither John nor I had talked to the press or shared details with anyone. I read that first story carefully to see what DOJ or the FBI was saying about me.

The article itself didn't actually lean one way or the other, aside from the fact that its existence was aimed at discrediting President Trump by discrediting me, simply because I was interrogated by the FBI. The mere statement that I was subpoenaed created an impression that a crime had occurred. But the facts were actually pretty accurate.

The part I found most interesting was the direct quotes from "three sources who do not want to comment publicly because of the sensitive nature of the sprawling federal investigation."[1] I figured those "three sources" were FBI or DOJ personnel—although I didn't know for sure—but I wanted to know what they thought. The article stated in part, when discussing my liability:

> "She is not criminally liable," the source said. "She is not going to be charged. She is not pointing fingers. She is simply a witness for the truth."[2]

As much as I hated the press writing about me in a way that made me look guilty of some unidentified crime, or an attempt to smear the President at my expense, I was very grateful for these few sentences. No one from my side would have the authority to make statements like that. How could any of us know if I was going to be charged? That had to have come from their side, either an FBI agent, a DOJ official, or someone connected to them. "She is not criminally liable"—I read it a thousand times. Although still nervous, I was relieved that DOJ or the FBI could at least see my role clearly.

The articles that spawned from the original NBC article were less accurate. Some suggested that I had "rolled" on President Trump and was now working to testify against him. Most of the later articles stated flatly that I had pointed fingers at my colleagues, even though the original sources said "she is not pointing fingers." Nothing I said incriminated any of my colleagues or the President, not even Evan. But that wasn't as exciting of a story, so they lied. Repeatedly.

After the story broke, I gave a few small statements to one or two outlets. One outlet that I had directly given statements to, and informed of the events surrounding the certification, disregarded what I said and lied about my involvement, claiming I had doctored the certification after it was signed. How could I have possibly even done that?! They printed it anyway. Other news outlets picked up on their story and repeated the lie, turning the next few days of the news cycle into a disgusting whirlwind of lies and derogatory speculation about my involvement.

More Lawfare

A few days later, as I drove to the gym in silence before the sun came up, the heaviness weighed on me; I didn't know how I'd find relief. During the workout, my coach told me to add more weight to the bar. "You can lift more than you think," he said. I was annoyed. I didn't want to lift more. I just wanted a nice little workout and then to get on with my life. But I added more weight.

When I returned home, I still felt out of sorts. How is it that American citizens are having to choose between voicing their political opinion and prison?!

As I stewed, there was a knock at my door. Expecting a package, I didn't bother to check the camera and just opened the door. It was another process server. This time, it was a subpoena for a lawsuit involving Rudy Giuliani. The Left had attacked him mercilessly because he stood by President Trump's side.

By this point, I had been subpoenaed by Smartmatic for their suit against Fox News, the US Marshals had shown up on my doorstep to issue a summons for me to appear before the January 6th House Committee, I'd been subpoenaed and interviewed by DOJ for the Mar-a-Lago case, I'd testified for the J6 committee . . . and I had been sued by Dominion Voting Systems for $1.6 billion, leaving a contentious defamation case hanging over my head.

Yet another subpoena meant yet another group of lawyers all trolling through my personal emails to determine what needs to be made public and what I can keep private. It's a violation of my privacy to repeatedly have attorneys going through my private communications, on a case that I have nothing to do with, just to decide what *they* say should be public.

When will this end? I thought. *When will the harassment stop?* I started to sink under the mounting pressure when I heard my coach's voice from that morning say, "You can lift more than you think."

I can handle more than I think. Like my weightlifting session that morning, I wasn't trying to figure out how much I can take. That fight came to me. I didn't want to know how much I was capable of, but I was about to find out anyway.

The Announcement

On November 15, 2022, a week after the midterm elections, President Trump held a party at Mar-a-Lago to announce his 2024 candidacy for President. As usual, the grand ballroom at the estate was lavishly decorated and packed full with guests and media stationed in the back on risers. American flags draped the platform and covered the walls, with the large Make America Great Again signs around the room.

Patriotism filled the room as his closest supporters jumped and cheered at the announcement. It was a fun, hope-filled event, with those in attendance discussing the prospects of a bright future.

Special Prosecutor Appointed

Like clockwork, just days after President Trump announced his candidacy for 2024, Biden's Department of Justice, led by Attorney General Merrick Garland, appointed special prosecutor Jack Smith to continue to investigate the Mar-a-Lago documents case. Garland claimed that now that President Trump had announced his candidacy, Joe Biden's cabinet should not be targeting his political opponent. In theory, the appointment of the special counsel made the investigation less political. In reality, it was nothing but political.

Back in 2013, the Internal Revenue Service made headlines for its scandal of illegally targeting conservative nonprofit organizations for tax "violations." The IRS Director of Exempt Organizations spearheaded the effort for two years as the IRS focused their enforcement efforts on conservative tea party groups. The DOJ official who had coordinated with the director on how to weaponize their respective offices to take down their political opponents was a guy named Jack Smith. The same Jack Smith had now been appointed special prosecutor to "investigate" Biden's political opponent. He picked up both the Mar-a-Lago documents and the January 6th investigations. Both political shams.

The irredeemably flawed January 6th congressional pseudo-committee had come up short at finding anything incriminating on Donald Trump. The only thing the committee could do was hold press conferences masquerading as public hearings. Those hearings were held simply to mislead the American people. They were held during prime time, and they got their media puppets to air them live, despite the fact that viewership tanked. Viewers were led to believe they were witnessing all of the testimony and hearing all of the evidence. They were not. They heard handpicked stories from planted witnesses.

I was subpoenaed to testify, and I did. My testimony was never played for the public to consider, because my testimony exonerated President Trump. So they buried it. They also buried Bernie Kerik, Donald Trump Jr., Rudy Giuliani, and a number of Trump staffers who provided the same information, all of which would lead an unbiased fact finder to conclude President Trump had nothing to do with any disruption on January 6th.

Most of the January 6th Committee members lost re-election in the 2022 midterms. Once Republicans took over the house, the committee died. So, Jack Smith turned his attention to the snipe hunt for nuclear secrets stashed at Mar-a-Lago.

CHAPTER 14

Presidents and Their Documents

The Mar-a-Lago documents case was a new, and apparently last-ditch, effort to try to discredit Donald Trump. In fact, the Presidential Records Act has no criminal penalty whatsoever. It's not a penal code. Not to be deterred, the Biden-Harris Administration would pretend it was a criminal code and ignore almost 250 years' worth of American history and Presidential transitions.

Jesse Watters and his staff at Fox News compiled the research of where the last few presidents had stored their documents and what became of them. When George H. W. Bush left the White House, he stored his documents in a strip mall with a bowling alley and a Chinese restaurant. Bill Clinton sent his documents to an abandoned car dealership in Little Rock, Arkansas. George W. Bush sent his documents to a warehouse in Texas. Apparently, according to Watters, George W. Bush kept several artifacts as well, like Saddam Hussein's 9-millimeter Glock. Barack Obama stored his documents at a defunct furniture store across the street from a McDonald's.

And of course, Joe Biden stored documents from his eight years as Vice President in an unsecured garage next to his car. Other documents were stored at his Penn-Biden Center think tank, which received funding from the Chinese Communist Party.

Watters noted in his show that none of these locations had security. In contrast, not only does Mar-a-Lago have private security guarding the grounds, but the United States Secret Service protects and patrols the grounds as well. Unquestionably, Donald Trump better secured his White House documents than any recent president. Did anything happen to the prior presidents? Nope. Nothing. They still have outstanding requests from NARA to return documents that are yet to be returned.

Don't forget about Hillary Clinton and the private email server that she had installed in her house to use for classified information when she was the US Secretary of State—notably *not* the President of the United States. Secretary Clinton's actions were expressly illegal, yet she faced no repercussions. President Trump's actions were expressly legal, and yet the full weight of the federal government pursued him criminally, simply because he was a formidable political foe.

The Presidential Records Act

The Presidential Records Act (PRA) governs the documents a president uses during his time in office and takes with him after leaving office. It is a civil statute with no criminal penalties. In other words, if DOJ wanted to prosecute a former president solely for taking records with him, they couldn't. It's not a crime.

In order for the Department of Justice to bring a charge against a former president, they would have to allege that he was doing something nefarious or illegal with the documents. Or, as we've seen DOJ try to argue, they have to allege that he committed some other crime in connection with the documents.

No former president has ever been charged with a crime. The Biden Administration made history by opening up a criminal investigation into Joe Biden's predecessor, and chief political opponent, for supposed misdeeds that Joe Biden himself was clearly guilty of. The whole situation was a mess, and it's clear that *no* crime was committed by Donald Trump—yet he was the one DOJ was hunting.

Judicial Watch actually filed a lawsuit and argued the issue of what a president is allowed to take with him back in 2012 when they tried to gain access to classified records Bill Clinton had taken with him after his time in office. After they were unsuccessful in gaining access to Clinton records through FOIA requests, the watchdog group sued, claiming that Bill Clinton and the Clinton archivist were required to turn over the information. They claimed Bill Clinton had mischaracterized his records as personal, but they were really presidential, meaning the public had a right to access them.

The case, *Judicial Watch v. National Archives and Records Administration*, more affectionately known as "the Clinton sock drawer case," was filed in Washington, DC, District Court and heard by Judge Amy Berman Jackson, an Obama appointee. The opinion states in part:

> Section 2203(a) of the PRA directs **the President, not the Archivist**, to take:
>
> all such steps as may be necessary to assure that the activities, deliberations, decisions, and policies that reflect the performance of his constitutional, statutory, or other official or ceremonial duties are adequately documented, and that such records are maintained as Presidential records pursuant to the requirements of this section . . . 44 U.S.C §2203(a). **The only reference in the entire statute to the designation of personal versus Presidential also calls for the decision to be made *by the executive [the President]*, and to be made during, and not after the presidency.** [emphasis added]

I recently spoke with the attorney from Judicial Watch who handled the Clinton sock drawer case. He told me that during the hearing, he argued to the judge that the public had a right to see the documents that Bill Clinton had taken with him. The judge sarcastically asked him something to the effect of, "Well, what do you want me to do about it? Have the FBI raid the Clinton residence and seize the documents?" All parties chuckled in 2012, recognizing that was a preposterous solution—and a very dangerous precedent to set. Give it ten years and Democrats would change their minds.

The opinion from the DC District Court, the only court to have heard this issue, clearly states that the PRA directs *the President* as the sole decision maker on what is a presidential record and what is a personal record. No one else, not even the National Archives, has a say in what the President keeps and what he returns. It was Donald Trump's decision alone.

President Trump's defense team argued this point in court. The judge rejected the argument, siding with the government that the charges were not for keeping presidential records, but for allegedly mishandling the records that he chose to keep.

Joe Biden's Classified Documents Problem

When news broke that classified documents had been "discovered" in Joe Biden's garage, next to his mechanic's wrench and spare oil filters, the media scrambled. Realizing that Joe Biden's possession of classified documents in unsecured locations was hypocritical to their coverage of Donald Trump, the media quickly started their choreographed routine. Headlines read: "Biden's Document Case Isn't Similar To Trump. It's More Like Hillary's."[1] They were right, it is more like Hillary's—both are criminally liable, neither of them was president, and both had the federal government cover it up. In contrast, Donald Trump does not actually have criminal liability. The headline, arguably, is correct—just not in the way the press intended it.

Another headline read: "The GOP Effort to Equate Biden and Trump on Classified Documents Is Working."[2] At the very least, Biden's retention of classified material muddied the Left's desire to prosecute Donald Trump for the crime Joe Biden committed. Think about it: Donald Trump had no criminal liability, but Joe Biden did. They prosecuted Donald Trump for the crime Joe Biden committed.

Another headline read: "Is it Fair to Compare Biden's and Trump's Classified Documents Scandal?"[3] The befuddled choreographed message of the American media was *Donald Trump is bad, so just keep hating him even though it doesn't make sense.*

The next schizophrenic message from the media was that Joe Biden cooperated and Donald Trump didn't, so that's why all of the illegal activity on the part of the federal government was justified. First of all, no. There's nothing true or virtuous about that message.

Donald Trump cooperated. He invited the FBI and Department of Justice into his home and told them to their faces that they were welcome to see whatever they wanted. He didn't have to do that. President Trump simply volunteered transparency with DOJ and allowed them access to his home.

They politely thanked him for the opportunity, toured the storage room, and left with no further requests. Two months later, they raided the place. No follow-up phone call saying, "Hey, we think there's more information," or "Could we please come see the boxes?" No. They went straight to raiding his personal residence despite President Trump personally inviting them to cooperate. So, the truth is, President Trump cooperated with DOJ and the FBI. DOJ and the FBI did not cooperate with President Trump.

Second of all, the federal government must always follow the law regardless of how cooperative someone is. Trying to fool the public into believing they were justified in their abuse of power by deceiving the court and insinuating that Donald Trump did not cooperate was untrue and potentially illegal. They abused their power, period.

Merrick Garland, Biden's Attorney General, had appointed Jack Smith to investigate Donald Trump. Someone now needed to investigate Joe Biden.

The Department of Justice was first notified of Biden's classified documents months before the news broke, back in early November 2022. To be clear, they were aware of Biden's criminal activity before the 2022 midterms, but collaborated with the media to hide the information from the public until after the midterm elections—*long* after the midterms; nearly two months.

The news broke in January 2023, and Garland reluctantly appointed a special counsel to investigate. Liberal media praised Garland for appointing Robert Hur "just hours after the news [of Biden's classified documents] broke."[4] But let's be clear, they waited *months* to break the news and only announced the appointment after the press refused to keep the story hidden—after the midterm elections. I believe that Garland would never have appointed a special counsel to investigate Joe Biden if the story hadn't become public.

Mike Pence Finds Documents Too

As if the circus Democrats created around classified documents wasn't ridiculous enough, Mike Pence then announced that he too had classified documents from his time as Vice President. Of course he did. They all do. Barack Obama rightly refused to allow investigators to search his property.

Mike Pence, being the imaginary Boy Scout that he is, appeared to be plagued by his conscience and volunteered his classified documents to investigators. President Trump quickly came to Pence's defense and put a statement out on social media saying that "Mike Pence is an innocent man. He never did anything knowingly dishonest in his life. Leave him alone!!"⁵

To me, Pence's announcement appeared to be one of those face-palm moments. No one cared what documents Mike Pence had. DOJ and the FBI were trying to find a reason to charge Donald Trump with a crime because they hate him politically. This entire investigation was political persecution and had nothing to do with actually protecting America. DOJ overreach is the biggest threat to our freedom this nation has ever experienced.

To add fuel to the fire, Jack Smith subpoenaed Mike Pence to testify before the grand jury investigating Donald Trump. Apparently, conservatives no longer have the benefit of Executive Privilege, or attorney-client privilege for that matter. Jack Smith also required Evan Corcoran to testify before the grand jury. DOJ didn't care about any crimes unless your name was Donald Trump, or you worked for him.

Remember, Evan is the attorney representing Donald Trump in this exact matter. DOJ required him to testify, and a judge in DC allowed it to happen. It's an affront to the legal profession like nothing I've seen in my career before. Conservatives do not have the same legal protections as liberals. There are now two tiers of justice in this nation. Donald Trump and those of us supporting him are subject to different rules and held to a different standard than liberals.

To say we are entering dangerous territory is an understatement.

CHAPTER 15

Testifying Before the Grand Jury

I had already gone through a meeting with the FBI at Mar-a-Lago, an eight-hour raid on Mar-a-Lago, and a subpoena-enforced interview with the FBI at their Washington field office. But they weren't done with me yet. In December 2022, my attorney, John Lauro, called to tell me DOJ still wanted me to testify before the grand jury in Washington, DC. Even though this case was supposed to be in Florida, I was headed back to Washington.

On January 5, 2023, I woke around 6:00 a.m., due to meet John in the lobby at 7:30. I took my time getting ready. My mind was focused on my imminent testimony, but I wasn't too worried about it. I had already met the DOJ attorneys and told them my story—I figured it would be similar to the meeting we had back in October. Only this time, there would be a jury watching.

John and I headed out of the hotel on Pennsylvania Avenue toward the courthouse, the same direction as the US Capitol. It was a beautiful, crisp January morning. We turned up Sixth Street NW and right on C Street to avoid the press. A minute or two later, one of the DOJ employees opened the door for us and led us in through the labyrinth of hallways. We went through a security screening and then were led up several floors on the elevator to the DOJ attorneys waiting for us.

Getting Started

Our escort knocked on the door of a small room where the DOJ attorneys were assembled. The male DOJ lawyer who had led my interview two months earlier stepped out and greeted us warmly.

"Good morning, great to see you," he said as he shook my hand.

"Good morning," I said, giving a slight smile. Although I completely disagreed with his political positions and objected to his apparent attempts to imprison his political opponents, I actually had come to like him as a person.

He greeted John and pointed us to a small room right next to theirs. "We've reserved this room for you here so you can talk privately. We should be starting in about fifteen minutes and will come back to get you."

"Thank you," John said as he closed the door.

John and I sat across the table from each other in the small conference room. It was tight with the two of us in the room. Any more and it would be uncomfortable.

"Remember, don't become an advocate," John said. "Just state the facts as you recall them. It's very easy for lawyers to switch into advocate mode. Once you start advocating, you can get into trouble. Stick to the facts."

"I know. I got it," I said.

John looked at me for a second. He knew I have a habit of fighting everyone on everything. So he just hoped for the best.

The DOJ attorney came back a few minutes later and led me just a few doors down to the grand jury room. He introduced me to the other prosecutors. I recognized the female DOJ attorney from my interview two months prior. There were two more attorneys I had not met, both men, one in his early forties and one a little bit older, maybe in his sixties. The lead DOJ lawyer explained they were from Jack Smith's office, the special prosecutor assigned to investigate President Trump. He then pointed me to a seat and said, "This is where you'll sit."

The room was about thirty feet by twenty feet, with amphitheater-style seating for the jury, while the panel of lawyers and the witness (that was me), sat at a long rectangular table at the front of the room. It looked like a typical college lecture class. The court reporter was all the way at the far end of the room from me, sitting at what would be the "L" in the table. Next to her was the older special prosecutor. Next to him was the younger special prosecutor, then the female DOJ lawyer, the lead DOJ lawyer, and then me as the witness.

The grand jury foreman closed the door as I sat down, the court reporter started her recording, and the lead DOJ attorney said, "We are now on the record." He asked the foreman to swear me in. I turned to the jury foreman who was seated in the first row, almost directly in front of me.

He said, "Ms. Bobb, do you swear or affirm that the evidence you are about to give will be the truth, the whole truth, and nothing but the truth?"

"Yes." I took my seat.

"Ms. Bobb," said the lead DOJ attorney, "You understand that you are under oath and you could be charged with a crime for lying?"

"Yes," I said.

Most of the questions—and my answers—covered the same ground I had lived and relived over the past six months. But there was one worrisome difference. Throughout the day, the younger special prosecutor would frequently jump in and say, "And who do you represent?" or "Who do you work for?" It was obvious he was trying to get me to implicate Donald Trump, even though the President had nothing to do with what I was talking about. He did it all day, and I had to frequently explain myself clearly; I wanted to be sure he couldn't twist what I said to somehow imply that President Trump had directed anything when he hadn't.

I mentioned that I had a direct relationship with President Trump, and the young special prosecutor asked me to describe what I meant. "He has your cell phone number?" he asked.

"Yes," I said.

"And you have his cell phone number?" he asked.

"Yes," I said.

"You call each other?"

"Yes."

"And the circle of people who can call him is very small?" He asked.

"It's not as small as it could be," I said. "He's very accessible." Some of the jurors chuckled at that. I wasn't trying to fight the young special prosecutor, but he was being so aggressive, it made me want to pump the brakes.

"Fine, but not everyone can just call Donald Trump, right?" he said.

"Correct," I responded.

"When was the last time you were with him?" asked the lead attorney.

"New Year's Eve," I said, five days ago.

"That was just for social reasons?" asked the lead attorney.

"Yes," I said. Sarcastically I thought to myself, *So glad we cleared up the fact that Donald Trump celebrates New Year's Eve. Good thing a grand jury is investigating his social schedule.*

Regaining control, the lead DOJ lawyer pulled out a stack of documents containing the text messages we had gone through two months prior. As he walked me through the phone call with Boris, the younger special prosecutor jumped in with a couple questions in a more antagonizing tone. Why was he coming at me? I was an easy witness for them.

Why was he being hostile with me? Had they changed their approach? Were they actually targeting *me?*

I answered questions—yet again—about my texts with Evan the evening before our June 3 meeting with the FBI.

The young special prosecutor interrupted again: "Do you think Mr. Corcoran was qualified to do this search?"

"I don't know what his qualifications are. I believe he used to be a prosecutor with the Department of Justice, so he *should* be qualified." But by this point, I had my doubts.

The young special prosecutor jumped in and aggressively pushed, "You have a security clearance, correct?"

"Yes."

"So you know whether these documents were classified," he pushed.

"I do not. Even if you showed me the documents, even if I saw classification markings on them, I could not verify that they are or are not classified. I understand there's a possibility that they were declassified. If they were declassified, the markings don't magically disappear. I wouldn't know one way or the other."

The lead attorney leaned forward and removed the exhibit of our text messages from the projector and replaced it with the exhibit of the signed certification. "Okay. Let's get back to the certification. Is this the certification you're referring to?" he asked.

"Yes," I said.

"Is this your signature?" he asked.

"Yes," I confirmed.

Before the lead attorney could continue to walk me through the rest of the phone call and the details surrounding the certification, the young special prosecutor jumped in again. He said, "Excuse me, I'd like to just establish a few things here."

"Okay," I said.

"So, when you received this certification, you just signed it." He made a signature motion with his hand. "You had no idea what was in it, didn't ask any questions. You just signed it, correct?" he asked in an oddly aggressive tone. "You didn't know Evan at all. You didn't know anything about the situation. You had no information, and you just signed it, correct?"

Where was he going with this? I didn't understand why he was pushing me to say that. I responded, "Well, not really. That's why there was a second certification."

"What do you mean there were two certifications?" he asked.

Did he not know my testimony? His questions put me on edge and made me feel that I needed to be careful. It felt like he was trying to trap me.

The young special prosecutor got out of his seat and walked over to the projector. He pointed to the certification and said, "This is the certification, correct?"

"This is the only certification that I signed, but it's the second version of the certification," I said.

The young special prosecutor paused for a second, looking confused. "Why is there a second version?"

"Because I asked him to make a change. I refused to sign the first version as-is."

"What did you change?" he asked.

The lead attorney flipped through the exhibits to the original certification to show that he had it.

"Can we go through it?" I leaned forward to look more closely at the certification.

"Hang on a second. We'll get there." The lead attorney indicated that he wanted to get through his line of questioning.

By now, I had real concerns that the young special prosecutor was trying to get me to admit things I didn't do. I wanted to make sure that I wasn't walking into a trap, so I asked, "Can we take a quick break?"

The lead attorney kindly said, "Sure," seeming to sense my uneasiness. We went off the record.

Sanity Check

I slipped out of the room and went back to the side room where John was working while I testified. I opened the door quickly, rushed in, and exclaimed, "They're after me, John. I don't understand what they're doing. This was supposed to be a simple testimony similar to the interview two months ago. I thought we were all in agreement that I didn't do anything wrong? Why are they coming after me?"

John was startled from the notes he was reading on his tablet. He took off his glasses as he looked at me and calmly said, "What's going on?"

Frantically, I said, "That younger special prosecutor is trying to get me to admit to things I didn't do! He's making a case that I was careless and negligent in how I responded. If I actually agree to what he's saying, they'd have a case against me. Are they targeting me?"

John furrowed his brows, concerned. He could tell I was very upset with how things were going. "No. They are not targeting you." Putting both his hands on the table he said, "Walk me through what's happening. Why do you think they're targeting you?"

I relayed to John the line of questioning. "Why are they trying to get me to admit to facts that they know aren't true? Why does he want me to say that I didn't read the certification? I told them I read it and made changes! John, I don't want to go to jail over this, just because I believed DOJ when they said I wasn't a target. Are they lying to me?" I was stressed.

"Go to jail? Christina, what are you talking about?!" John leaned his elbows on the table calmly trying to bring me back on track.

"Christina," John said, looking at me intently, "It sounds to me like he's unprepared for the interview." He waited for my reaction, but

I just stared at him. "He didn't read the briefing memo and he has no idea what you're going to say. He sounds like an arrogant prosecutor who thinks he knows everything and assumed he knew what you were going to say. He got it wrong. Honestly, I think that's it."

I sat there for a second before responding, "Can you please confirm they are not targeting me?"

"Absolutely," John said.

After John met with the DOJ lawyers, he spoke with me briefly to let me know everything was fine. If I was comfortable, he was comfortable with me finishing my testimony. I walked back to the grand jury room to finish my testimony.

The lead DOJ attorney resumed the questions and we continued to go through the sequence of events, all while the younger special prosecutor kept interrupting to ask questions that were out of the sequence. I realized John was right and this guy just was not prepared at all for this discussion. It was annoying, because the questions could have been very simple and established the facts they wanted, but I (and the other DOJ attorneys) needed to get him up to speed *on the record*. He should have just kept his mouth shut so he didn't sound unprepared. Now there's a record of it.

We continued to walk through my time with Evan before the FBI arrived and how I declined the opportunity to search the boxes myself.

"Why did you decline to search the boxes?" asked the young special prosecutor.

"Because I had already signed the certification saying that I was not part of the search and review, and I didn't want to blur any lines. I wanted to be precise. My security clearance wasn't active, and I didn't want to be accused of illegally accessing classified materials. Also, I didn't have time to do a real search anyway, so there was no reason for me to even attempt to conduct a search at that point," I said.

The young special prosecutor pushed me on this point, arguing that Evan offered to tell the FBI to wait. Why didn't I take the opportunity to search while the FBI waited? We went back and forth on this point for a couple rounds before I got frustrated. I threw my hands up, shrugged and said, "What do you want me to do? I didn't feel I could properly search with the FBI waiting in the living room. I didn't want to do that, so I declined!"

Eventually, we got to the point where President Trump had personally offered full cooperation. "So, let me get this straight." The young special prosecutor was leaning over with his hand pointing into the table. "So you're saying the President wanted to fully cooperate, but it was *Evan* who didn't want to cooperate fully."

"Correct. That's what he said," I answered. I wanted to point out the fact that Evan even told that to DOJ at the meeting. When Mr. Bratt asked Evan if they could see the storage room, Evan said, "If it were up to me, I'd say no, but President Trump gave clear instructions that you can see whatever you want. So, if you want to see the storage room, I'll take you to the storage room." Evan specifically told them it was President Trump who wanted them to have access and that *he, Evan,* didn't want to give them access. But I never got the opportunity to raise that point to the grand jury.

"Tell me about the discussion with the FBI and DOJ attorney," said the lead attorney. "How did that conversation go? Did the DOJ attorney then ask you who did do the search?"

"Yes," I said. "When he asked me that, I didn't respond but turned to Evan and asked him how he'd like to respond."

The young special prosecutor jumped in and said, "Isn't it true that the way Mr. Corcoran answered that question led the FBI agents to believe that more than one person did the search?"

"I don't know what the FBI agents believed. However, they *could have* believed that based on his response," I said. He pushed me one or two more times to try to get me to say that Evan misled the FBI agents into believing more than one person did the search. I stood firm that I had no idea what the agents believed. I did not believe Evan's answer was intentionally misleading.

The young special prosecutor jumped in again: "Would you agree now that your certification was wrong?"

"I wouldn't say it was wrong," I said. "You can say it's inaccurate if you want to, but I can't say that. Based on all of the information that I have personal knowledge of, the certification is true. I understand that many people believe it's inaccurate, and that's fine, but I don't have personal knowledge of what was seized from Mar-a-Lago."

The young special prosecutor lightly scoffed at me and said, "You don't know that the certification is inaccurate? You know we've recovered classified documents from Mar-a-Lago. How can you say you don't know it's wrong?"

"You never showed me the documents! I have no idea what you seized from Mar-a-Lago. I know what *you've told me* you seized from Mar-a-Lago, and that's fine," I said, implying that fact would be hearsay if I testified to it. "That's why I say *you* can say it's inaccurate. But I can't say that. I've never seen the documents. I do not have personal knowledge of what you took from Mar-a-Lago. Even if you did show me the documents, I couldn't verify whether they were classified. Were they declassified at any point? I don't know. I don't have personal knowledge of that. There are a lot of unanswered questions about these documents, and all I'm saying is I don't personally have the answer."

Surprising Discovery

"Now, let's go to the day of the raid. Actually, let me be more specific. I'll offer that I informed you that we recovered classified documents, and you were surprised. Why were you surprised?" asked the lead attorney.

"I was surprised because I had been told that a diligent search had been conducted and that all responsive documents had been turned over."

"Did you call Evan after I informed you that we were seizing classified documents?"

"Yes," I said.

"And what was his reaction?" asked the lead attorney.

"He said, 'Oh. That's not good.'" I paused for a moment and looked at the lead attorney. Then I said, "That's the understatement of the century." Some of the jurors chuckled.

I continued to answer questions about the raid, my role, and my impressions. But there was nothing new here, I had told this story so many times before, it was becoming old hat.

Questions from the Jurors

After the DOJ attorneys and the special prosecutors were done with their questions, the lead attorney asked the jurors if they had any questions for me. There were about twenty jurors in the room, and about ten of them had masks on. By January 2023, the medical mask had become a reliable signal that the wearer was a staunch liberal. I thought most of the jurors in the room hated Donald Trump, and probably hated me by extension. Still, they all seemed relaxed and laid-back.

The first juror to ask a question was a white male in his early fifties. He had a kind demeanor, which helped set me at ease, and he was not wearing a mask. He stated, "Thank you for your candor and providing your testimony today. Did you ever consider pulling back your certification and not allowing them to use it?"

"When I received the first draft of the certification that did not have the qualifying language in it, I was concerned. I knew it was a very tricky situation that needed to be handled carefully. At that point, I knew that if I did not sign the certification, they would have found another staffer to do it. That staffer would have been younger, less experienced, and less capable of navigating the situation. I consciously decided at that point that I would handle the situation, because I did not want to put a junior staff member in a difficult position that could expose them to liability."

The gentleman seemed satisfied with that answer and another juror raised her hand. She was Asian and looked about thirty years old, but she had a mask on so it was hard to tell. "After you arrived to Mar-a-Lago and saw all of these red flags, did you ever consider pulling your certification back at that point?"

"The FBI and DOJ were already there. There would have been other consequences if I had done that. Either way there were consequences, so I never really had the option to do that."

Another white mask-less gentleman in his fifties asked if President Trump, when he stopped by the meeting with the FBI, could see the container of documents that Evan had turned over. Was it on the table? Was it clearly visible that it was a relatively small number of documents that was being turned over?

"The agent took the container and was trying to put it in the courier bag. When it didn't fit, she left the bag unzipped, and set it next to her chair like this," I said as I motioned with my hands as if I were setting a bag down at my feet.

Both the juror and the lead attorney said, "Oh! It was on the floor!"

Another white gentleman in his fifties or sixties responded by asking: "Did the FBI ever push back on having the opportunity to look in the boxes? Was there any dialogue about that? Or did they just take no for an answer?"

"There was no further discussion about it. Once Evan told them not to go through the boxes, they did not ask about it again," I responded.

The jury foreman, a white middle-aged man, asked me whether the boxes were sealed when I went down to the storage room with Evan.

I started to answer and then realized I didn't know what he meant by "sealed," so I asked him to explain. He simply meant taped closed. He wanted to know if I could tell if Evan had actually conducted a search or not.

"Oh, I'm not sure. The boxes that I saw were open. I could see into them and saw newspaper articles and magazines. I didn't examine all of them, so I don't really know."

With that, the lead attorney dismissed me and asked me to wait with John until they were certain there were no further questions. I stepped out of the room and my grand jury testimony was over.

CHAPTER 16

Squeezing Team Trump

By March 2023, the Department of Justice was scrambling to convince the public that Donald Trump had mishandled classified materials. Maybe he was selling nuclear secrets? Or maybe he was doing something else nefarious? He was in lawful possession of the documents, so in order to charge him with a crime, there had to be some illegal activity connected to his handling of the documents. But they had no evidence of any crime. All they had was that Donald Trump took documents with him from the White House to Mar-a-Lago, which is perfectly legal, classified or not.

So, they developed a new theory, and Evan Corcoran, President Trump's attorney in the matter, became their new obsession. They decided that Donald Trump had instructed his attorney, Evan, to lie to the FBI and hide his documents—the documents that he was legally allowed to have. Did they have evidence of that? No.

They needed Evan, who now potentially had his own criminal exposure for misrepresenting facts to the FBI and DOJ, to say that the President made him do it. Which presented another problem: As the President's lawyer, Evan is *not allowed* to share information or conversations he had with his client; it is covered by attorney-client privilege.

Not to be deterred, DOJ went to a DC judge and asked for a court order to allow them to breach attorney-client privilege and order Evan to testify and turn over all his records based on the "crime-fraud exception." This exception basically says communications between an attorney and client are not privileged if they are made for the purpose of furthering a crime.

The DC court went along with this farce, ruling that Evan's missteps with the documents were clearly signs of criminal activity, and allowed DOJ to order Evan to testify at the DC grand jury and to turn over his records and cell phone records.

Donald Trump was stripped of his right to confidentiality with his lawyer—a lawyer who had made mistakes handling the case and could possibly face his own prosecution. Or, he could testify against Donald Trump and say the President made him do it.

Targeting a Navy Vet

DOJ had another problem. They were trying to claim that Donald Trump had mishandled classified documents. But Donald Trump never handled *any* documents. He doesn't pack his own boxes, nor does he clean out his own closet. Donald Trump never did anything DOJ was alleging. So in order to charge President Trump with a crime, DOJ concocted yet another story: that the staff who packed and moved the boxes were doing so at the direction of Donald Trump and that Trump specifically instructed them to commit crimes on his behalf.

Who could they blame for "mishandling" classified materials that the President never handled? They set their sights on Walt Nauta. Walt is a US Naval Academy graduate, Navy veteran, President Trump's personal valet, and a friend of mine. He is one of the kindest, purest souls I know, and I cannot say enough nice things about him. Everyone who knows Walt loves him.

DOJ needed to create a co-conspirator to further their conspiracy theory about nefarious dealings with classified documents. There are lots of big personalities in Trumpworld. Many are very public polarizing personalities whom people either love or hate. Many of President Trump's most loyal staffers have been targeted by the media for their dogged advocacy for the President. If DOJ wanted to sacrifice someone on the altar of public outrage, they had options.

They picked Walt?! DOJ claimed Walt Nauta was President Trump's co-conspirator who supposedly hid classified materials from the FBI (the materials he was lawfully in possession of). Walt is probably the only person in President Trump's circle about whom *nobody* would say a negative word. He's honest. He works hard. He's responsible. Patriotic. Kind. And *that's* who DOJ chose to paint as some sort of criminal henchman? Good grief.

Pressuring His Lawyer[1]

The story gets even more outrageous as DOJ turned its attention to Walt's attorney, Stanley Woodward. At DOJ's insistence, Woodward agreed to meet with prosecutors in person at DOJ Headquarters ("Main Justice") in Washington, DC. The purpose of the meeting was supposed to be to discuss Walt's prior FBI interview and concerns DOJ had over his testimony.

On August 24, 2022, Woodward entered an ornate conference room to find three prosecutors working with Jack Smith's team present at the table, and one appearing via video conference.[2] Instead of asking Woodard about his client, as Stanley expected, the DOJ attorney leading the investigation pulled out a file on Stanley Woodward himself. Why would they have a file on Woodward? This meeting was supposed to be about Walt Nauta.

The lead DOJ attorney opened the file, revealing contents of Stanley Woodward's professional career. "Specifically, [the lead DOJ attorney] remarked that he was aware of the fact that Mr. Woodward had been recommended for a Presidential nomination to the Superior Court of the District of Columbia."[3] DOJ stated to Woodward that their case against Walt "was strong." Woodward was told to tell Walt that he needed to "[give] up a lifestyle of private planes and private golf courses," and that it would "behoove" Walt to cooperate with the government.

Then, the lead DOJ attorney played a shocking card. He stated to Woodward, "[You're] not a . . . 'Trump attorney,' "[you'll] do the right thing." DOJ then implied that Woodward's potential judicial nomination to the Superior Court would be impacted by whether or not Walt—*Woodward's client*—decided to cooperate with the government. In closing the discussion, the lead DOJ attorney remarked about Woodward's potential nomination: "I wouldn't want you to do anything to mess that up."

This is corrupt abuse of power at its most venal. DOJ needed a witness against Donald Trump to lie and say he committed a crime that never happened. DOJ picked Walt Nauta, and then tried to get Walt's own lawyer to pressure him into lying about President Trump in exchange for a judicial nomination. They tried to squeeze Walt and Woodward. Neither one buckled. Walt never lied and he never provided negative information about Donald Trump. So DOJ indicted him as Donald Trump's co-conspirator.

DOJ disputes this story. They admit the meeting and discussion took place, but they claim that no intimidation or coercion was implied or expressed at the meeting. In a now unsealed response, DOJ argues that Woodward's story was not credible, because Woodward did not object during the meeting or in follow-up discussions, but had waited to file a motion with the court months later.[4] According to DOJ, there was no threat.

Woodward's recommendation for judicial nomination remained open from November 23, 2020, until it expired in March 2025—lasting the entire Biden Administration. Walt never rolled on the President, and Woodward never received his judicial nomination. It appears that not only did DOJ threaten Woodward in the conversation, but they made good on that threat.

Manufacturing a Crime

The Mar-a-Lago case was completely fake. No one committed any crimes. No one breached any security protocols. No one mishandled national security documents. Big fat nothingburger. President Trump was lawfully in possession of the documents he took from the White House, and no one has authority to tell him what he can and can't take (*Judicial Watch v. NARA*).

That didn't stop DOJ and the FBI from terrorizing the Trump Team. They went after all of us, including junior staff—kids in their twenties. Everyone on Donald Trump's team from the President himself all the way down to the most junior staff were threatened with subpoenas, indictments, searches, privacy violations, and negative press. It was a disgusting, abusive overreach of government authority for the purpose of eliminating a political opponent.

CHAPTER 17

Surprises and Betrayals

With the Mar-a-Lago grand jury testimony behind me, I closed the books on a year of harassment and fear and tried to look ahead. After five different subpoenas (at that time), several encounters with the FBI and DOJ, the drama at Mar-a-Lago, countless meetings with attorneys, and a lawsuit for $1.6 billion, I was ready to say good riddance to 2022. Maybe 2023 would be a better year; honestly, it couldn't be much worse. Or so I thought.

I had just returned from the Michigan GOP convention in February 2023 when I received an email from one of my lawyers. One of the attorneys representing me in a matter from my time at One America News (OAN) emailed me, effectively telling me to secure my own counsel and that they were withdrawing from the case.

What?! I thought. This particular matter was very small, and I wasn't even a party to the case. Because I had done so much reporting for OAN on 2020 election irregularities, several election-related lawsuits had subpoenaed me for my information. This was one of those cases. As a reporter at OAN, their insurance coverage provided me with legal representation. Until now.

The lawyers the insurance company had hired to represent me with the subpoenas were now unilaterally withdrawing, telling me they recommended the insurer no longer cover my expenses. This particular case had been especially onerous, with the plaintiff demanding that I turn over every single note I had ever made as a reporter and writer. We had already been to court numerous times fighting their discovery demands and arguing that what they were asking for was unreasonable. Now my attorneys were pulling out just four days before discovery was due.

But even worse than the sudden withdrawal was their excuse: They told me that they believed I was about to get sued for publishing my first book, *Stealing Your Vote* (which had nothing to do with the matter at hand). Because, in their opinion, I was likely to get sued, they now had a conflict of interest.

By the time my book was published, I was no longer a reporter for OAN, so my book was not covered by OAN's insurance. But this case had nothing to do with my book. Furthermore, I had not been sued about my book, and never did get sued. I wasn't sued then, and I haven't been sued now about the book. There was no actual conflict. The reason they gave was simply that I could potentially be sued.

OAN was well aware that I was publishing *Stealing Your Vote*. In fact, the CEO, Robert Herring, even gave me a blurb to use to promote the book. It's still on the back of the book to this day.

"Christina"—the lead attorney used an unnecessarily condescending tone—"you chose to write this book. No one made you do it. And that's your right, but you have live with your decision. You brought this on yourself," he said.

I brought this on myself? I thought. Brought what? This subpoena was a direct result of my investigative work for OAN. I was not a party to the lawsuit, because I never reported on, nor even investigated, the party who filed the subpoena. I did not have any information relevant to this litigation. This should be a very simple discovery matter.

"Your assessment is completely wrong," I said. "There is no actual conflict, and this subpoena is a direct result of my employment at OAN. My book has nothing to do with it."

"We believe your lawsuit is imminent, which creates a conflict for us," said the lead attorney. He then spent the next three days trying to convince me that I was on the verge of a massive lawsuit that would ruin me financially, easily costing a million dollars just to defend.

"Large democrat donors, like George Soros, are going to fund this suit to try to take you and your book down. They don't care that they have no case and can't win. They just want to harm anyone working for Donald Trump," he said.

George Soros? George Soros is not mentioned in my book, and neither is any phantom plaintiff that my attorneys seemed convinced was going to take me for everything I own. I don't even tangentially allude to Soros in any conceivable way—and they think he wants to sue me?! This is absolute insanity. These attorneys were supposed to be representing me in a simple discovery matter that should be resolved very quickly. Now, my own lawyers are trying to convince me I'm getting sued by George Soros? Bananas.

"This doesn't make any sense," I said, trying to figure out what I was going to do without counsel. "I do not consent to your immediate withdraw, and I do not agree that this subpoena is not related to my employment with OAN."

"Christina, you're a lawyer," the lead attorney said with a level of disdain. "Why don't you just represent yourself?"

I figured it was best not to respond as I wanted to, so I just didn't say anything.

OAN's Response

The sense of abandonment was piercing, but the threat of frivolous litigation stunned me. My lawyers were acting contrary to my best interest and I needed new counsel immediately. I was also struggling to figure out how what they were saying could possibly be true. It didn't make any sense.

One America News, the Herrings (owners of OAN), and I had been through war together. They encouraged me to pursue the election story and travel the country gathering evidence. I was disparaged, ridiculed, and mocked by all the major news networks for staying with the 2020 election story. Every time I took a public beating, OAN received publicity. We'd been through worse things than a minor discovery dispute. We had each other's backs, right?

In fact, in *Stealing Your Vote*, I mentioned the Herring Family and how supportive they were to me. I credited them with so much of their support to me and had made very gracious remarks about them. Was I wrong? The book had been published for less than thirty days before my attorneys abandoned me.

Since leaving OAN, I had maintained a close personal relationship with the Herrings and many of the reporters. Naturally, I called OAN leadership to figure out what was going on from their perspective. No answer. I tried again. No answer. I tried the next day. No answer. I sent an email. No answer. I sent another email. No answer.

The message was clear—you're on your own.

I knew they were probably just following the advice of their stupid lawyers, but even that was hurtful. The wave of betrayal overwhelmed me like a flash flood. I wanted to hide away in anger and resentment, but I didn't have time. I needed to get a new lawyer—fast. If my current lawyers were right that I was facing an imminent lawsuit from Soros or a phantom liberal billionaire, I needed a fighter—fast. (Thank God they were wrong.)

I also needed to figure out how to pay for a lawyer, but that would come later. A frivolous lawsuit would cost hundreds of thousands of dollars to defend, which I didn't have. It could potentially cost over a million dollars if the judge didn't stop it quickly.

The fact that the insurance defense lawyers went out of their way to scare me into believing any number of crazy liberal billionaires would sue me frivolously—that was gratuitous. It was simply their excuse for unilaterally withdrawing, but it caused me significant angst as I hustled to try to figure out how to first defend the subpoena, and then prepare in case the lawyers were right.

I know that OAN leadership was simply following the advice of counsel. Their attorneys (who were also my attorneys for this matter) had convinced them that they needed to cut ties with me for their own safety, and they complied. This is one of the reasons lawfare works. It causes fractures among allies. OAN and I have always had a good relationship, and I am still grateful for my time with them. Lawyers ruin everything.

How is it possible that this nation has *so many* lawyers yet so little justice? As a profession, we can do better.

Calls for Help

My first call went to a lawyer who could negotiate with the insurance company for me to secure new counsel.

My next call was to Susie Wiles. She didn't really have a role in any of this, but I trusted her. I just wanted to talk to someone and make sure I wasn't getting washed away in the flood of emotions I felt. Her response was amazing.

"Anything you need help with, let me know," she said. "You're not in this alone." She was as appalled as I was by the backstabbing, cowardice, and betrayal by those who supposedly represented me. "Christina, you've got people who care about you and support you. Fight your fight, but don't be afraid to call me if you need me." Her words were a balm to my wounds. My feet suddenly found solid ground.

These moments of abandonment and betrayal (there were a few) were the lowest points throughout this entire process. It's no exaggeration to say that it was easier for me to navigate discussions with DOJ lawyers—lawyers who would like to throw me in jail—than it was for me to work with some of the attorneys on my own side. It was more painful for me to face the fact that my supposed allies would stab me in the back without batting an eye than it was getting interrogated by the FBI.

It took several weeks before I learned that the insurance company was not dropping me from their coverage after all. Thankfully, I was allowed to fire this firm and retain new counsel.

Fani Willis Gets Involved

My new counsel quickly filed a motion to quash the subpoena. He and I assumed plaintiff's counsel would contact us to meet and confer about the discovery. They didn't.

Instead, it appears that this plaintiff's lawyers tried a new and nasty tactic of harassment: They reached out to the Fulton County, Georgia, special prosecutor investigating Donald Trump and tried to embroil me in yet another unrelated criminal matter.

District Attorney Fani Willis had appointed a special prosecutor to investigate Donald Trump and others regarding imaginary crimes surrounding the 2020 election in Georgia. The investigation took over nine months and seventy-five witnesses, none of which mentioned my name. The grand jury for this case had already adjourned.

Yet, just a couple days after filing our motion to quash the subpoena, this special prosecutor reached out to my attorney asking to talk to me. Why, after such a lengthy investigation, was the special prosecutor now suddenly interested in interviewing me? My attorney called the special prosecutor, and he tells me the conversation went something like this.

"Why are you now interested in interviewing my client?" my attorney asked the special prosecutor.

"I've received information that she has valuable information that I should know about," he responded.

"What information do you believe that she has?" John asked.

"I have no idea. I don't know what she knows but would like to talk to her and find out," he said.

"You had to hear her name from somewhere. Something had to lead you to believe that she had information. What do you believe that she knows?" my attorney insisted.

"I don't know!" The special prosecutor pushed back. "I've received information that she is involved and I need to talk to her. That's it," he said.

"Did an attorney call you and ask you to interview her?" my attorney asked.

"I did receive a phone call from an attorney suggesting that I talk to Ms. Bobb. The attorney was not affiliated with any political action committee," he said, which means it most likely was plaintiff's counsel from the OAN case.

Unbelievable. These leftist groups have become so aggressive that they are now coordinating with government officials to combine civil and criminal efforts against a political opponent. As a reminder, I was not a party to the lawsuit with this plaintiff. I had zero involvement with any of these people whatsoever. They hated me because I support Donald Trump, so they used every legal avenue they could think of to harass and disparage me.

I can only guess, since I don't have access to the special prosecutor's investigation, but I believe the plaintiff's lawyers encouraged the special prosecutor to intimidate me into an interview that I wasn't consenting to with this plaintiff. Maybe the prosecutor could get information about me that they could use against me, or at least make my life hell. They potentially used the criminal process, which grossly infringes on personal liberties, to secretly gain information that they could use against their political opponents. It's un-American and possibly illegal.

My attorney politely declined the opportunity for me to get interrogated. Since the grand jury was over and they couldn't subpoena me, that was the end of the discussion.

Meanwhile, the discovery issue in the OAN case ended up being the simple issue that we suspected it would be. And no, George Soros never sued me. He probably doesn't even know who I am. All the pain and anguish my own lawyers caused was meaningless.

CHAPTER 18

More Harassment

In June 2023, about five months after my grand jury testimony, I received an email from the California bar informing me that I was now under investigation by the state bar and in jeopardy of losing my law license.

Let me get this straight. Attorneys from DOJ and the FBI (1) misled a federal court about President Trump's level of cooperation (2) to obtain an unprecedented warrant to search the private residence of an American President, where they (3) exceeded the scope of the warrant by taking personal effects (which they ultimately had to return), (4) breached the attorney-client privilege by seizing privileged information, (5) shamed him publicly, causing a chilling effect in the political process nationally, and then (6) tried to intimidate co-defendant's counsel into securing a witness against the President. And *I'm* the one defending *my* bar license?! Unbelievable.

My heart sank at the thought of another attack. Why are these people coming after me? I was desperate for help, so I called John Lauro, my criminal defense attorney in the case.

"John," I said panicky, "The California bar opened an investigation into me about the Mar-a-Lago case. How do I end this as quickly as possible?! I didn't do anything wrong."

John paused longer than I expected him to. "Oh, Christina, I'm so sorry this is happening to you. I'm sure that once the bar finds out your role, they'll close this case quickly. You didn't do anything unethical," he said. But he didn't sound as reassuring as he had in the past.

"You already have the facts and information; it would save me a lot of money if you could represent me in this matter. Hopefully it'll be as small as you think it will be," I said.

"No!" John responded quickly and sharply. It caught me off guard. "No," he said, "I can't represent you in this matter. You need someone in California to help you."

I tried to convince John that he was the best person to represent me, but he firmly pushed back. "Christina, I can't represent you. I have a conflict for this matter."

"A conflict? What do you mean you have a conflict? You've represented me for close to a year on these facts. How do you now have a conflict?!"

By June 2023, the Trump Team was well aware that DOJ was trying to indict the President on facts relating to January 6th in order to prevent him from being eligible to hold office. The democrat establishment knew they couldn't beat Donald Trump in an election. He was too popular, so they were trying to make him ineligible.

I had recommended that John Lauro be brought on to help with the litigation. In part due to my recommendation, John Lauro was hired to prepare for and defend any potential indictment of Donald Trump relating to January 6th.

Due to John now representing the President, I had unintentionally lost the chance for him to represent me in ongoing matters. John said, "I'm now working on the President's case, and you work for the President. I can't afford any conflict."

"They are two totally different, unrelated cases. It's a completely different set of facts!" I argued, not wanting to have to get another new lawyer. "On that note, don't you think it's weird that the bar complaint just came in *now*?" I asked. "I mean, it's been over *a year* since I met with the FBI at Mar-a-Lago, and ten months since the raid. Why are they just now investigating me?"

"I don't know, Christina," John sounded annoyed. "You just need a California lawyer."

Frustrated that I needed *another* attorney due to *another* baseless attack, I reached out to my former boss at the firm I had worked at in San Diego, Steve Cologne.

Help from Old Friends

"Christina!" Steve greeted me as an old friend would. "How are you? I've seen you in the news." He laughed playfully, "Are you doing okay?"

"Hi, Steve!" I responded, so deeply grateful for a friendly voice. "Ugh," I joked. "I'm okay. I've been worse and I've been better. I'm not in jail, so that's something to be grateful for," I joked, referring to my run-in with DOJ.

I updated Steve on my predicament with the California bar. Over the next few days, he looped in his partner, who I also knew from my time at the firm, Paul Pfingst. Paul was a well-respected criminal defense attorney in San Diego. Prior to that, he was elected the Republican District Attorney for San Diego, so he understood politics, which I greatly appreciated.

"Why does the California bar believe they need to be involved in a matter that occurred entirely in Florida involving someone (you) who was not acting as an attorney, but as a custodian of records?" Paul asked. *Great question!*

"I don't know," I said. "I'm sure they're salivating over the idea of disbarring another Trump attorney," referencing John Eastman. The lawyers investigating me were the same lawyers who had disbarred John Eastman, a very well-respected Constitutional lawyer who provided counsel to Rudy Giuliani and Donald Trump in the post-2020 election challenges. By my assessment, John Eastman had not done anything wrong, certainly nothing that warranted disbarment. As far as I could tell, he was disbarred as retaliation for supporting Donald Trump.

Paul spent the next several weeks negotiating with the California bar. He drafted a great summary of my case and sent it to John for approval and edits. John was still my criminal defense attorney in the case, so I needed him to approve anything I took ownership of to ensure I wasn't running afoul of my role with DOJ.

Several months later, Paul notified me that the California bar had completed their preliminary investigation but needed me to sit for a deposition before they could decide if they were going to refer my case to trial or close it out. *Yet another deposition*, I thought. More legal fees, more insulting questions, more wasted time, and more anxiety. But I had to go through it to avoid losing my right to practice law in California.

The first phase of a bar complaint in the state of California is simply the bar investigating a complaint against an attorney. The attorney does not get to see the complaint levied against her until the bar decides to refer the case to trial. If the case goes to trial, the lawyer gets to see the accusations and is given an opportunity to defend herself at trial. In my case, I was hoping the bar would simply close my case without a trial, which also meant I'd never get to see the complaint filed against me.

The deposition went as expected. The state bar attorney conducting the deposition was kind and professional, but I still felt like he was looking for a reason to accuse me in some way. He never said that, and was very polite throughout the process, but he focused on details that made me feel he was trying to "catch me" in something. For me, the entire process was excruciating. Was I going to lose my law license and career simply because the bar hated my boss?

It was both gratifying—and terrifying—to hear Paul reach the same conclusions I had. Here's the way Paul described the case: "It became obvious that the bar investigation was part of the Democrat strategy to make attorneys fearful of representing Donald Trump. The message is: We WILL make your life miserable and require you to pay for representation if you provide legal services to Donald Trump. In almost fifty years of legal work, I have never seen anything like it."

Weeks after the deposition, I still didn't have a response. Nearly another month went by with no response from the bar. Paul continued to follow up and answer any questions they had. Finally, on November 22, 2023, the California bar closed their investigation and found no misconduct. I was *so* grateful! Finally, I could move on, or so I thought.

Jack Smith Subpoenas Me *Again*

In June 2023, at the same time the California bar opened their investigation, the Department of Justice reached out to John Lauro to subpoena me on the January 6th investigation Jack Smith had opened. With John insisting he had a conflict and could no longer represent me, he introduced me to his friend and fellow federal criminal defense attorney, Jeff Neiman.

Jeff was based in South Florida, and I made at least one trip to Fort Lauderdale to meet with him and his team of lawyers. Anything and everything I had written in email, text, notes, documents, or any other type of recording was searched and subpoenaed. Jeff and his team knew everything about my life from November 2020 to the present day. They had charts and reports laying out all of my communications.

During the 2020 election, I was a reporter and also volunteered to help Rudy Giuliani investigate the election irregularities when President Trump's lawyers all quit around the same time. It was my role with Rudy that DOJ was interested in.

"All right," said Jeff, "we've been through your materials and realize there's been a lot of investigation into your role already."

I nodded.

"You've already testified under oath before Congress, you've provided a production of documents related to your congressional subpoena, you've been deposed in a civil suit, you've conducted discovery in a separate civil suit involving the same time frame, you've written a book about your involvement in January 6th . . ." Jeff rattled off a list of landmines I needed to navigate.

"Uh huh," I said, looking at him like *What am I supposed to do about it?* I'd make all these inquiries stop if I could.

Jeff walked me through a number of scenarios, asked me any and every question possible surrounding January 6th.

"Christina," Jeff said with a serious tone, "these prosecutors are looking for a reason to indict you."

I nodded at him. "I'm aware."

After walking me through specifics of accusations DOJ could make, he said, "You still have your Fifth Amendment rights, which you've never invoked. I think you need to invoke your Fifth Amendment rights on this one."

I immediately hated the idea. Even though they're not supposed to, everyone assumes you're guilty of something if you invoke your rights. I hadn't done anything and had nothing to hide. I also knew they were hunting me and looking for anyone close to Donald Trump to destroy.

"What will happen if I invoke?" I asked.

"Well, a couple things could happen," Jeff said. "If they really want to target you, they may push back and give us a hard time since you've already testified before Congress, and more specifically, you've already produced records to Congress."

"They lost my records," I said.

"What do you mean they lost your records?" Jeff asked.

"The January 6th Committee made all of their records public. It's available online, but my documents are missing. They didn't produce my records."

"How do you know they lost them?" Jeff asked.

"Well, they either lost them, or intentionally didn't publish them for the public to see," I said. "Maybe they didn't want the public to realize no crimes had been committed. Who knows?"

"Is there anything in them you wouldn't want them to have?" Jeff asked the obvious question.

"I don't want them to have *any* of my private records. I don't want my own lawyers to have my records! It's such an invasion of privacy. It's humiliating. But, here we are, dissecting my every thought. Would you want all of your personal emails posted on the Internet by the United States Congress? I don't want *any* of it public," I said.

Jeff nodded understanding and said, "Right, but I mean is there anything in them that we haven't seen?"

"No. Of course not. You have all of my records. You've seen everything they have."

"Okay. Good," Jeff said. "Well, getting back on track. If you invoke your right against self-incrimination, I actually expect them to just accept it and leave you alone."

"Why do you think that?" I asked.

"Because I don't believe you have anything to offer them. More likely than not, they are trying to rule you out as a defense witness. They just want to make sure that you're not going to testify on behalf of the defense, and if you are, they want to know what you're going to say," Jeff explained.

"Think about it," he said. "They're running out of time. They want to get a conviction before the election. They don't want to waste time. They are simply trying to rule you out as a defense witness. If that's *not* what they do, we'll see how they respond and handle it then."

As I debated whether or not to invoke my Fifth Amendment right, Jeff's partner, Kate Meyer, reminded me that the United States Supreme Court states that "the [Fifth Amendment] protects the innocent as well as the guilty" (*Ohio v. Reiner, 532 U.S. 17 [2001]*). That helped. I've grown to love our Constitutional rights more than I ever thought I would, especially when it's painful to use them. I was grateful to Kate for sending me that case.

"Okay," I told Jeff. "Please let them know I'm invoking my Fifth Amendment rights."

Jeff notified DOJ I was invoking my rights. He was right. They didn't want to waste time on me and quickly wanted my invocation in writing. It was a Tuesday. July 4, 2023. I'm probably one of the few Americans who can say I invoked my Fifth Amendment rights on the Fourth of July. #America! DOJ left me alone for the remainder of the J6 case.

CHAPTER 19

America's Mayor Under Attack

One of the reasons the Left uses lawfare is because it causes chaos and suspicion. Driving a wedge between allies, creating doubt, spreading rumors—it's all designed to break our spirit and our commitment to the truth. If they make things difficult enough, maybe we will just fold up our tents and go home. For the fighters who wouldn't quit, that just drew more fire.

As I fought legal battles on several fronts and from several different directions, I was attacked with accusations that I had "flipped," whatever that was supposed to mean. I don't think anyone truly believed it, but it still caused frustration and suspicion. Whom can I trust? Who trusts me? How do I work with my colleagues if they're reading that I lied? Or worse—are *they saying* I lied?

There were days when I truly got discouraged, feeling persecuted and alone. But I would remind myself: There is someone I know who has suffered much worse. Despite all the heartache, fear, anxiety, and expense I suffered, it paled in comparison to the lawfare waged against Rudy Giuliani.

Rudy Giuliani Exposes Corruption

Rudy Giuliani was one of the most successful and transformative leaders in New York City history. And he was a thorn in the side of the progressive Left for decades, starting with his law-and-order revolution that transformed New York City into a safe and thriving center after many years of rampant crime. But once Rudy started to destabilize the Left's stranglehold on power, their pushback turned into a firestorm. The Left didn't want to just beat him, they didn't want to just silence him, they wanted to destroy him.

Burisma

Even before the 2020 election, Rudy was prominent in uncovering the Left's criminal behavior. Back in 2019, Rudy played a key role in exposing the Biden family's financial schemes with the Ukrainian oil company, Burisma. A handful of witnesses reached out to him to provide the details of the Biden financial situation. He vetted each one and arranged to go to Ukraine to personally interview each whistleblower and retrieve recordings of Joe Biden bribing then-Ukrainian President Petro Poroshenko.

On the tapes, Joe Biden threatens Poroshenko to withhold $1 billion in aid money to Ukraine unless Poroshenko fires then-Prosecutor General Viktor Shokin. Shokin had opened a criminal investigation into the oil and gas company Burisma (the same company that had Hunter Biden on their board and was paying him handsomely), and Vice President Joe Biden wanted the investigation shut down, which he later bragged about successfully doing.[1]

"The Ukrainian government didn't try to stop you from getting those tapes?" I asked Rudy one night as we caught up after a dinner party.

"They didn't know I was there, or what I was there for." Rudy smiled a mischievous grin. "A source tipped me off to the fact that they were going to stop us at the airport when we arrived the next morning for our 10:00 a.m. flight home. So, we hurried and left as soon as we could. Erik Prince's team was providing protection for us and managed to book us a private plane out of Ukraine a few hours later at 11:00 p.m. As we drove to the airport, we noticed a car following us. Later, I was told that as we were taking off, government officials were arriving trying to stop our departure."

"Were they going to arrest you?" I asked.

"I don't know," Rudy said matter-of-factly and then laughed like a schoolboy before saying, "I didn't want to find out!"

More than anyone else, Rudy exposed the Biden Family corruption, and was becoming a pain in the neck to those in power. The details of his findings are in his book *The Biden Crime Family*.

The Secret Grand Jury Investigation

"So, when did the FBI start targeting you?" I asked Rudy as I joined him and his entourage in the dining area of their hotel suite at the Willard. "Was it because you challenged the 2020 election?"

"Oh gosh, no. It was way before that," Rudy said, thinking back to when it began. "They started investigating me when I first represented Donald Trump in 2018, but I didn't find out about it until 2019. I later found out that they opened a grand jury investigation into me and gained access to my iCloud account. They were watching all my communications, even privileged communications."

"What was the grand jury investigation about?" I asked.

"I don't know. I never found out what they were investigating me for. Some people speculated it was some alleged FARA [Foreign Agents Registration Act] violation or tax issue, but nothing was ever confirmed. They eventually closed the grand jury. The prosecutors admitted in a letter that they didn't have probable cause to continue the probe, so they closed the investigation. That was great, but if they didn't have probable cause, by their own admission, how did they get a search warrant to search my iCloud account and then eventually my home?" Rudy chuckled at the obvious contradiction but was clearly frustrated by the apparent unlawful intrusion. "They executed search warrants on my home, my law practice, and my private business, completely violating attorney-client confidentiality." Rudy stopped a second and shook his head.

"You know, when the FBI raids your law practice and private business violating attorney-client privilege, that's bad for business. It absolutely destroyed my business. I had built a security business that, if I were to sell it, would have been worth about fifty million. Overnight, it was worthless. They destroyed my business for nothing. They found nothing."

"Why do you believe they were working so hard to hurt you?" I asked.

"Joe Biden," he said matter-of-factly. "When Joe Biden announced he was running for President in 2019, he sent a letter to all of the major networks telling them not to let me on the air and not to give me any credibility. I found out about the letter when George Stephanopoulos asked me about it when he received the letter. It was a surprise to me. But after that, the media just unleashed on me."

I started to ask another question, but Rudy continued: "Remember, they'd been monitoring my iCloud account for about a year at this point. I think they originally started monitoring me because they were looking for information on Donald Trump. I don't think I was originally their target. But once they knew all the evidence I had on Joe Biden, particularly from Ukraine and the witnesses that came forward, then they had to destroy me."

Mark Zuckerberg Makes a Phone Call

The attacks on Rudy came from all sides.

"Why did your law partners force you out of your firm?" I asked.

"My firm had a very substantial practice group in Silicon Valley. They represented a lot of the large Silicon Valley companies. I wasn't part of that group, but my partners were. My partners told me that Mark Zuckerberg called them and said they needed to kick me out of the firm or he would take all the Silicon Valley business somewhere else," Rudy said.

"Mark Zuckerberg?" I asked, surprised. Why the heck was he involved? "Was he a client of yours?"

"Not mine, no," Rudy said. "I'm not even sure if he was a client of my partners or if he just had a lot of sway over their Silicon Valley clients. I didn't bother to ask. It was clear that if I didn't leave the firm, Mark Zuckerberg would end my partners' Silicon Valley business," Rudy said.

Why would Mark Zuckerberg care about Rudy Giuliani's law firm? Did someone ask him to make the call? Does someone now owe Zuckerberg a favor? Have they repaid? This raised lots of questions for me but provided no answers.

Hunter Biden's Laptop

Rudy was undeterred. Just weeks before the 2020 election, Rudy dropped what should have been the biggest story of the election cycle. Giuliani had obtained a copy of Hunter Biden's laptop, with all the emails discussing "10% for the Big Guy," prostitutes, drugs, and a slew of other material that no potential First Family would want public.

By all accounts, the laptop appeared to prove the Biden family, managed by Hunter Biden, was involved in illegal activity, making millions of dollars by selling their political influence to foreign nations. That should have ended Joe Biden's election hopes. Instead, CIA and intelligence officials went to work at the direction of Antony Blinken, Biden's soon-to-be Secretary of State, to convince the American public the laptop was Russian disinformation.[2] It wasn't. The CIA had no reason to believe that it was. They simply lied to the American public to keep the Biden Crime Family in power.[3] The only voice they couldn't quiet, however, was Rudy's.

"At first I just had a lot of witnesses and interviews I'd done of Ukrainian whistleblowers. I had recorded Zoom interviews with whistleblowers like Viktor Shokin, the fired Prosecutor General investigating Burisma. I went to Lindsey Graham first with the information, because I thought the senate should investigate the situation, but he didn't want to hear it."

"What do you mean 'he didn't want to hear it'?" I asked, confused. As a prominent Republican US Senator, wouldn't Lindsey Graham want to know?

"Graham told me he wasn't interested 'because Joe Biden was a US senator,'" Rudy said.

"What does that mean?" I asked.

"I took it to mean that he didn't believe a US senator could be so compromised. He didn't believe the allegations and wouldn't even entertain them," Rudy said, without elaborating. It was unclear to me if that was Graham's intent, or if he meant that he didn't want to break some unwritten code among senators. "Once Graham refused, the witnesses I'd interviewed—my informants—all told me not to take the story to the FBI, because they believed the FBI was 'in on it.'" Rudy shrugged as if he didn't share the informant's concerns about the FBI.

Then he laughed. "I didn't know it at the time, but the FBI already had the laptop anyway. So I guess the informants were right in a way. I sent the information to John Solomon [former editor-in-chief of the *Washington Times*, columnist for the *Hill*, and founder of *Just the News*] who re-vetted all my sources himself and went through the allegations very carefully. John and I went on Sean Hannity's show around February 2019.

"In October 2020, I got the hard drive itself. That's when I pitched it to the *New York Post*, the *Wall Street Journal*, the *Daily Mail*, and Steve

Bannon. The *Journal* and the *Daily Mail* declined the story. Miranda Devine picked it up for the *Post* and really pursued the story well. She vetted everything carefully and really did a great job." Miranda Devine also published the bestselling book *Laptop from Hell.* "Bannon published the story too," Rudy added.

The 2020 Election

The mainstream media, of course, buried or ignored the stories of Biden family corruption, and Joe Biden went on to become President. Meanwhile, the Swamp doubled down on their campaign of misinformation. In November 2020, the media message across almost every network and platform was synced: *This was the most secure election in US history. There is no evidence of fraud.* Anyone who deviated from that message was censored, silenced, sued, and ridiculed. The machine behind that message was massive and rolling full steam ahead with the even more ridiculous claim that *Joe Biden received the most votes in American history. Joe Biden is the most popular president in US history.*

Almost no one was willing to deviate from the narrative, even conservative news personalities. Anyone who questioned the election outcome was labeled a "conspiracy theorist" and discredited, so most news personalities refused to challenge the narrative. They wouldn't even report on findings of potential election fraud or corruption. (I know, because whenever I appeared on the media, most networks refused to allow me to even mention the existence of my book, *Stealing Your Vote*, never mind speak about what I had found in researching it.) Who in their right mind would take on the media establishment? Rudy Giuliani.

Rudy spoke out relentlessly and worked tirelessly to try to expose the errors of the 2020 election. He asked for several public hearings with state legislatures to expose the evidence that citizens were bringing forward, and spent countless hours contesting "the narrative" publicly.

As Rudy persisted in arguing these cases and challenging their narrative, the Establishment began to realize Rudy's information could help turn the tide of the 2024 election (as I believe it did). They needed to discredit him, silence him, and punish him. To permanently take down Donald Trump, they needed to get rid of Rudy Giuliani.

CHAPTER 20

Unleashing the Hounds

"In 2021, after Joe Biden was in office, the FBI executed a search warrant at my home," Rudy reflected as he leaned back in his chair. "It was early in the morning, about six a.m. Bang! Bang! Bang! on the door of my apartment in New York. I got out of bed and opened the door. There were about eight FBI agents lining the hall, mostly male. The lead agent said, 'I'm really sorry that we have to do this, but I have to execute a search warrant on your home.'" Rudy looked at me in disbelief, like he still couldn't believe it happened.

"What did they say they were looking for?" I asked.

"Electronics. I let them in and they went straight to my nightstand in my bedroom and took my phone. They compiled all my electronics, I showed them where they all were, and they laid them out on my dining room table. I explained to them what each item was. They took everything. It was really weird. They took my ex-wife's old desktop from 2002. Just really bizarre stuff.

"Then I asked them, 'Do you want the incriminating stuff?'" Rudy said with his mischievous grin. "They said, 'Oh yeah, yeah.' They were interested," Rudy said. "So I had them follow me and I pulled out Hunter Biden's hard drive," Rudy said, still grinning, "I told them, I have two versions. 'Do you want the version with child porn? Or the one I've cleaned up and removed the child porn?'" Rudy had indicated he didn't want to distribute the compromised material when he gave copies of the hard drive to the reporters, so he created a clean version.

"They jumped back with their hands up and said, 'Oh no no! we can't take that! That's not what we're here for!'" Rudy exaggerated while laughing. "They wouldn't take the hard drives!"

"Did Hunter Biden really have child porn on his hard drive?" I asked.

"Uh-huh." Rudy nodded. "Nothing of sexual acts with children. It was all mild, mostly provocative posing of children, but it did meet the definition of child porn." Rudy paused and then emphasized, "My point is, the FBI should have wanted to take it, but they refused."

The Mayor Reacts

"Were you surprised by the way DOJ and the FBI treated you?" I asked.

"Very," he said without missing a beat. "I would never have thought the Southern District of New York would have been willing to allow that level of abuse against me. I was by far their best known, most successful, most distinguished attorney. I crushed the mafia, Wall Street crimes, prosecuted more political corruption than all the US attorneys before me combined. I was the first to use RICO [the Racketeer Influenced and Corrupt Organizations Act] against the mob and businesses. I prosecuted two Nazis and sent them back to Europe. I prosecuted terrorists, drug dealers, got a receivership on the Teamsters' union, I got a judge to remove the entire board of the Teamsters' union. We put in our own board until they were disengaged with the mafia and Las Vegas. It was through the Teamsters union's pension fund that the mafia laundered money to Las Vegas, originally set up by Jimmy Hoffa.

"I couldn't imagine anyone would think I'm dishonest! I spent my whole life being obsessive about my honesty. I wouldn't even take the ring from George Steinbrenner when the Yankees won in 1996. I sent it back to him. After I left office, I paid for the ring. He presented me with three more rings after I left. I said I'll only take them if I pay for them. I had my secretary document everything. I even went to the jeweler and asked what the players pay when they lose a ring. I paid the same rate as the players for a replacement ring. I bought all four World Series rings offered to me from my time as mayor."

The Bar Targets Rudy

The Left filed bar complaints against Rudy in New York and Washington, DC. Both bars suspended his license without a hearing, which is unheard of in the legal profession, especially against someone with such a distinguished history.

Finally, in December 2022, the DC bar decided to give him his hearing. The crux of the complaint was that Rudy Giuliani somehow acted unethically by representing President Trump in Pennsylvania when he presented the facts exactly as they were. He had more than three hundred affidavits from Pennsylvania witnesses, and all of his information was based on sworn eyewitness statements. Rudy Giuliani had called me a few weeks earlier to see if I would be willing to testify on his behalf at the DC bar. My testimony would be to confirm that, when I was working for Rudy on the post-2020 election cases, Rudy actually did acquire the information prior to arguing it in court—which is true. What Rudy Giuliani argued to the court in Pennsylvania was an accurate representation of the evidence he had acquired from witnesses in Pennsylvania.

It's also worth noting that the judge in the Pennsylvania case never accused *any* of the attorneys of wrongdoing. Oftentimes, a judge is the one who raises the issue of potential malpractice and the bar will get involved later. In this case, political activists who wanted to destroy America's Mayor started the process.

The hearing took place the week of December 5, 2022. My testimony wasn't until Wednesday, so I watched short bursts of the hearing when I had time. Like most legal proceedings, it was boring. Like most targeted political accusations, this was an assault on Rudy Giuliani's character.

At one point, they were questioning him for disagreeing with a Pennsylvania Supreme Court's decision, accusing him of running contrary to the law, because he argued the Pennsylvania Supreme Court erred in its opinion. The questions were derogatory and condescending, aimed at making America's Mayor out to be a traitor.

Rudy responded saying in effect, "I recently saw you on television talking about the *Dobbs* decision, which overturned *Roe v. Wade*. Correct?" The attorney acknowledged he'd been on TV to discuss *Dobbs*. "You mentioned that you thought the decision was wrongly decided and that the United States Supreme Court made a mistake in its ruling." Rudy paused for effect. "Was that treasonous of you to make those statements on television? Were you violating the law by questioning the Supreme Court's decision?" Giuliani beautifully pointed out the hypocrisy for which the liberal activists had no response.

It's only considered "malpractice" when conservatives question a ruling; Democrats can apparently do whatever they want with impunity. Rudy made his point, saying, "Questioning a court's decision is not treasonous. Arguing that a case was wrongly decided is not a violation of the law. That's how you practice law. It's what lawyers do. There was nothing wrong with me questioning the Pennsylvania Supreme Court, just like there was nothing wrong with you questioning the United States Supreme Court."

At another point in the hearing, one of the DC bar lawyers questioned Rudy's argument that it's actually the state legislators who determine the electors for their respective states. "So, you argue that the state legislators have the authority to determine a state's electors, is that right?" he said.

Rudy responded confidently, "One hundred percent. That's correct."

The attorney responded, "So, you're arguing the 'independent legislature theory'?"

Rudy looked confused for a moment and then said "I don't know it as that."

"What do you know it as?" asked the DC lawyer.

"Article 2, section 1, clause 2 of the United States Constitution. It's stated plainly," said Rudy. Article 2, section 1, clause 2 of the United States Constitution states in its entirety:

> Each State shall appoint, ***in such Manner as the Legislature thereof may direct***, a Number of Electors, equal to the whole Number of Senators and Representatives to which the State may be entitled in the Congress: but no Senator or Representative, or Person holding an Office of Trust or Profit under the United States, shall be appointed an Elector. [emphasis added]

This issue of the elections clause went before the United States Supreme Court in *Moore v. Harper*, which was heard the same day as Rudy's hearings. Meaning, at the same time political activists were trying to disbar Rudy Giuliani for holding a different opinion than theirs about the elections clause, another set of lawyers were arguing the different opinions before the United States Supreme Court.

Rudy's hearing wrapped up three days later after five of us—Corey Lewandowski, John Droz Jr., me, Bernie Kerik, and Rudy—testified that Rudy's actions were honest and an accurate reflection of the information available at that time. He was disbarred anyway.

The Brutal Attacks on Rudy

Second only to Donald Trump himself, Rudy Giuliani faced a fierce backlash for his support of the President.

"How many cases did they bring against you?" I asked.

He shrugged and waved as if I'd asked him to guess how many marbles were in a jar. "I've lost count. It's been a lot." He thought for a second and said, "You know who represented those ladies from Georgia who sued me?"

"Who?" I asked

"Michael Gottlieb," he said. He chuckled as he said, "He was Hunter Biden's former partner and he used to represent Burisma." He laughed as he shook his head. "You can't make this stuff up."

Rudy Giuliani is a fighter and not easily taken down. But that's not for lack of trying. During the four years between the 2020 election and Donald Trump's victory in 2024, the Establishment waged a massive campaign of lawfare and harassment against Rudy, including:

- A defamation lawsuit by Dominion—pending
- A defamation lawsuit from Smartmatic—settled out of court
- A lawsuit by Rep. Eric Swalwell (D-CA) for damages relating to January 6, 2021—case dismissed
- A defamation lawsuit from election workers in Georgia— settled out of court
- A subpoena to testify before the J6 committee—he testified
- Lawsuit alleging misconduct and harassment by a former associate—still pending
- Giuliani was listed as an unindicted co-conspirator in the federal case of Trump's alleged attempt to overturn 2020—this case was dismissed without prejudice in November 2024
- Giuliani is indicted in *The State of Georgia v. Donald J. Trump*—still pending
- Hunter Biden sued Giuliani for "hacking into, tampering with, manipulating, copying, disseminating, and generally obsessing

over data that they were given that was taken or stolen from" his devices[1]—Hunter Biden eventually dropped the case

- Giuliani indicted in Arizona on nine counts of forgery and conspiracy (he's my co-defendant)—still pending
- Giuliani disbarred in New York state
- Giuliani disbarred in DC

Giuliani has had some legal wins in litigation and investigations against him, though they are scant relief compared with the barrage unleashed against him. Federal prosecutors dropped an investigation in 2022 into whether Giuliani followed foreign lobbying laws without bringing any charges,[2] and a federal judge dismissed a lawsuit against Giuliani that sought to hold him liable for the January 6, 2021, riot at the Capitol building.[3] The ruling found that Giuliani's speech before the riot, in which he called for "trial by combat," clearly referred to the voting machines being compared against the results, not actual combat of people, and was protected speech.

Throughout it all, the media has piled on, constantly portraying Rudy as someone not to be trusted. The truth is that Rudy Giuliani is and always has been an American hero. The public legal campaign against him is one of the darkest stains throughout this period of history. Rudy Giuliani loves this nation and has sacrificed personally and professionally to ensure Americans have the information they need to prevent a tyrannical take over. He was demonized for it and deserves to be restored.

CHAPTER 21

January 6th—The Federal Government Targets Americans

Going after Rudy Giuliani was, perhaps, not surprising, given his high profile and his very vocal advocacy for the rule of law in the face of a tidal wave of corruption and abuse of power. Even going after me was, sadly, par for the course, as I had worked for President Trump and aggressively advocated for transparency and fairness in our elections—two things the Left seemed determined to oppose. But most of America was shocked when the Establishment went after ordinary citizens, mobilizing both the Department of Justice and the mainstream media to destroy the lives of more than 1,500 regular citizens.

Four years after the fateful events of January 6, 2021, many Americans still believe that violent extremists stormed the Capitol and threatened democracy. The facts tell a much different story and provide a sad chapter in the history of lawfare. While the media loves to paint all the J6 "insurrectionists" as violent extremists, none of them was actually charged with insurrection.[1] Only 174 of the 1,583 people prosecuted were charged with crimes of assaulting or impeding an officer using a weapon or inflicting bodily harm.[2] A little over a third of those prosecuted were alleged to have assaulted or impeded an officer, but without a weapon or doing harm.³ In other words, nearly two-thirds of those prosecuted were merely charged with trespassing, unlawful entry, or parading. That's a far cry from the idea that everyone there that day was a violent right-wing extremist. Legally speaking, there was no insurrection.

While there will no doubt be countless books describing the events of January 6th, my goal is not to provide a blow-by-blow account of what happened, but to give you a look behind the curtain at the shocking weaponization of justice against regular American citizens. The stories that follow, of the Praying Grandma, the Shaman, and the Oath Keepers, are just three of the hundreds of cases of lawfare waged by the Establishment against voices that dared to challenge "the narrative." These three cases represent the full gamut of cases against the J6 defendants—from the least severe to the most extreme, and everything in between.

The "Praying Grandma"

Rebecca Lavrenz, "the Praying Grandma," a seventy-two-year-old resident of Colorado described the event like this: "I didn't touch anything," Lavrenz said. "I was swept up with the crowd. It was like a big rush going into the Capitol. There on the video, Capitol footage video, there's a gentleman, a police officer, right beside me, almost like a door greeter at Walmart, just saying hi to me, and I was just talking to him. He never told me to leave the building. And so I didn't think I was doing anything wrong. I really didn't."⁴ When asked why she thought it was okay to enter the Capitol, she said that the doors were opened from the inside—the police opened the doors and allowed them in.⁵

The judge sentenced her to six months home confinement, a year of probation, and a fine of $103,000.⁶

Lavrenz's version of events matches the video footage of her presence in the Capitol and that of many others. The police opened the doors and allowed the protesters in, leading them to believe they were lawfully allowed to be there.

Most of the 1,583 protesters prosecuted by DOJ had similar stories to Lavrenz, despite the media's narrative that they were dangerous. They just weren't. That's likely why the Establishment fought so hard to keep the public from seeing the surveillance videos—for years—because those inside were *not* violent.

Jacob Chansley—The Shaman

Another January 6th victim of lawfare was Jacob Chansley, better known as "The Shaman." Chansley was charged with obstructing an official proceeding.[7] According to the Department of Justice:

> Chansley "was shirtless, wearing a Viking hat with fur and horns, covered in red, white, and blue face paint, and carrying an American flag tied to a pole with a sharp object at the tip and a bullhorn. He . . . then entered the Upper West Terrace . . . as the certification proceedings were still under way. Chansley . . . reach[ed] the Gallery of the Senate and then the Senate floor. He then scaled the Senate dais, taking the seat that Vice President Mike Pence had occupied an hour earlier. Chansley proceeded to take pictures of himself on the dais and ***refused to vacate the seat when asked to do so by law enforcement***. Instead, he stated that "Mike Pence is a f----ing traitor" and wrote a note on available paper on the dais, stating "It's Only A Matter of Time. Justice Is Coming!" He further called other rioters up to the dais and led them in an incantation over his bullhorn.[8] [emphasis added]

He pled guilty and was sentenced to forty-one months in prison.[9]

But in March 2023, then-Fox News Host Tucker Carlson managed to obtain footage of the closed caption TV footage from inside the Capitol on January 6th. Trump supporters had been trying to obtain the CCTV footage *for years*, but Congress prevented its release. Surely, if the CCTV footage showed massive riots, looting, and vandalism, wouldn't Congress want the public to see the damage Trump supporters were doing? Didn't DOJ want to use the footage in trial? The problem was, the CCTV footage didn't match the narrative that Congress, the J6 Committee, Jack Smith, DOJ, and the media were pushing. The protesters were peaceful.

In fact, the video footage showed Capitol Police *escorting* Jacob Chansley through the building and directing him to the Senate Chambers.[10] Chansley's conduct in the videos did not match the allegations brought by DOJ of his interactions with Capitol Police.

Chansley's attorney, Albert S. Watkins, told the *Washington Times*: "The government had a duty to release material video footage, not just video footage that supported the government's prosecutorial narrative."[11] Prosecutors are required to turn over exculpatory evidence, known as *Brady evidence*, to defendants so that they can meaningfully defend themselves. They didn't.

DOJ withheld the evidence from the defense and sent Chansley to prison without him knowing that video evidence existed contradicting the government's claims. A few weeks after Tucker released the video, Chansley's sentence was cut fourteen months short, supposedly for good behavior, having nothing to do with the release of the video.[12] Chansely's defense attorney called for sanctions against the DOJ prosecutors for withholding the evidence.[13]

The Oath Keepers

Another high-profile target of the J6 prosecutors were the Oath Keepers, a group of mostly former military, founded by Elmer Stewart Rhodes, a former Army paratrooper and Yale lawyer.[14] They have over 35,000 dues-paying members, and "more than a decade's worth of a spotless record, providing disaster relief and security services during riots and other large events. They had never once been accused or charged with a crime in thousands of operations."[15]

Rhodes's role in January 6th, according to DOJ, was that of a planner and organizer. "At approximately 2:30 p.m., according to the government's evidence, Oath Keepers and affiliates—many wearing paramilitary clothing and patches with the Oath Keepers name, logo, and insignia—marched in a 'stack' formation up the east steps of the Capitol, joined a mob, and made their way into the Capitol. Rhodes remained outside, coordinating activities."[16]

His trial included charges of leading teams of Oath Keepers "prepared to rapidly transport firearms and other weapons into Washington, DC, in support of operations aimed at using force" on the Capitol.[17] But in fact, no weapons ever came into DC, and it doesn't appear that Rhodes tried to deploy them. But, according to DOJ, Rhodes had them staged and available if needed.

Rhodes was eventually convicted of seditious conspiracy and sentenced in May 2023 to eighteen years in prison with three years of supervised release—the longest sentence of any J6 defendant.[18] A handful of other Oath Keepers were also convicted of seditious conspiracy and received lighter sentences. Leftists called the Oath Keepers "domestic terrorists" and explained why everyone should fear them.[19] So, justice was served, right?

Steve Baker Uncovers the Inconvenient Truth

Enter Steve Baker, an investigative reporter with The Blaze. In 2023, Baker obtained copies of a batch of released closed-circuit TV footage from inside the Capitol on January 6th. His first report on his review of the CCTV footage was October 4, 2023—almost three years after

January 6th—titled "Analysis: Did Nancy Pelosi's security chief perjure himself in Oath Keeper's trial?"[20]

In his report, Baker details down to the minute the location of the police officers and matches it up with their testimonies at the Oath Keepers trials. He explains that 1,700 security cameras inside the capitol produced more than 41,000 minutes of footage of the event, most of which was kept from defense counsel.[21] Again, the government is required to turn over exculpatory evidence, *Brady evidence*, to the defense so that they can defend themselves against the government's accusations. They didn't.

At trial, rather than playing all of the videos for the jury to make up their own minds about the guilt or innocence of the Oath Keepers, the prosecutors instead decided to rely on testimony of police officers—trusted bulwarks of society—to tell the jury the truth about what happened. They used carefully selected pieces of the video to support the testimony, withholding anything that contradicted their version of events. The key pieces of evidence to support the claims of seditious intent came from the testimony of police officers.[22]

According to Baker's review of the CCTV footage, "The problem with [the officer's] testimony about this significant event is that, according to direct video evidence the jury never saw, *it never happened.*"[23] [emphasis added] Baker's article states: "The Capitol Police officer . . . appears to have given false testimony about his whereabouts during a key encounter with members of the Oath Keepers . . ."[24] Maybe the officer just forgot or misremembered? Or worse. Either way, his testimony didn't match the video. Baker's article marked the beginning of a series of "analyzing the video evidence recently made available to the public."[25]

Surely once DOJ leadership was made aware of Baker's report, the prosecutors then worked diligently to ensure the rights of the accused were protected, right? Any wrongs committed by the prosecution should be corrected, right? No. What did they do? *The FBI arrested Steve Baker!*

In 2024, after Baker had been reporting on the injustice for a few months, the FBI arrested him, in handcuffs, charged him with four misdemeanors, and booked him for prosecution. The charges were related to his presence, *as a journalist*, at the Capitol on January 6, 2021. He, like many journalists (myself included), were present to report on the events of the day. The FBI showed no interest in him for three years but arrested him in 2024 after he reported on how the CCTV footage does not match the testimony of police officers in the Oath Keepers trial.

Baker was scheduled for a trial in November 2024 after Donald Trump had already won the 2024 election. In order "to avoid the shaming exercise of a trial," Baker plead guilty to charges of trespassing and disorderly conduct, maintaining that he did not do anything wrong and was being prosecuted for his journalism.[26] He would have been sentenced on March 6, 2025, but instead received a pardon from President Trump in January 2025.

Wrongful Convictions

The Praying Grandma, The Shaman, and the founder of Oath Keepers were just three of the more than 1,500 victims of lawfare. Some were sentenced to weeks or months in jail, some were convicted but not sentenced to jail time—and some were imprisoned for years without any chance for justice at all, as they were held without trial.

For example, Jake Lang, from New York, was arrested ten days after the J6 events in January 2021. He was held in prison *without trial* for four years until he received a pardon from Donald Trump and was released.[27] Not only was he held without trial, but he was also frequently placed in solitary confinement—a form of torture and psychological abuse.

To be clear, Lang was imprisoned for four years in Washington, DC, and has never been convicted of any crime. Lang has by far been the most outspoken J6 defendant of the abuses of the system. DOJ has not publicized how many defendants were held in pre-trial confinement and never actually received their trial, so the total number is not known. This was weaponization of justice at its most evil—more reminiscent of a Soviet Gulag than the US judicial system.

President Trump Pardons the J6ers

Due process in America requires a timely and fair trial—not imprisonment for years without a trial, manufactured charges, suppression of evidence, and perjury. The entire spectrum of January 6th investigations was irredeemably compromised from the beginning. Justice was not served and does not appear to have been the goal. Rather, punishing political opponents (the very definition of tyranny and abuse of power) seems to have been the driving motivation for an unprecedented abuse of power against ordinary citizens.

When President Trump announced his intentions to pardon the January 6ers as political prisoners, the media erupted with criticism.[28] The gross mishandling of the evidence and witness testimony by DOJ to unfairly manufacture convictions required complete pardons.

Had there been some semblance of justice in the nearly 1,600 cases, perhaps President Trump could have resolved the wrongs individually. The breadth of injustice provided no such opportunity. The only remedy to ensure people were not wrongly convicted was a blanket pardon. Rather than a scalpel, President Trump used a wrecking ball. He rightfully pardoned every single J6er.

CHAPTER 22

Keeping Donald Trump off the Ballot

For more than four years, the Left conducted their "investigations" into the events of January 6, 2021, and yet Americans remain heatedly divided about what transpired on that day. Surely a thorough investigation would put the issue to bed, right? How can there still be so many misconceptions and disagreements about what actually happened? The answer: Because the "investigations" were never a search for truth.

From the beginning, the aim of the investigations was to prevent Donald Trump from ever holding office again. Democrats and the political class aggressively and unfairly targeted Americans and threw them in jail—some without trial—for years to try to discourage people from supporting Donald Trump.[1] Americans who went to Washington, DC, to "peacefully and patriotically make [their] voices heard" ended up as targets of the federal government.[2] But why?

January 11, 2021
Merely five days after the events of January 6th, the House of Representatives, led by Democrats, impeached President Donald J.

Trump—who had only nine days left in office. Clearly there was not enough time to complete an investigation, hear witnesses, examine evidence, or anything else that could fairly establish a finding of guilt.

President Trump supposedly "incited violence," but how? Surely Congress doesn't expect us to believe that his speech on the Ellipse convinced the listeners (unarmed and unprepared) to spontaneously storm the Capitol? If not that, then what? What did he actually *do* to organize an insurrection? Congress couldn't be bothered with facts, so the House moved with uncharacteristic speed to rush Donald Trump through impeachment with nine days left in office. What was the urgency? After all, he'd be out of office in less than two weeks anyway.

The second sentence under Article 1 of the impeachment reveals their true goal: "Further, section 3 of the 14th Amendment to the Constitution *prohibits any person* who has 'engaged in insurrection or rebellion against' the United States *from hold[ing] any office* . . . under the United States"[emphasis added]. January 6th was always about preventing Donald Trump from returning to office.

Just in case you missed it, the last sentence of the very short impeachment document repeats the point: "Donald John Trump thus warrants impeachment and trial, removal from office, and *disqualification to hold and enjoy any office* of honor, trust, or profit under the United States" [emphasis added]. They didn't want Donald Trump to ever hold office again. They failed.

January 6th Committee

But even after this last-minute impeachment failed, they were not done trying. The Democrat-controlled House of Representatives created a Select Committee for the purposes of investigating the January 6th attack.[3] Republicans said the committee was illegitimate for several reasons, but the most glaring was the blatant violation of the House

Committee Rule that required thirteen committee members to be appointed by the Speaker of the House (Nancy Pelosi [D-CA]) and five to be appointed by the Minority Leader (Kevin McCarthy [R-CA]).

McCarthy appointed Jim Banks (R-IN) to serve as Ranking Member, along with Jim Jordan (R-OH), Rodney Davis (R-IL), Kelley Armstrong (R-ND), and Troy Nehls (R-TX).[4]

Pelosi rejected Jim Jordan and Jim Banks and selected the two Republicans that *she* wanted on the committee, Adam Kinzinger (R-IL) and Liz Cheney (R-WY), violating the House rules and proper procedure to constitute a committee. McCarthy then withdrew his other nominees in protest, claiming the committee was not properly constituted. That left the committee without a proper Ranking Member or minority members, rendering it illegitimate.

President Trump's Offer of Assistance

The committee's so-called investigations overlooked all of the exculpatory facts showing that President Trump tried to make Washington more secure on January 6th. On New Year's Eve, DC Mayor Muriel Bowser sent a request to the Department of Defense for additional support.[5] Defense Secretary Chris Miller testified before Congress that President Trump's response was to "fill [her request] and do whatever is necessary to protect" the city.[6]

As President, prior to January 6th, he offered 10,000 troops to DC Mayor Bowser to help secure the city, but that was declined.[7] The Trump White House went to the Department of Defense and requested a Quick Reaction Force to be ready in case it was needed.[8] Kash Patel, the Chief of Staff at the Department of Defense at that time, testified before the J6 Committee that the Trump White House had authorized 10,000 to 20,000 troops for support.[9]

When the Capitol was breached, White House Chief of Staff Mark Meadows called Secretary of Defense Chris Miller to activate the

Quick Reaction Force.[10] Meadows said to Miller, "Get them in here. Get them in here to secure the Capitol now!"[11]

All of this information was readily available to the J6 Committee and comes from transcripts from their own hearings.[12] In fact, "an early transcribed interview conducted by the committee" included precisely this same evidence "from a key source."[13] Liz Cheney (R-WY), Nancy Pelosi's replacement from the lawfully nominated Republicans, and other committee and staff members, attended and personally participated in the interview.[14] Yet, the final report issued by the J6 Committee stated that there was "no evidence" that Trump offered 10,000 troops in support of securing the city.[15] The Committee lied.

Another strange fact that the Committee overlooked was the fact that Donald Trump's tweets were censored. Once the Capitol had been breached, Donald Trump posted a video to his Twitter page telling everyone to remain peaceful and to go home.[16] The tweet was censored by Twitter, taken down, and the public was prevented from seeing it. Why? It's almost like they were trying to frame him for insurrection so that he could never hold office again and they didn't want his side of the story available.

The "Un-select" committee, as called by Donald Trump due to its improper formation, spent nearly two years parading their investigation around prime-time television. They held several hearings of selected witnesses to testify on prime-time news networks.

I can tell you from experience that those public hearings were misleading. I know, because I was summoned to testify. The committee's legislative counsel interrogated me for about six hours, asking me bizarre questions about email chains I wasn't even on, hoping I'd say something that they could use to make the President or Rudy Giuliani look bad. I didn't. They pulled memes I had retweeted asking me to explain the significance of the memes. The attorneys used their position of authority to try to pressure me about memes.

Yes. Congress actually conducted an investigation into the memes I retweeted.

The story fed to the public was not the reality of the J6 committee. The committee only held public hearings of cherry-picked witnesses for the nation to see.[17] Several other witnesses, myself included, testified behind closed doors away from the view of the public. Then, when the committee publicized their report on December 22, 2022, they deleted much of the information provided by witnesses that tended to exonerate the President.[18] The public only saw the witnesses the committee wanted them to see.[19] The entire production appeared to be an attempt to defame Donald Trump and convince the public he was bad and should never hold office again. They failed.

The J6 Grand Jury

As it became glaringly apparent that the J6 Committee was a paper tiger, Biden's Attorney General, Merrick Garland, decided to appoint a Special Prosecutor to complete what the J6 Committee couldn't. Smith's appointment would later be deemed an unconstitutional violation of the Appointments Clause by Judge Cannon in the Florida case.[20] Until then, Smith was given a nearly unlimited budget with no oversight,[21] all to target the Biden Administration's chief political opponent.

A conviction for insurrection was the holy grail to ensure Donald Trump couldn't hold office again, and Jack Smith was their chosen knight. However, even Jack Smith couldn't shoehorn the facts of January 6th into a case for insurrection. There was no evidence that Donald Trump participated in or orchestrated an insurrection, and Smith couldn't find a way to say that he did.

Neither the original indictment nor the superseding indictment against Donald Trump included a charge for insurrection.[22]

Without a conviction of Donald Trump for insurrection, the Establishment backing Jack Smith didn't have a mechanism to prevent

Donald Trump from winning the White House. The best they could hope for was that the negative press surrounding the Smith investigations would discourage the public from voting for him. They failed.

The Playbook

By the time the 2024 election rolled around, DOJ was prosecuting people who didn't deserve to be prosecuted, apparently manipulating facts by allowing their witnesses to mislead the jury, arresting the journalists exposing them, hiding exculpatory evidence, hiding video evidence, and manufacturing convictions—all to fit the narrative that Donald Trump had instigated and orchestrated an insurrection.

This was all in addition to the slew of other lawfare aimed at taking down Donald Trump, including prosecution by the New York Attorney General and Manhattan District Attorney, the classified documents case, the Fani Willis criminal charges in Georgia, and the myriad cases involving the 2020 election. Don't forget about the Russia and Ukraine hoaxes, and all the false accusations levied against President Trump during his first term. Every single one of these cases was aimed at keeping Donald Trump out of the White House. By 2024, they were getting more desperate and more direct.

States Try to Remove Donald Trump from the 2024 Ballot

In another Hail Mary attempt to keep Donald Trump out of office, political opponents in several blue states creatively tried to exclude Donald Trump from the 2024 ballot, declaring him an insurrectionist (without a criminal trial).[23] Litigation ensued that quickly wound its way to the United States Supreme Court. In March 2024, the Supreme Court *unanimously* ruled in *Trump v. Anderson*, a case from Colorado, that the states could not exclude Donald Trump from the ballot. They failed again.

On November 5, 2024, Donald Trump won the Presidential election, including the popular vote, and was due to be sworn in as the forty-seventh President on the afternoon of January 20, 2025. With Donald Trump about to return to the White House, it appears that the Establishment hacks who had been relentlessly abusing the justice system to try to end President Trump's political career got scared. Joe Biden still had a few more weeks in office, and so they ran to Uncle Joe for cover.

Joe Biden Pardon's the J6 Committee and Capitol Police

On the morning of January 20, 2025, Joe Biden's last morning in office, he—or whoever controlled the autopen—issued preemptive pardons to every member of the January 6th Committee and their staff. He also pardoned four police officers, two Capitol Police officers, and two DC Metro Police officers who had testified before the January 6th Committee.

Joe Biden and his administration claim the pardons were to ensure the J6 Committee members, their staff, the Capitol Police, and the DC Metro Police were not unfairly targeted for political prosecutions by the Trump Administration. Maybe. Or maybe they knew they had exposure to criminal liability and would need pardons. Maybe they lied under oath. Maybe their conduct was not above reproach as they wanted us all to believe.

Why Do They Want Him Out of Office?

Why was the Establishment hell-bent on keeping Donald Trump out of the White House? Because he's doing exactly what they feared. He's exposing the billions, likely trillions, in slush funds of government checks with no accountability. The corruption likely runs deeper than we could have even imagined, but Donald Trump is exposing it. Those benefiting from the unaccountable blank checks from the government don't want Trump to turn the spigot off and return the money to the American people, where it belongs. He's ending the reign of the billionaire political class, and they hate him for it.

One More Thing

In January 2024, I received another subpoena from a civil matter against Donald Trump relating to January 6th. Once again, I called my lawyer (Jeff), to relay the news of yet another bullet aimed in my direction. This subpoena largely covered the same thing as the previous DOJ subpoena about January 6th, so the decision to invoke my Fifth Amendment rights again was obvious. I was grateful for Jeff and his team's quick response in handling the situation. I also hoped it would be the last time I'd need their help. It wasn't.

CHAPTER 23

Amateur Hour

Ding. Ding. Ding. The three-toned alert from my Ring doorbell broke my concentration. I paused the email I was writing and looked at my phone. A Palm Beach County Sheriff's Deputy stood at my door with papers in his hand. *You've got to be kidding me! What the hell does he want?* This was my ninth encounter with some type of law enforcement, criminal investigation, or process server in less than three years. Constantly having police officers, the US Marshals, the FBI, or process servers show up at my home gets very old very quickly—which is why they do it.

Every time a police officer knocks on your door with a warrant, subpoena, or whatever, it's very expensive and very scary. Attorneys spend hundreds of hours poring over your personal information, emails, thoughts, anything you've done for years just trying to figure out how you could get thrown in prison or owe millions of dollars to someone you've never even heard of. Surely, I'd done something wrong and they were determined to find it.

Even though I'd made it through the previous three years without liability, I'd racked up hundreds of thousands, maybe millions of dollars in legal fees defending myself to prove I'd done nothing wrong.

Some of the attorneys' fees were covered by insurance, some covered by
my employer, some were covered by a generous donor, but it's always
terrifying. What if I'm not covered? I'd be financially ruined. My enemies had already made multiple attacks on my law license. Would they
try again? For what? Just to destroy my career.

I sat at my desk in my home office trying to figure out what this
could possibly be about. The FBI had already shown up to my home
regarding the Mar-a-Lago raid. This wouldn't be related to that. No
other incidents had occurred in Florida, to my knowledge. Certainly
nothing that I was a part of. What on earth is the Palm Beach County
Sheriff's office doing here? How hard should I make this for the deputy? Having been through this eight times prior, I decided to just open
the door and figure out what he wanted.

"Hello. I'm looking for Christina Bobb," the officer said.

"What's this about?" I asked, not acknowledging his question.

"Well," he said, somewhat evasively, "I have a subpoena here for
grand jury testimony." The officer looked to be in his forties, fit, blond
hair, tan skin (like everyone in Florida). He quickly added, "It says
you're not under investigation, they just want documents and your testimony." He seemed to be kind and wanted to put me at ease, but he
didn't. Even nice police officers can ruin your life.

"What's this about?" I asked again.

"Well." He paused. "It's from Arizona." He shrugged a bit. He never
said it, but we both knew that meant the subpoena was not enforceable
in Florida. Arizona does not have jurisdiction in Palm Beach County,
Florida.

My blood was boiling. *Who the hell does the Arizona Attorney
General think she is? She knows she doesn't have jurisdiction in Florida,
but she's still going to make me spend my time and money defending this
bullshit subpoena anyway. All because I reported on how messed up the*

Arizona elections were. It's a complete abuse of power. I didn't say anything but continued to stare at the police officer.

He looked at me for a second and said, "Did you witness a murder or something?" He paused to gauge my reaction.

"No," I said flatly.

He clearly didn't know what was going on and continued "It's really unusual to see something like this from out of state. This isn't really . . ." he trailed off, then regrouped. "It doesn't say what crime they are investigating. It just says they want you to show up to testify and to bring documents, but it doesn't say what documents." He reached out to hand me the paper. "Do you have any idea what this is about?"

"I work for Donald Trump," I said, attempting to signal that whatever he was serving me with was bullshit. He may or may not have agreed. He didn't show it.

I locked the door behind him and walked back to my desk to look at the subpoena. *Office of the Arizona Attorney General—Criminal Division.* The subpoena contained the seal of the Arizona Attorney General and simply stated when and where to appear. Then, in all caps, in large, bold lettering centered on the page it stated:

**IF YOU FAIL TO APPEAR AS ORDERED,
A WARRANT WILL BE ISSUED FOR YOUR ARREST.**

How on earth is this legal?! Arizona can't arrest me in Florida! They didn't bother to domesticate this subpoena, meaning getting a Florida court to bless it and make it enforceable in Florida. They didn't domesticate it either because they didn't know how, or they knew a Florida court would never grant their request. Are they really threatening to arrest me? For what?

A letter accompanied the subpoena and said in full:

Dear Ms. Bobb:

You have been subpoenaed to appear before the State Grand Jury at 1:00 p.m. on Monday March, 18, 2024. I am supplying this letter to provide helpful background information about the State Grand Jury. The State Grand Jury consists of from 12 to 16 persons selected from the entire State of Arizona. It is the State Grand Jury's responsibility to inquire into State crimes within its jurisdiction.

As a State Grand Jury witness you will be asked to testify and answer questions, and you also may be asked to produce records and documents. Only the members of the State Grand Jury, attorneys from the Arizona Attorney General's office, and a court reporter are permitted in the grand jury room while you testify. If you have an attorney, your attorney must wait outside the grand jury room while you testify.

You are not a person under investigation by the State Grand Jury [emphasis added]. Nevertheless, as a witness before the State Grand Jury you may refuse to answer any question if a truthful answer to the question would tend to incriminate you. Anything that you do or say may be used in a subsequent legal proceeding.

Please contact me at 602-xxx-xxxx if you have any questions.

Sincerely,
Nicholas Klingerman
Division Chief Counsel
Criminal Division

No wonder the Palm Beach County Sheriff's deputy thought I'd witnessed a murder. There was less than zero information in this letter. I was being ordered, on the threat of arrest, to appear 2,500 miles away to answer criminal questions and bring documents for . . . what? What crime are we talking about here? It was February 29, 2024, and they expected me to be in Arizona in a couple weeks. My lawyers needed to shut this down quickly.

Was This All About 2020?

Even though the subpoena gave no hint as to what case I was being dragged in to testify on, I had a pretty good idea I knew. It no doubt related to the 2020 election. In November 2020, Donald Trump and his supporters, myself included, were convinced that the election had been rigged in favor of Joe Biden. The media initiated a full-court press denying any evidence of election fraud without even looking for it. The only acceptable narrative in the mainstream press was *There is no evidence of election fraud. This was the most secure election in US history.* How the media knew that to be true just days after the election is still a mystery. Anyone deviating from the narrative was deemed a conspiracy theorist.

Not to be intimidated, between November 3, 2020 (election day) and January 6, 2021 (the day the US Congress certified the election), Donald Trump challenged the results in seven states: Pennsylvania, Georgia, Michigan, Wisconsin, Nevada, New Mexico . . . and Arizona.

Which brings us to the thorny issue of state electors. Federal law requires that individual states certify their elections on December 14. Thus, every four years, on December 14, state electors in every state must meet in order to comply with this federal law to certify their results.

Each state has a set number of electors equal to the electoral college votes assigned to that state. Arizona has eleven electoral college votes, and therefore eleven electors who vote and sign the certification for their victorious candidate. Each political party pre-determines the electors who will sign the certification, so two sets of electors (Republican and Democrat) are chosen in advance, and then everyone waits for election day to see the results.

The Republican Party, through the Arizona GOP, held a vote earlier in the year to select the eleven individuals to serve as Trump electors in the event Donald Trump won the state of Arizona. The Democrat Party held the same process, each party hoping that their respective candidate would win the votes in the state on November 3, granting the right to their respective electors to cast eleven electors ballots on behalf of the winning candidate. Only the winning candidate's slate of electors counts.

There's a catch though. Several states, including Arizona, had ongoing legal challenges in late 2020 that were unlikely to be resolved by the December 14 deadline but which had the potential to change the outcome of the state's election. If Donald Trump won his legal challenge in Arizona on, say, December 20, Arizona would need a new (Trump-based) slate of electors. However, they would have missed the December 14 deadline required by law.

Therefore, on December 14, 2020, the Trump slate of electors met to sign a document known as the "Trump slate." The Trump electors were *required by federal law* to meet on December 14 to sign the document, preserving a Trump ballot that would comply with federal law and could be counted on January 6, 2021, when Congress would meet to certify the winner of the Presidential election. This "alternate slate" of electors was to be used as exactly that, an alternate slate in the event the election challenges were successful.

Despite media reports, this was neither unprecedented nor illegal. In the 1960 presidential election, Richard Nixon originally won the state of Hawaii's three electors. However, John F. Kennedy challenged the results of Hawaii's election. That challenge went past December 14, and so the three Kennedy electors had to sign a document creating an alternate slate of electors in case Kennedy was ultimately successful. He was, and the alternate slate of electors was used to certify the state of Hawaii for Kennedy.

President Trump's legal team (led by Rudy Giuliani) needed to have an alternate slate of electors ready for each state, including Arizona, in case they were successful in any of their challenges. The alternate electors—in accordance with federal law—preserved President Trump's ability to use their state's electoral votes in the event he won his challenges. That's it. That's all that happened.

Liberals were upset that conservatives didn't concede the suspicious election and started bullying the electors. Pundits claimed the move was illegal, despite the fact that there was legal and historical precedent for it. Several media outlets published articles and had "experts" explain how the 2020 electors differed from 1960. It was a feat of mental gymnastics to try to distinguish between what happened in 1960 and what happened in 2020. In reality, there was no meaningful difference.

As far as I know, liberals have not come out and explained why they targeted the alternate electors so aggressively. From my perspective, it was an attempt to scare conservatives out of fighting for the election and to prevent any type of challenges in the future.

In addition to the fact that all the actions taken by the alternate electors and Rudy Giuliani's team of attorneys were completely legal, I personally had nothing to do with it. I had come down with a severe case of COVID and was bedridden and quarantined in my home (then in Washington, DC) until December 12.

I learned for the first time on two back-to-back phone calls on December 12 that, as a matter of procedure, electors needed to meet. The call participants (I didn't know who they were at the time—and still don't) summarized the progress of finalizing the alternate slate of electors. I emailed Mike Roman, the RNC's Election Day Operations Director, in Pennsylvania, with my notes from the call. The email goes like this:

> Hi Mike,
> Here are my notes from the call. I'm not sure who else was on the call, so please either forward it to them, or send me their contact info and I will make sure they get it. Thank you!!
>   . . . [discussed the other states] . . .
>   Arizona—All 11 electors are prepared to meet for Monday. Kelli Ward will be there. Access shouldn't be a problem. AZ law does not demand a specific location, so they can change location if building is closed.

I was never in Arizona during the election period, never spoke with anyone in Arizona regarding the electors' certification, never emailed anyone in Arizona about the electors, and never drafted, planned, or coordinated anything associated with Arizona's electors. All I had done was summarize a phone call discussing proper legal procedure. To my knowledge, no one on the call was in Arizona, and my recap email went to Mike—in Pennsylvania. From the context of my email, it's clear the alternate electors were trying to *follow the law*, not break it.

Kelli Ward was the Arizona GOP Chairwoman. As a reporter, I had requested to interview her a handful of times about the election. We never spoke about the electors, and I didn't know that she *was* an elector until this criminal case popped up. She was not on the call referenced above.

So, why was the Arizona Attorney General sending a sheriff to my home in Florida with a subpoena?

My Lawyers Call the Arizona AG's Office

By February 2024, I'd had multiple sets of criminal lawyers. Funny, but if you had asked me five years ago if I had any regrets in life, I would have told you that I regretted never rebelling or pushing the boundaries. Raised in a conservative Christian home, I attended a Christian school, never experimented with drugs, never smoked a cigarette, and never really "broke the rules." I remember one time in high school coming home past curfew—totally sober—just watched a movie with friends and came home late. My mom went berserk, and it never happened again. Did I miss out? Should I have been more rebellious?

Well, now that I'd received my eighth subpoena, the fourth criminal subpoena, someone clearly thought I was a chronic rule-breaker. I had my criminal defense attorneys on speed dial. Time to call them again.

I called my lawyer, Jeff Neiman, to fill him in, and ask: "Is this even enforceable?"

"No," he said flatly. "Arizona doesn't have jurisdiction in Florida, and this subpoena isn't domesticated. You can basically ignore this."

I definitely wanted to ignore it. But I had learned better. "Can you please just call the AG's office and coordinate with them? I'm not inclined to participate when I'm not required to, but I also don't want them messing with my life just because they're on a power trip. Please call and figure out what they think they gain by subpoenaing me. What are they after?" I asked. "I will likely be traveling to Arizona for the campaign, and I want to make sure I'm not going to get arrested when I arrive in the state."

"Will do."

A day or two later, Jeff called me back. He said, "The AG's office acknowledged that they don't have jurisdiction. They acknowledged that they didn't get the subpoena domesticated and that the document is unenforceable."

"What is this case about? Is it the Arizona electors, like the other states?" I asked.

"Yeah," he confirmed. "Arizona is copying other states and going after the alternate electors from 2020."

I was furious. There was nothing illegal about anything that the electors did in 2020. This was an attempt to smear Donald Trump prior to the November 2024 election, and they would destroy the lives of innocent people just to score political points.

"Did they sound embarrassed?" I asked annoyed. "They should be humiliated for how stupid they look."

"No. I don't think they know they look stupid," Jeff said. "He did acknowledge that your subpoena's not enforceable, but they were hoping that you'd just comply with it and participate anyway."

"Why would I do that?" I asked honestly. "I mean, what incentive do I have for doing that? Nothing good can come from me talking to the Arizona AG. They are looking for a reason to prosecute me and right now they don't have one. Why would I participate?"

"You're exactly right. They didn't offer any good reason for you to participate," Jeff said.

"Am I under investigation? The subpoena says I'm not under investigation," I said. "Do I need to be worried that they're trying to target me?"

"No. He confirmed that you are not under investigation. They know you didn't have anything to do with the alternate electors, they just want to know what you know," Jeff said, relaying the prosecutor's perspective.

"First of all, I don't have any information, and they should know that," I started.

"They do know that," Jeff inserted.

"Second, if they really wanted something from me, why didn't they try to negotiate by making an offer? I have no reason to cooperate with them." If they really thought I had information that they needed, they would have negotiated. They didn't.

"Yeah. They didn't offer anything," said Jeff. "They just said that you're not under investigation, but if you don't cooperate, we'll see what happens."

That didn't sound great. "Are they threatening to indict me if I don't waive jurisdictional requirements and my constitutional rights?" I asked, shocked at the audacity of the AG's office.

"They can't indict you without evidence," my lawyer said, "and right now they don't have any evidence. So, as long as you don't speak with them, they shouldn't have any evidence against you, and shouldn't be able to indict you. I don't know what they're doing, though. They did sound like they were trying to threaten you."

"So now what?" I asked. "Wait and see?"

"Yeah," said Jeff, "wait and see."

My Role in Arizona

At the time of the 2020 election, I was a reporter for One America News in Washington, DC. I closely covered the progress of President Trump's challenges and reported on the progress of both the litigation and the effort to certify the election for Joe Biden.

Due to political and financial pressure, most of President Trump's law firms had bailed on him, refusing to support his challenges to the election. Rudy Giuliani stepped up to defend Donald Trump, his long-time personal friend. Through media contacts, I reached out to Giuliani and offered to volunteer and help him since so many of the lawyers refused to investigate the 2020 election. The story is captured in my book *Stealing Your Vote*.

The Establishment, however you want to define it, has mastered the art of crippling their opponents through frivolous and needless lawsuits and criminal charges. Whether baseless lawsuits, criminal charges, or subpoenas, defending yourself against any of it is expensive.

By the time I was served with this latest unenforceable subpoena, I had been sued for $1.6 billion in a lawsuit that was still lingering and had been for three years at this point. I had been served with a subpoena to testify before Congress with their illegal "unselect" January 6th Committee, only to have my testimony buried. I had been subpoenaed four times in litigation for which I was not a party, but nonetheless needed lawyers to ensure I didn't become a party. US Marshals, the FBI, and the Jupiter Police had all been to my home. Teams of lawyers have scoured everything on my cell phone, in my email, and on my personal devices.

So when the Palm Beach County Sheriff's Deputy arrived at my house for this latest round of unconstitutional lawfare by the Arizona Attorney General, I knew the game. At least the Arizona Attorney General's office had been expressly clear that I was not a target for indictment. But that, unfortunately, wasn't true.

CHAPTER 24

The Indictment

In mid-March 2024, about two weeks after the Palm Beach County Sheriff's office dropped by with the Arizona latest subpoena, the Chief of Staff at the RNC called and asked me to help the Trump campaign take over the Republican National Committee. Division had grown between the Trump grassroots movement (the MAGA movement) and the more established political elites running the RNC, and President Trump wanted to unify his campaign with the RNC. I was thrilled to transition over to the RNC and help "MAGAfy" the organization, so I quickly moved back to DC and went to work at the RNC headquarters.

The Trump Campaign and the new leadership at the RNC announced my new role as Senior Counsel for Election Integrity at the RNC in a public statement, and the liberal media lost their minds. The Democratic National Committee issued multiple public multi-paged statements from their War Room saying among other things:

> Christina Bobb is a self-described "conspiracy theorist" who will fit right in with the far-right extremists and election deniers who make up the new MAGA senior leadership at the RNC.[1]

The *Washington Post* reported:

> LaCivita is installing Christina Bobb—**a former OAN reporter who has espoused false claims that the 2020 election was stolen**—as senior counsel for election integrity. Bobb is the author of a book called "Stealing Your Vote: The Inside Story of the 2020 Election and What It Means for 2024" and promoted the audit of Arizona elections. [emphasis added][2]

Media Matters reported:

> Bobb, who joined Trump's legal team last year, was previously an anchor for the far-right One America News Network. While at OAN, Bobb was a **prolific spreader of false claims that the 2020 presidential election was rigged**, and she financially supported the sham "audit" of ballots cast in 2020 in Maricopa County, Arizona. [emphasis added][3]

CNN,[4] MSNBC,[5] the *Washington Post*,[6] *New York Times*,[7] ABC News,[8] and several other outlets all reported with renewed fervor that I was a terrible choice and trashed me. Obviously, I was nuts for believing that Joe Biden was *not* the most popular president in US history. (This was still five months before Democrats initiated a coup against their own candidate, the sitting President of the United States, to force his withdrawal from the Presidential race and install someone whom no one had voted for.)

For nearly a week, the liberal press hammered the new RNC leadership for their takeover and trashed me as their choice for Senior Counsel for Election Integrity. I didn't think much of it.

Bearer of Bad News

I should have known better. Less than a month later, in April 2024, I received a text from my attorney, Jeff. *Hey. How are you? Let me know when you have a minute to chat.*

I thought, *Ugh. This isn't going to be good.* I called him and he looped in the other two attorneys on the team, Kate and Derick.

"Hey, Christina," he said, "how are you?"

"I was fine until I got your text," I said a bit sarcastically. "What's going on?"

"Yeah, I'm really sorry to be the bearer of bad news, but you've been indicted in Arizona," he said.

I'd been indicted. The gravity of those words stopped time and made my head spin. Nothing in life prepared me for what it's like to be hunted by my own government. Disgust. Anguish. Fear. Helplessness. Injustice. It's a horrible cocktail of emotions. I gathered myself together as best I could.

"For what? I didn't do anything in Arizona." I said, shocked at the turn of events.

"I know. We've been through all your emails, and you didn't have anything to do with the alternate electors. They looped you in with the entire group of eighteen defendants on conspiracy to commit forgery."

Forgery? What on earth? Nine felony counts of conspiracy to commit forgery would basically ensure that I'd spend the rest of my life in prison. I'd be financially ruined and pretty much lose everything. These people are evil.

"How on earth is this a forgery case? What are they claiming happened?" I asked.

"Well, they're basically saying that the alternate slate of electors is a forged document created for the purpose of deceiving state officials and Congress into believing Donald Trump actually won the election," he said. "They're arguing that the whole purpose of the alternate slate was a deception campaign to trick officials into declaring Donald Trump the winner of the 2020 election."

"How are they going to prove that? What evidence do they have to argue deception?" I asked.

"I don't know," said Jeff, "but they argue that the alternate slate of electors was not an enforceable government document, so by creating it, the only possible intent was deception, which makes the document a forgery, according to their logic."

"Well, based on that logic, their fake subpoena that they had delivered to me at home by a Palm Beach County Sheriff's Deputy was also a forged document. It was an unenforceable document, that *they knew was unenforceable*, containing the seal of approval from the State of Arizona, created for the purpose of deceiving me into believing I needed to comply with it. By their own admission, they told you that they hoped I'd just go along with it. By their logic, isn't that a forged document? In order to prosecute me for forgery, they did exactly what they're accusing me of doing," I argued to my lawyer.

How is one document legal and the other illegal? They were both exactly what they purported to be—unenforceable documents. The difference between the two was that the AG actually did create the document with the intent to deceive me, by their own admission. The alternate electors never intended to deceive anyone.

"Yep. Pretty much. They did exactly what they are accusing the alternate electors of doing," said Jeff.

Unbelievable.

"What's the evidence they are claiming to have against me?" I asked.

"We haven't seen it, yet but will let you know," my attorney said. "They probably don't have any. I've seen everything on your phone, email, and hard drives. You had nothing to do with the alternate electors at all, let alone any deception objectives. My guess is the AG is hoping you'll get scared that you're indicted and be willing to say something incriminating against Rudy Giuliani, Mark Meadows, or someone else. We'll see."

The Arizona Attorney General's office was nothing more than the latest activist prosecutor's office engaging in political grandstanding. Like a handful of prosecutors across the country, AG Mayes and her attorneys were on a power trip and demanded I play along. She hoped I would fear her, bow to pressure, and say whatever she wanted me to say to incriminate completely innocent people. I refused.

Arizona Attorney General Kris Mayes

This was not my first introduction to Arizona's Attorney General. Kris Mayes became the Arizona Attorney General following the controversial 2022 election in which she beat Republican candidate Abe Hamadeh by 280 votes in a race with over 2.5 million votes cast.[9] Democrats had typically higher voter turnout during early voting, while Republicans overwhelmingly voted on election day. In Maricopa County, the voting machines worked fine throughout the election . . . until election day . . . when Republicans typically vote.

On election day, at least 36 percent of the machines malfunctioned and were unable to accept votes.[10] The county offered voters the option of casting their ballots into "secure boxes" called "Door 3," where the votes would be cast later by someone else.[11] Voters were outraged. After waiting in line for hours and hours to try to vote, all they could do was leave their ballots behind and hope someone else would eventually cast their ballots for them.

I was on the ground in Arizona supporting gubernatorial candidate Kari Lake and began calling voters to figure out what was happening. These "secure boxes," as I was told, filled up quickly with thousands of ballots, because there were so many election day voters, likely Republicans. Once "Door 3" filled up, voters were told to put their ballots in Rubbermaid bins and were promised someone would eventually cast their ballot for them.

Conservatives in the state erupted with claims of fraud. How could the machines work fine for early voting, when Democrats vote, but suddenly malfunction on election day, when Republicans vote? This is the same election where the Democrat secretary of state (responsible for running the election) was running for governor. The situation reeked of foul play. At best, the election was run completely incompetently. Unsurprisingly, Democrats benefitted from the errors. It was this botched election that took control from Arizona Republicans and transferred power to a Democrat governor, secretary of state, and attorney general.

Abe Hamadeh filed a lawsuit contesting the results of the elections, claiming the Democrat secretary of state counted hundreds of thousands of mail-in ballots that did not meet the requirements of Arizona law due to lacking a proper voter registration file.[12]

Rather than comparing the signature on the mail-in ballot to a proper voter registration file, the signatures were instead compared to the affidavit signed by the person casting the ballot, not a confirmed lawful voter file.[13] That means that at no point in the voting process was the person casting the ballot ever confirmed to be the lawful registered voter they purported to be.

According to the complaint, "Maricopa County tabulated a material number of approximately 1.3 million mail-in ballots by verifying them without any reference to lawful signatures on voters' 'registration records.'"[14] The original result of the election had Kris Mayes ahead of Abe Hamadeh by 511 votes, which prompted a mandatory recount.[15] The recount dwindled Mayes's lead down to 280 votes when Pinal County found 507 votes that they forgot to count originally.[16] Oopsies.

Hamadeh argued to his supporters that 9,000 provisional ballots remained uncounted, and that if the state actually counted the provisional ballots, he would be the rightful Attorney General.[17]

Provisional ballots are those that require closer examination by officials to determine whether the voter is properly registered. Maybe the voter forgot his ID, or the information didn't match registration. Hamadeh appeared to argue that the state was purposefully not doing the secondary examination of the remaining 9,000 ballots, because allowing them to be cast would have changed the outcome of the election.

Hamadeh ultimately lost the series of cases on appeal with a 2–1 split decision from the Arizona Court of Appeals. The Chief Judge David Gass acknowledged in his opinion that "a virtual firestorm of challenges followed the 2022 general election."[18] Plenty of people in Arizona were angry, as they did not believe that Kris Mayes was lawfully elected as the Arizona Attorney General.

What did Kris Mayes do to try to quell her constituents' anger and convince them that she was lawfully elected to protect the laws and citizens of Arizona? She quickly went to work to try to throw anyone who questioned the results of elections into prison. And I had just become her latest target.

A Case Riddled with Holes

Immediately the press went to work to defame and slander me, telling the world how I was indicted on nine felony counts in Arizona. Pundits started talking about how I could spend the rest of my life in prison.[19] The jackals that make up the liberal press pool cackled with glee at the dire situation I was in, happily predicting my demise.

Haters on social media sent me terrible comments wishing that my life be ruined. All for what? Because I supported Donald Trump? Because I reported on the rigged election in Arizona? Because I took a new job with the RNC? What exactly was my crime? It certainly wasn't conspiracy to commit *forgery*.

After a couple grueling weeks of slanderous stories in the news, I had to fly to Arizona to be officially arrested and booked at the

Maricopa County Sheriff's Office. I got to the Sheriff's Office right as they opened, sneaking past the crew of news outlets stationed outside—they didn't seem to notice me walk in. The gentleman working that day took me back and took my mugshot and fingerprints.

He showed me my mugshot and I couldn't help but say, "Oh my gosh!" I looked *pissed*. "I look like I murdered someone and buried their body in the desert!"

He laughed and nodded saying, "Yeah. Actually, you do."

I wasn't trying to *look* angry, but I was. It was all over my face. Turns out my face is pretty intense. I was okay with that.

I made my way up to the fourth floor of the courthouse to the courtroom for the arraignment. It was the first time I had seen several of my co-defendants in years. Kelli Ward and Anthony Kern, among others, were present in the courtroom. Rudy Giuliani, Mark Meadows, John Eastman, Mike Roman, and several other out-of-state defendants appeared remotely via Zoom. Kelli and I quickly embraced and wished each other well. Same with Anthony Kern. Several members of the press were present to watch the hearing.

Invisible Injustice Is Worse

As I watched various media outlets file into the courtroom, I started to panic about what they would write and say, knowing nine felony indictments would destroy my reputation and my life as I knew it.

My attorney seemed to sense my unease. "What's wrong? What are you thinking?" he asked.

"The media is going to ruin my life, my reputation, any credibility I have. My career is over. My life is over. They're going to destroy me," I said, somewhat matter-of-factly.

"No. Don't think that way," my attorney said, trying to reassure me. "Don't worry. They're not here to hurt you. They want to hurt

Rudy. He's the big name. They'll leave you alone. Don't worry." He tried to reassure me that the media wasn't interested in me.

Oh my gosh, I thought. *That's worse!* It's bad enough to be defamed publicly, but at least some people will see the injustice I'm going through. If no one reports on it, I'm just getting destroyed for my political beliefs and no one cares. Like being buried alive and no one hears your screams.

How many people does this happen to and we don't even know about it? How many people suffer abuse at the hands of rogue prosecutors, but they aren't affiliated with Donald Trump, so the public never even hears about it? As much as I hated what the media was about to do to me, I was grateful people would at least see. I felt sick for those victims of injustice that no one hears screaming for help.

CHAPTER 25

Nine Felony Counts Against Me

The judge eventually called my name, and I made my way forward to stand at the counsel's table with my attorney. She asked me to state my name and a few basic identifying questions. I waived the reading of the charges against me, promised not to flee the country, to stay in contact with my attorney, and to make all required court appearances. The experience was surreal. It was quite a humiliating and degrading process, all highlighted by the media and used to defame my reputation unfairly and untruthfully.

As my attorney and I exited the courthouse, I was accosted by a mob of reporters all looking for a statement from me. I had every intention of speaking to the press, but they swarmed very close to me physically, shoving microphones and cameras in my face. "Christina! Do you regret your involvement?" "Christina! Are you going to flip?" "Are you ashamed of yourself?" "Christina! How could you betray your country?" "Christina! Are you thankful you're not being tried for treason?" The questions were nasty and aimed to provoke me. The process was overwhelming and I couldn't get out of there fast enough. Just get to the car. Forget the statement.

One reporter was extremely aggressive, clearly trying to get me to punch him. He pushed his large, oversized camera in my face and would scream "Assault!" as I pushed it out of my way so I could walk. Having just been arraigned, I wondered if Arizona law enforcement were crazy enough to buy his bullshit. Was I now going to get arrested for walking to my car?! Thankfully, the mob of reporters stopped following me at the end of the courthouse property and my attorney and I escaped to a coffee shop a few blocks away to debrief.

The Debrief

The Arizona Attorney General's office had confirmed in their written letter to me in February 2024 that I was not under investigation by the Grand Jury. They also confirmed to my attorney, when he called to figure out what they were trying to do with an undomesticated unenforceable subpoena, that I was not under investigation and they just wanted a statement from me. But none of that had been true.

We'd find out later in the case (from the grand jury transcript), that not only was I under investigation, but I was *a target for indictment* before they ever served that subpoena. The prosecutors had lied. In writing and over the phone. They lied to me and to my lawyers to deceive me into hopefully incriminating myself—which I never did. That's illegal and unethical. Those prosecutors need to be investigated and disbarred.

Prosecutors are supposed to protect the public. That is their sole purpose. However, by 2024 it was apparent that many prosecutors had become a militant arm of the far left to crush political opposition. Prosecutors in Georgia, Michigan, Wisconsin, Nevada, New York, Washington, DC, and Arizona had all used their offices to target anyone they deemed a political threat. That's what I was facing in Arizona.

"Tom, I didn't do anything illegal. I certainly didn't commit *forgery*." Tom was my new Arizona attorney, and I was eager to hear his assessment.

Tom Jacobs is a well-established criminal defense attorney from Tucson, Arizona. He's taken cases all the way to the United State Supreme Court and defended accused criminals for over thirty years. A mutual friend introduced us via email. We had spoken on the phone, but this was our first private in-person conversation. I hoped he would share my perspective that this was a baseless case aimed at hurting political opponents.

"Christina, this case is unjust. The fact that they charged you with forgery proves that." Tom was calm and collected as he sipped his coffee. "If you or any of the other defendants had committed a crime in your election efforts, there would be a crime called 'unlawful electioneering,' 'election fraud,' or something along those lines. The fact that they had to shoehorn this into a supposed 'conspiracy to commit forgery' charge demonstrates that your activity was not criminal. Nothing about these efforts had anything to do with forgery."

Tom continued, "It's clear to anyone who has glanced at this case that all of the activity surrounding the alternate electors was an effort to *follow* the law, not to break it. Not only was it perfectly legal electioneering activity, but it's constitutionally protected activity. The Arizona Attorney General is targeting everyone for political reasons, and she's going to end up regretting this." Tom's experience comforted me. He spoke like he knew what he was talking about, and his appearance led me to believe that he was not a novice, but an experienced criminal defense attorney who knew how to navigate this case.

"Why do you think she'll regret it?" I asked. I agreed, but I wanted to know why Tom thought so.

"She's not even going to be able to get this to trial. I can think of five or six motions to file that should get this dismissed. Even if she did manage to get this to trial, which she won't, there's not a jury in this state that will convict any one of you. This is a politically motivated prosecution and she can't escape it. The prosecutors will be lucky to keep their bar licenses by the time this is over."

"They should all get disbarred," I said. Tom nodded, understanding my anger. "First of all, no one—none of the eighteen defendants—committed any crime," I said. Tom continued to nod. "Furthermore," I added, "I didn't have anything to do with the alternate electors. I didn't even know about it until they were executing the alternate certification."

"What *were* you doing? How were you involved?" Tom asked.

"I was a *reporter!*" I said, shocked that I'd been indicted for my reporting.

"Well, they can't indict you for your activity in the media," Tom stated the obvious.

"I know! That's what I'm saying!" I protested. "I never spoke to an elector. I never coordinated anything. I didn't draft anything. I didn't even know others were coordinating anything until they were executing the alternate certification."

"They believe you were working for Rudy Giuliani to execute this plan," Tom said. "One of the few specifics about you in the indictment says that you were 'closely associated with Rudy Giuliani.'" Tom looked at me to explain myself.

"Yes. I am close to Rudy Giuliani. He's a good friend. Is that illegal?" I looked back at Tom as he smirked.

"You do have a fundamental right to freely associate with Rudy Giuliani. So, what *did* you do for Rudy?"

"Right after the election, I was helping Rudy arrange public hearings for state legislators, which my network—not me—reported on and aired live. I helped arrange the public hearings. I also acted as a point of contact for the litigators the Trump team hired to challenge the election. Rudy was difficult to get a hold of, so I was the point person for litigators in Arizona, New Mexico, and Michigan. I basically relayed information between Rudy and the litigators. None of it had anything to do with electors, certifications, or Congress."

"When was the first time you heard that they wanted to create an alternate slate of electors?" Tom asked.

"A day or two before they created the alternate slate. I received a calendar invite for a phone call. I joined the call, but never said anything on the call and no one said anything to me. The only thing they said on the call was that they needed the alternate slate of electors in case the litigation was successful. Arizona law and federal law are specific about how the slate is to be created and they wanted to ensure they followed the law to prevent the slate being thrown out on procedural grounds in the event the litigation was successful. That's the only time I ever heard anything about it."

"Hmmm," Tom said. "We'll have to see what evidence they turn over related to you. I'm not sure how they're planning on roping you into this. The indictment is painfully thin on you. Nothing in the indictment actually links you to a crime, so they still need to explain what they believe your criminal activity is. You're charged with *conspiracy* so they have to prove that you knew of a criminal conspiracy and took some action in furtherance of the conspiracy. Merely knowing about it is not sufficient to make you a participant."

"I don't even *know* of a criminal conspiracy! As far as I know, everyone was trying to *follow* the law, not break it," I said.

Nine Felony Counts Out of Thin Air

The case against me was so flimsy, it was laughable. But when you have nine felony charges brought against you, carrying the threat of many years in prison, it's hard to laugh. The full indictment against me and my seventeen "co-conspirators" was fifty-eight pages long, but there was very little referring specifically to me. In fact, the entirety of the allegations against me as detailed in the indictment was as follows:

1. Christina Bobb was an attorney for the Trump campaign and worked closely with Rudy Giuliani. Bobb lobbied Arizona's Republican legislators after the 2020 presidential election to disregard the popular vote in Arizona. She additionally helped organize the false Arizona Republican electors' votes on December 14, 2020.

2. Christina Bobb and Kelli Ward posted on social media on December 6, 2020 the following:

3. Jason Miller texted Justin Clark, White House attorney Eric Herschmann, and campaign communications director Tim Murtaugh:

"Just got a call from Rudy: [discussion on Wisconsin] He also said Boris [Epshteyn] has been coordinating state elector whip efforts and I should connect with he and Christina Bobb."

[Note: I am not on this text thread, they are just talking about me].

4. Rudy Giuliani scheduled a conference call to discuss with Bobb and Ellis, and others, which was shared in the text message thread to which Herschmann responded "certifying illegal votes."

[Note: I was not on this thread; they were just discussing if I could help. This call never happened].

That's it—the sum total of my alleged illegal activity. Based on this, I was charged with nine felony counts, including one count of conspiracy, one count of fraudulent schemes and artifices, one count of fraudulent schemes and practices, and six counts of forgery.

"Do I even have a chance at a fair trial?" I asked my lawyer.

"Yes. Of course," he said, "I'll make sure of it." Tom was calm and assured that he could wrangle a rogue attorney general and her minion political hacks posing as prosecutors. I wasn't quite so sure, but his confidence was reassuring.

"I'm worried this whole thing is rigged. The prosecutors will rig the jury," I started to rattle off a list of my concerns but he cut me off.

"Rig the jury?!" He tilted his head at me like he couldn't believe what I was saying. "And how exactly are they going to do that?"

"I don't know!" I admitted but was confident they would. "They do it all the time! They're doing it in New York right now with Donald Trump!"

"This isn't New York and you're not Donald Trump," he said kindly to reassure me. "Maricopa County is a conservative county. Seventy-five percent of your jury will be conservative. Not a chance they'll be able to get a unanimous conviction. I mean, good grief! They couldn't even get a unanimous *grand* jury verdict! The grand jury voted nine to three to indict. If they can't get a unanimous grand jury, they don't stand a chance at being able to convict anyone in this case."

I didn't want to get on my election soapbox with my lawyer, but I've been saying for years that there's a problem with Arizona's elections. If the jury pools are conservative, so are the voters. Yet Democrats took the top of the ticket in 2020 and 2022. So Democrats vote in huge numbers through mail in ballots but never appear for jury duty? I'm not sure if that made me feel better or worse. They cheat. If they can cheat in elections, they can rig a jury. I didn't know how, but I believed they would try.

"I don't like our judge," I said changing the subject and looking at the paperwork the court handed me. The paperwork showed that the case was assigned to Judge Daniel Martin.

Tom looked surprised that I knew the judge and said, "Do you know him? What do you know about him?"

"This is the same judge that was assigned to hear the post-2020-election Arizona audit litigation. I wrote about him in my book *Stealing Your Vote*. The audit was obviously contentious, and Daniel Martin ruled on those cases." I looked at Tom to see if he was reading between the lines.

"That's interesting." He didn't show whether he shared my concern.

"How many judges are there in Maricopa County?" I asked.

"Oh, I don't know, in criminal court?" Tom paused to think, but I cut him off.

"No. The entire bench," I said. "The Arizona audit wasn't a criminal case. It was in civil court. So, Judge Martin had to switch from the civil bench to the criminal bench."

Tom was kind, but sighed a little as if he wasn't buying where I was going with this. "I don't know, but Maricopa County is very big."

I did a quick Google search. "There's about one hundred judges throughout the entire county for every type of court. One hundred judges. And we just so happen to get the exact same judge twice?" I asked him, implying the system was rigged and not to be trusted. "I don't believe that's an accident. What are the odds of that happening at random?"

Tom looked at me like my tinfoil hat was showing. "Well, we can challenge the judge if we need to. Let's take it one step at a time."

Turns out we didn't need to. Another defendant, apparently as skeptical as I was, challenged the judge before I even spoke with Tom again and the case was reassigned to Judge Bruce Cohen.

CHAPTER 26

Judicial Corruption Run Amok

In 2022, Arizona amended its Anti-SLAPP (Strategic Lawsuit Against Public Participation) statute to include criminal prosecutions. That means criminal defendants can challenge an indictment on the grounds that the prosecution is aimed at punishing constitutionally protected activities, like political activity and free speech. Defendants must demonstrate that the case against them was substantially motivated by a desire to deter, retaliate against, or prevent the lawful exercise of a constitutional right.[1]

As far as I'm concerned, our case was a classic example of political prosecution. If we proved that, then the State would be required to prove this was not a novel matter targeting political opponents. Arizona would have to affirmatively prove that they have prosecuted similar cases in the past and that this case was not a "creative" interpretation of the criminal code, which they could not possibly prove. Judge Cohen heard oral arguments in August 2024.

I appeared remotely at the hearing via video conference and listened as the new judge addressed the parties. My heart sank listening to him. One of the first things he said was something to the effect of, "There are so many pleadings in this case with eighteen defendants that I debated about just waiting to watch the movie about this case. Hahaha." *Watch the movie?! Oh my gosh, he thinks this case is going to drag out and be dramatic!* I hated the judge immediately. He sounded like a liberal hack and I didn't trust him.

The Anti-SLAPP arguments were lengthy. With eighteen defendants it ended up taking three days to get through all of the arguments. When it came to me, Tom argued in addition to the constitutional arguments raised by the other defendants, I also had First Amendment protections as a reporter and that this indictment was inappropriately based on my reporting activities. In their initial disclosure, the prosecutors listed media reports as evidence against me.

The prosecutors argued to the court that I physically went to Arizona to arrange the electors, which was untrue. Not only did I not go to Arizona, I had medical records and employment records documenting that I was quarantined in Washington, DC, with a severe case of COVID at all relevant times. I was bedridden at home, but Tom didn't tell them that at that time. He gave them rope to continue lying to the court.

The prosecutors then tried to argue that I went to *New Mexico* to supposedly hand out ballots? What?! First of all—no. I never went to New Mexico to hand out ballots. I was quarantined in Washington, DC, the entire time. Second, even if I had, what does that have to do with Arizona? And how is that illegal?

In January 2024, the New Mexico attorney general had investigated and issued a report indicating that no illegal activity took place in New Mexico surrounding the alternate electors.[2] So, apparently, the Arizona prosecutors were arguing to the court that I did something in New Mexico (which I didn't) that was not illegal in New Mexico, but if I had done this supposed activity (which I never actually did) in Arizona, then it *would have been* illegal in Arizona . . . but it never happened in Arizona . . . or in New Mexico for that matter. WTAF?!

"How on earth is this real, Tom?!" I yelled into the phone once the hearings were over. "This is a circus! How can they be allowed to slander and defame me, leading the nation to believe that I'm a criminal when this is the best they've got?! This is absolute bullshit. *THEY* should be prosecuted!"

Tom was very good about letting me rant and be angry—which happened a lot throughout this case. He listened as I unloaded on the illegal and unethical actions of these rogue prosecutors. "Yes. Their case against you is very weak. I expect this judge to rule in our favor on this motion in the next week or two."

"This judge is an absolute hack! He wants to *watch the movie!*" I mocked the judge for his comments. "No way. He's going to let this linger forever so that all of us defendants bleed to death. He's going to force us to lose everything we own paying legal fees for months needlessly when the law requires that he throw this case out." I was so angry I was ready to burst.

"Well, let's just wait and see. The statute requires the judge to rule quickly to avoid exactly what you're talking about. So, we'll know soon."

"I don't think we'll ever get a fair trial. I don't know how they keep rigging the system to give the prosecutors these unethical judges, but they do," I said.

"You don't know that yet," Tom pointed out. "Let's wait and see. We should know before the end of the month." It was August 2024.

By November 2024, the election was over and we still didn't have a ruling. Tom called me, "Well, I'm afraid you're right." No ruling yet.

"Tom, will I ever get a fair process? This shouldn't go to trial, but I need a fair judge to look at this, and I'm not convinced I can get that." I pleaded, hoping Tom could give me a glimmer of hope for justice.

"It's proving harder than I thought it would be." Tom didn't want to admit that the system was clearly rigged against us defendants. "I still believe you'll get justice, but it's difficult to work that out when the court is flat out denying you a ruling."

Judge Bruce Cohen Humiliates Himself

A few days after the 2024 election, a local independent reporter in Arizona broke a big story after they obtained several emails sent by my judge.[3] Apparently, Judge Bruce Cohen had emailed all of the judges and commissioners in Maricopa County and demanded that they speak out against any critics of Kamala Harris.

According to the *Arizona Daily Independent*, "Cohen equated Harris' critics to the Nazis, and said that those who refused to stand up for Harris as well as other females and 'colleagues who identify as being a person of color' were as bad as those who allowed the evil of the Holocaust to take place."[4]

That explains why my judge felt comfortable denying me and every single one of my co-defendants justice. He believes we're just as bad as the Nazis. My grandparents were Holocaust survivors, imprisoned, and Polish-Catholic slave laborers to the Nazis. According to my judge, my support for Donald Trump renders me just as evil and unworthy of justice and basic civil rights as the Nazis who tortured my family.

All of the defendants immediately filed motions to recuse Judge Cohen from our case. Judge Cohen didn't even bother to wait for the motion to be ruled on. He recused himself in utter humiliation. Bruce Cohen had an ethical obligation to disclose to the defendants that he was incapable of being impartial and actively campaigning against us to the entire Maricopa County bench. He refused to do so and used his position of authority to deny us all justice for months, forcing our case to linger past the 2024 election. He forced us all to spend tens of thousands of dollars over the wasted months. While he has since retired from the bench, he still deserves to be investigated by the Judicial

Council and state bar and should be disbarred. He should never be allowed to work in the legal profession again.

Judge Cohen's recusal forced yet another delay, as another judge had to be assigned to the case, which pushed the case into 2025. What should have been an open-and-shut dismissal to protect the rights of the accused turned into a slow bleed where the defendants were left to fend for ourselves for almost a year at that point.

Is the system rigged? Are prosecutors and judges politically biased? The media loves to paint me as a tinfoil-hat-wearing conspiracy theorist. Maybe, but I'm right a lot. My judge recused himself from the case in utter humiliation for being a covert political hack who got caught.

Misleading the Grand Jury

The case against me was so ridiculous, I could not believe it was still ongoing. My lawyer filed a "Rule 12.9 motion," which challenges an indictment on the grounds that the defendant (me) was denied a substantial procedural right. We challenged the indictment for four specific reasons:

1. The State presented misleading incomplete and/or inaccurate instructions on the law to the grand jury.
2. The State presented misleading and/or false testimony to the grand jury.
3. The State engaged in prosecutorial misconduct by allowing its investigator witness to avoid direct inquiries presented by the grand jury regarding my role and lack of involvement.
4. The State failed to instruct the grand jury to consider the allegations to each charge against me individually and separate from the other accused parties.

The prosecutors argued to the grand jury that I was a Trump attorney and senior Trump advisor and a former reporter. At all relevant times of the facts in question, I was not. I was a reporter. I didn't become a Trump attorney or advisor until 2022. They intentionally confused the jury about my *current* role, misleading them into believing I held that role at the time. I did not. Prosecutors also told the grand jury that prosecutors planned on having me testify despite the fact that I was a target of their investigation, which prejudiced me when I did not testify.

When the grand jury expressed confusion over my involvement and asked the state's investigator, a detective, to explain my role, the prosecutors allowed the detective to offer his opinion rather than evidence. How was I involved in this conspiracy? The detective simply responded that Christina Bobb was "deeply involved" in the alternate elector plan and misled the jury into believing I physically went to Arizona to orchestrate some conspiracy. I did not, and they did not have any evidence to suggest that I did. I *did* have evidence that I was quarantined in Washington, DC, and couldn't have gone to Arizona.

At one point, a grand juror said, *"I just threw her name up there. I didn't know where else to put her for now."* Meaning, they didn't understand how I was involved, but they just "threw my name [on the indictment]" because the prosecutors asked them to. Unethical.

The detective could not identify one single action I took, or one incriminating piece of evidence, but instead simply said that I was "deeply involved" hoping to convince the jury to indict me—and the prosecutors let him. The prosecutors also did not have the jury consider my case independently from the other defendants. The jurors simply voted on whether to indict all eighteen of us as a group without considering our individual involvement, or lack thereof.

This case reeked from the beginning.

Arizona Claims States United Democracy Center Represents Them in a Criminal Case

In November 2024, while we were languishing for relief from the court, The Daily Signal broke the story that the Arizona Attorney General had secretly partnered with a liberal nonprofit to prosecute all of us Trump supporters.[5] States United Democracy Center is a far-left nonprofit organization that was founded in 2020 "to coordinate left-leaning advocacy groups and Democratic campaign committees in the event that then-President Donald Trump lost and subsequently contested the results of the 2020 Presidential Election."[6] To be clear, one of the original purposes of the organization was to resist anyone or any group contesting or even questioning the results of the 2020 election.

Norm Eisen, the "Ethics Czar of the Obama White House," founded the organization.[7] "Eisen is a Trump critic who worked for the House committee that helped investigate what became Trump's first impeachment in 2019."[8] One of the highest paid contractors for the group is Mark Elias,[9] probably the most prominent Democrat attorney in the nation. His website defines his work: "Elias Law Group is a mission-driven firm committed to helping Democrats win, citizens vote, and progressives make change."[10]

States United received over half a million dollars for a research project on "state election disinformation mitigation and violence prevention" from the Institute for Strategic Dialogue (ISD).[11] ISD's parent organization receives funds from the Bill and Melinda Gates Foundation and George Soros's Open Society Foundation, among other liberal nonprofits.[12]

And I'm supposed to believe this prosecution isn't political?

My attorneys became aware of States United's involvement in my criminal matter when we received a copy of a memo written by the organization detailing how to target and prosecute Trump electors and supporters. The Arizona AG's office accidentally attached the memo to a request for a search warrant. The AG apparently thought that this memo would convince the judge to force Google to turn over all our personal emails and private information. To be clear, they were using a liberal nonprofit to justify why they should be granted access to all our private communications, including privileged information. The AG's office admitted that the memo was given to *and considered by* the judge when choosing to authorize a search warrant.

Once the AG's office realized they had disclosed the memo, they sent an email to the defense attorneys saying:

> As discussed, the State did not intend to provide the July 25, 2023 memorandum, instead, the State intended to provide a publicly-available memorandum from States United. However, because it was submitted and relied upon by the Court, it was properly disclosed under Rule 15 as part of discovery.
>
> However, the State maintains that this was not a waiver of the attorney-client privilege. The State will not provide additional information from States United because of the attorney-client privilege.

The prosecution intended to hide the fact that they partnered with a political advocacy group from the defendants. Why are all these prosecutors allowing liberal nonprofits to dictate their actions? This is what happened to me in Georgia when a liberal nonprofit encouraged the Georgia special prosecutor to investigate me, and the prosecutor obeyed.

Incredibly, the Arizona Attorney General's office actually forgot to request the search warrant until *after* they had indicted all of us, giving us a chance to fight it. To be clear, the prosecutors indicted all of us before they requested a search warrant for the alleged "evidence" they were looking for from our personal email accounts. From my perspective, it looked like they thought they could indict us and then just worry about getting the evidence later. We were indicted in April 2024. The 2024 election was just a few months away. If they wanted these indictments to sway the election, they didn't have time to wait for the evidence or a search warrant.

The defense attorneys jumped into action, filing motions to quash the search warrant and disclosure of private information. To Google's credit, they did not release our emails or information as requested in the search warrant, but are still waiting for an order from the court. At the time this book went to press, Google had not released any of my emails, which means that the one email from me mentioned above, which the Arizona prosecutors had, must have been turned over by someone else. I have never turned over *anything* to the Arizona Attorney General.

On our side, we demanded all of the communications between the AG's office and this liberal nonprofit. How involved was this group with trying to jail their political opponents? How much involvement was the Arizona Attorney General's office allowing them in this prosecution? The whole thing reeked of political manipulation.

During a meet-and-confer conference between defense counsel and the Arizona Attorney General's office, and later to the court, the prosecutors claimed that States United Democracy Center *represented the Arizona AG's office in this criminal matter* and they had attorney-client privilege with them and would not agree to turn over their communication or association with the organization.

slow blink Yes. They actually argued this in court.

To be clear, the AG's office took the position that a liberal nonprofit represented the AG's office, as counsel, in the criminal matter of *The State of Arizona v. Kelli Ward et al* (my case). A liberal nonprofit represents the AG's office in a criminal matter?

We did get a copy of the "engagement letter" (although we don't believe it met the requirements of an engagement letter) and States United agreed to provide work to the AG's office pro bono—meaning without getting paid. That means a political nonprofit agreed to work for free to help the Arizona Attorney General prosecute their political opponents—and the Attorney General let them.

If the Attorney General wants to receive information from an advocacy group, she can. But she can't then pretend that information is privileged and refuse to share it with the people she's prosecuting.

Additionally, Arizona Governor Katie Hobbs hired her "top attorney" from States United.[13] The attorney worked for Hobbs when she was secretary of state, left to work for States United, and returned to work for Hobbs once she became governor. Then, the attorney "signed a retainer agreement with States United that would continue the group's influence in Arizona."[14] All pro bono, of course.

To be clear, outside groups do not represent the attorney general's office in *any* criminal matters. The attorney general is where the buck stops when it comes to prosecutions in any state (or federal) court. An attorney general can appoint a special prosecutor, as we've seen Merrick Garland do, or District Attorney Fani Willis. But an elected official (the Attorney General) cannot covertly cede her authority to an unelected, politically motivated nonprofit who dictates which political opponents to prosecute and how. Yet that's what the prosecutors argued to the judge. As if it were normal.

Naturally, the defense attorneys pushed back and refused to concede any imaginary attorney-client relationship between the AG's office and this nonprofit. Yet again, we'd have to wait for the judge to decide the motion. Normally, this would be a slam dunk. But by this time, I'd lost all faith that any of the judges would give me a fair ruling.

Once our last judge disgraced himself, the court appointed a new judge, Sam Myers. Judge Myers was appointed to the bench in 2007 by then-Governor Janet Napolitano, who now sits on the advisory board of—you guessed it—States United Democracy Center. Just to be clear, a member of the advisory board of the liberal group prosecuting me appointed my judge.

We challenged the fake attorney-client relationship in November 2024. As this book goes to print in June 2025, the judge has not ruled on whether attorney-client privilege applies and has not given the defense access to the communications the attorney general had with a far-left political advocacy group with a stated mission to target Trump supporters. Don't forget, we also still have an anti-SLAPP motion pending since June 2024, arguing that this was a political prosecution. The emails between the AG's office and States United, no doubt, are extremely relevant to that motion. Yet, we have received no relief.

CHAPTER 27

The Cancer Spreads

The American judicial system is designed to protect Americans from a rogue government. There are checks and balances in place to ensure "the little guy" isn't unfairly crushed by antidemocratic tyrants, either in Congress or the White House. Our criminal justice system is sacrosanct and always tips in favor of the accused. Innocent until proven guilty, right?

But what happens when the judiciary becomes politicized? When, instead of standing as a bulwark against abuse of power, the judicial branch is weaponized to protect and empower the very arms of government it is supposed to restrain? Across the country, it's clear that our system of checks and balances has broken. The political class, funded by the elites, has taken over the judiciary.

So many judges have washed their hands of actually acting as a counterbalance not only in political cases like mine, but in any other case where prosecutors may be biased for some other reason. It's easier to look the other way and hope the case washes out through a jury. The tragedy is that innocent people are forced into a trial they should never have to face, while civil courts bankrupt people and ruin lives.

I wish Arizona Attorney General Kris Mayes were a lone, crazed prosecutor and the case of the Arizona electors was one of a kind. It's not, and Americans are in danger of losing our freedoms due to the lack of checks and balances coming from feckless judges refusing to pull their weight.

If President Trump's team had really committed egregious crimes when creating the alternate slate of electors, surely the numerous criminal cases concerning electors would have resulted in many convictions or judgments against these "criminals," right? Surely at least *one* of the cases would have resulted in guilty verdicts by a jury, right? Surely at least *one* of the cases would have produced a "win" for the prosecution, right? Surely at least *one* of these cases would have put on display the horrific crimes committed and allowed the public to rightly judge the offenses, right? Nope. Not a single one.

Georgia got four defendants and Arizona got one defendant to plead guilty for a punishment of probation (in Arizona, *unsupervised* probation) in exchange for their freedom and avoiding the pain of a costly and humiliating process. Technically, a guilty plea is a conviction, but a far cry from a "win." Unsupervised probation. Michigan had one defendant "cooperate," so they dropped the charges completely.[1]

In order to have a respectable reputation, a prosecutor should have over a 90 percent conviction rate. They are, after all, the ones who determine which cases to prosecute, so they should only be bringing cases they can win. Activist prosecutors in Georgia, Nevada, Wisconsin, Michigan, and Arizona all filed charges against the Trump electors who created alternate slates in case Trump won his challenges. Combined, these prosecutors indicted about sixty different people (some indicted multiple times in multiple states) relating to this particular set of facts. How many terrible criminals have they sent to prison of the sixty? Zero.

Remember, these cases are billed as a matter of national security, because the electors were supposedly attempting to deceive the United States Congress into seating the wrong president. Not a small accusation. And *nobody* has been found guilty by a jury? *Nobody* has been sent to prison? *Nobody* who cooperated got more than probation?

Not only have they won zero cases, but Donald Trump went on to win all of those states in the 2024 election.

Oppo Research in Georgia

While the Arizona Attorney General used the creative charge of forgery to indict me and seventeen others for the Arizona alternate elector slate, Fulton County District Attorney Fani Willis made history when she shoehorned a supposed election crime into a RICO—racketeering— charge in Georgia in 2023. She indicted Donald Trump and eighteen others as well, including some of the electors.[2] It was this case that gave Donald Trump the mug shot heard 'round the world, which he ended up using in his winning campaign.

Willis also indicted America's Mayor Rudy Giuliani, Mark Meadows, John Eastman, and a number of well respected, highly regarded Americans to fan the flames in this case. One of the people she indicted was my good friend Mike Roman.

Mike is known throughout conservative politics as one of the best opposition researchers in the business, and he served as President Trump's Election Day Operations coordinator in 2020. Why Fani Willis included him in the indictment is a mystery, but she likely wanted to create a huge splash by indicting a large number of people, so she indicted Mike. It would be her downfall.

When Fani Willis put Mike Roman in a position where he had to fight for his freedom, he did. He began researching Fani Willis the way he would any political opponent, and he found the goods.

In January 2024, Mike's attorney, Ashleigh Merchant, filed a motion to dismiss the indictment and disqualify Fani Willis for further prosecutions due to her improper romantic relationship with the appointed prosecutor, Nathan Wade. Mike's motion alleged that Willis and Wade were in a romantic relationship, and were profiting financially from the taxpayer-funded prosecution by overpayments to Wade that they would then use for cruises, vacations, and other luxuries.[3]

Over the next year, Wade and Willis were both required to testify under oath, in court, and on camera, as to the nature of their relationship. Those testimonies will likely go down as the most humiliating display of any prosecutor in American history. Clips started going viral. Willis admitted to keeping cash from her political campaign, which appears to be a campaign finance violation.[4] Concerns rose that she lied under oath about the timing of her relationship with Wade and the source of funding for their lavish excursions—which she says she paid for in cash.[5] Willis lost her cool and seemed so flustered that she even wore her dress backwards.[6]

The judge, apparently not wanting to upset the political powers that be, relieved only Nathan Wade from the case, but allowed Fani Willis to remain on the case, meaning the unfair and partisan prosecution could continue.[7] Split the baby and leave the innocent defendants to languish further as their lives are ripped apart by false accusations.

The Georgia case turned from focusing on the defendants' alleged racketeering into an investigation of Willis's professional conduct, or misconduct. Mike Roman again, through his attorney Ashleigh Merchant, challenged Willis's refusal to turn over documents she was required to produce. Merchant won her arguments at the Georgia Supreme Court, which forced Willis not only to turn over the undisclosed documents, but also to pay Mike Roman's legal fees on that issue.[8]

The public hearings surrounding Fani Willis and Nathan Wade were so alarming due to their lack of professionalism that the House Judiciary Committee opened an investigation and required Nathan

Wade to testify before Congress. Wade admits that he had multiple White House meetings with the Biden Administration,[9] which raises several concerns about the Biden Administration interfering, or possibly directing, the prosecution of Joe Biden's political opponent.

The Georgia Senate Special Committee subpoenaed Willis, but she refused to comply. In February 2025, the court denied Willis's request to quash the Georgia Senate subpoenas.[10] In December 2024, the Georgia Court of Appeals found that Fani Willis was disqualified from prosecuting the case, due to her conflict of interest with Nathan Wade. The Appeals Court found "an appearance of impropriety," and determined that "this is the rare case in which disqualification is mandated and no other remedy will suffice to restore public confidence in the integrity of these proceedings."[11] Fani Willis appealed the decision to the Georgia Supreme Court, which has not yet granted review as of May 2025.

As this book goes to print, the open proceedings in the Georgia case all center on Willis's misconduct, not that of the defendants. With both prosecutors disqualified, this case will get dismissed unless the Georgia Supreme Court reverses the Court of Appeals, or another prosector wants to step in and clean up Willis's mess. It's unclear at this point if Willis will be able to work her way out of this. I doubt it.

Fani Willis has proven herself to be an incompetent (at best) prosecutor and looks like she may need to ultimately defend her bar license. The case has devolved from a supposed racketeering case to a constant airing of potential prosecutorial misconduct. Needless to say, the case isn't going well for Fani Willis. I hope that the remaining defendants who did not buckle under pressure will be fully exonerated and their case dismissed.

Forgery in Carson City

The Nevada Attorney General charged the state's six electors with "uttering a forged document," a felony in Nevada.[12] All of the events surrounding the creation of the alternate slate of electors took place in Carson City, the state capital.

The state likely did not want to bring charges in Carson City, because in 2020 Donald Trump won over 54 percent of the vote in Carson City, and Joe Biden only won about 42 percent of the vote. It would be very difficult for the attorney general to get a conviction there. So, contrary to jurisdictional requirements, the attorney general filed criminal charges against all six electors in Las Vegas, Clark County, the bluest county in the state.

The defense attorneys went to work to file a motion to dismiss due to improper venue. The court granted the defense motion finding that the attorney general had improperly filed the case in Las Vegas.[13] Finally, a court with a spine. However, days before the statute of limitations expired, the Nevada Attorney General refiled the charges against all six republicans in Carson City.

If things stay as they are, I don't see how the AG could possibly get a conviction in Carson City. But the process is the punishment. These cases scare the public from getting involved in the political process, making it easier for tyrants to get away with whatever they want. The thought of being prosecuted due to your political beliefs is a huge deterrent. So even though the Democrat AG can't possibly win this case without some crazy new development, he still wins by deterring Republicans from opposing the political machine in Nevada.

Michigan: A "Blueprint" for Taking Down Republicans

Michigan was the first state to indict the 2020 electors without drawing Donald Trump or his team of advisors into the case. In July 2023, Michigan Attorney General Dana Nessel announced charges against the sixteen alternate Trump electors for conspiracy to commit forgery. Liberals praised her efforts as a "blueprint" for how to take down

Republicans across the nation, and several states followed suit.[14] Thus, the fake forgery charges began.

Nessel wasn't satisfied with simply charging the Trump electors. She also brought a case against attorney Matt DePerno and a few others for bringing challenges to the election in Michigan in 2020. In 2023, she charged DePerno and others with illegally accessing voting machines, which of course all the defendants disputed. Maybe it was just a coincidence, but months before his indictment, DePerno was the Republican attorney challenging Nessel for the role of attorney general in the 2022 election. Once Nessel won, she promptly prosecuted her political opponent. Some may call that a deterrent from challenging her power.

By June 2025, twenty-two months after the indictment, Matt's case was still sitting before the judge waiting for a preliminary hearing. Nearly two years after the indictment, the court still had not made a finding of probable cause to believe Matt had committed a crime. The prosecution clearly wasn't in a hurry to try this case. Letting Matt and the others slowly bleed through the criminal "justice" system was victory enough. If they can't get a conviction, at least they can inflict as much harm as possible to deter other attorneys or electors from challenging the results of elections, or worse, from challenging the attorney general in an election.

As this book goes to print, not one single elector or attorney in Michigan has been tried or convicted for forgery. They've been struggling through the criminal court system for years without relief as the Left ruins their reputations and finances—with nothing to show for it. But the message is clear: Do not challenge the established political class.

Ten Felony Counts in Wisconsin

The Wisconsin indictment is the worst of all of them. In 2022, the Wisconsin Election Commission heard a complaint brought against the Republican electors, but the commission rejected the complaint.[15] In its rejection, the commission *"attached a letter from the Wisconsin Department of Justice that said that Republicans who attempted to cast the state's 10 electoral college votes for Trump did not break any election laws."*[16] [emphasis added] "The state Justice Department concluded that Republicans were legitimately trying to preserve Trump's legal standing as courts were deciding if he or Biden won the election."[17]

Just months before the 2024 election, the Wisconsin Department of Justice announced that they were potentially going to indict Trump allies, despite their earlier findings that no crime had occurred. Their announcement appears to be an attempt to affect the 2024 election in Wisconsin.

Fast forward to December 2024, *after* Donald Trump won the 2024 election, the attorney general of Wisconsin, Josh Kaul (who is the head of the Wisconsin Department of Justice), indicted Mike Roman, Ken Chesboro, and Jim Troupis on ten felony charges alleging conspiracy to commit forgery.[18]

Jim Troupis, a former judge and attorney who is alleged to have recommended the alternate slate, made a statement at his hearing: "On this very day four years ago, we publicly announced in advance that we had recommended an alternate slate of electors to meet in order to preserve President Trump's constitutional rights of appeal," he said. "And four years ago this very day, Attorney General Josh Kaul was told about the claim and he approved it."[19]

Attorney General Josh Kaul is on record in a letter and in discussion with the Trump attorneys in Wisconsin approving of the plan and need for the alternate electors to meet and preserve President Trump's slate of electors should he eventually win his challenges in the state. Then, Kaul indicted the very people whose plan he approved anyway. What Josh Kaul has put good people through is unconscionable—and all for what? Why go through the political theater that destroys lives and families? The political gamesmanship these rogue attorneys general are playing is evil and they must be stopped.

None of the cases in any of the states has amounted to "wins" for the liberal prosecutors. So why are they all bringing these loser cases? Because it punishes their political enemies. These alternate elector cases have never been about justice. They inflict pain, deter political participation, and further the liberal agenda.

Colorado Jails Gold Star Mom

Tina Peters was the Mesa County Clerk in Colorado from 2019 to 2023. She is a cancer survivor and Gold Star Mom of a Navy SEAL who served multiple tours in Iraq and Afghanistan before he was killed in 2017 at the age of twenty-seven.[20] In the wake of the 2020 election, Peters said "hundreds of citizens" came to her with "their experiences of significant election irregularities."[21] As the county clerk, Peters was responsible for safety and security of the election, so she began to investigate and speak publicly about the concerns she saw in Colorado's election. Rather than address the concerns she raised, Colorado opted to prosecute Ms. Peters.

"On August 12, [2024], a Mesa County jury found her guilty of three felony counts of attempting to influence a public servant, one felony count of conspiracy to commit criminal impersonation, one misdemeanor count of official misconduct, one misdemeanor count of violation of duty in elections, and one misdemeanor count of failure to comply with the secretary of state. She was acquitted on two felony counts of criminal impersonation and one count of identity theft."[22]

Ms. Peters was sentenced to nine years in prison.[23] As this book goes to print, Tina Peters, sixty-nine years old, is sitting in prison in Colorado. President Trump has publicly called for her release, stating that she "is an innocent Political Prisoner being horribly and unjustly punished in the form of Cruel and Unusual Punishment."

These prosecutions don't protect the public. They protect those in power by scaring everyone else from challenging their authority.

CHAPTER 28

The Attorney General Doubles Down

On November 5, 2024, I breathed a huge sigh of relief. Donald Trump had won the 2024 election. Not only did he decisively win, but he decisively won the state of Arizona and every other contested state from 2020, which should have sent a huge message to Attorney General Kris Mayes that her case was in trouble. Good luck getting a unanimous conviction in a state that just elected Donald Trump. Maybe she would follow Jack Smith's lead and dismiss the indictments against us?

Nope. She made a statement shortly following the election saying she was determined to continue the prosecution.[1] These people are evil. The election was over, and their little plan failed. Give us our lives back already! My life was held hostage by her pride.

Now that the election was over, I'd be out of a job in a matter of days. Under normal circumstances, I'd have several amazing opportunities. However, I had nine felony charges hanging over my head. I'd decided not to go into the Administration and needed to land somewhere. Whenever I spoke with someone in media or law, the response was, "Good luck on your case! Let me know when it's over."

If I didn't get out of this case soon, I'd bleed to death for lack of work. I couldn't start my own business, because I couldn't take on clients with the possibility that I wouldn't be able to complete their cases. I was stuck and needed out ASAP.

"Tom, this case is going to destroy me. At this pace, even if I win, I'll lose everything I've built because I can't work," I said to my attorney.

"Let me talk to the prosecutors about dismissing you. I've sent them several emails that they've ignored. With your permission, let me talk to the prosecutors face-to-face at the next hearing about getting a dismissal," Tom said.

"Do you think they'd even be open to it?" I asked. "Why would they even consider dismissing me for nothing? I'll never cooperate with them. I'll never be a witness. Would they dismiss me even if I offer them nothing?"

"Well," Tom chuckled, "that's a hard sell. But, in this case, I do think it's the right move. You make their case worse. They don't have a single piece of evidence connecting you to the conspiracy of forgery that they have alleged. Not a single witness at the grand jury identified you as being involved with the electors. Also, we have a pending motion to remand [Rule 12.9], which I think we're actually going to win. More importantly, I think the AG's office thinks we have a shot at winning that motion, which will look *really* badly for them."

In addition to the 12.9 motion, we still awaited the ruling on the anti-SLAPP motion, which should have already disposed of the case. Tom was prepared to also challenge jurisdiction, file a motion to dismiss, and a series of other motions with a good chance of success, if the judge treated me fairly. If the prosecutors were being honest with themselves, they should want me out of the case. I had a good chance of winning a number of motions, all of which would be a terrible blow to their case.

I was one of sixteen remaining defendants, all of whom had equally strong defenses and aggressive attorneys who each filed multiple motions. Quite simply, the Arizona Attorney General had bit off more than she could chew. Tom's goal was to get her to spit me out.

Their Best Effort

Tom pressed the prosecutors to dismiss me from the case, pointing out they didn't actually have any evidence against me. In the course of his discussions with the Attorney General's office, he asked me to talk to the prosecutors to help clear up their obvious misunderstandings about my role at the time. I agreed to talk to them directly, hoping to clarify questions they had about my involvement—or lack thereof.

So, in early December 2024, I met with the Arizona prosecutors over Zoom. I was shocked at their questions. They had indicted me for nine felonies and knew absolutely *nothing* about their own case.

They didn't know that I didn't work for President Trump at the time of the 2020 election. They didn't know I was actively a reporter at the time. They didn't know I didn't have access to the White House, had never spoken with President Trump, and had no communication with him whatsoever at that time. They didn't know I didn't begin working for the President until 2022. They didn't know I wasn't in Arizona. They didn't know I was quarantined in DC with severe COVID. What *did* they know about the case? Not much. They believed I worked for President Trump as an attorney in Arizona in 2020 and spoke with him about Arizona electors, despite the fact that they *had no evidence* of it. So they lied to a grand jury and indicted me anyway for a make-believe crime that never occurred.

Finally they asked me, "Do you know Ben Howell[2]?"

"Ummm. Yes?" That's weird. Why on earth are they asking me about him?

"Who is he?" the lead prosecutor asked in a serious tone.

I couldn't help but laugh at the question as I answered, "A guy I went to kindergarten with. We grew up together and were in class together from about kindergarten through high school. Why?" I asked, not even trying to hide my laughter. *Is this the best they can do?!*

The prosecutor laughed a little too, maybe unsure how to respond to me. "That's what it seemed like." He explained that they accessed my then-Twitter account and went through all of my direct messages. Ben Howell had DM'd me on November 30, 2020, saying, "Love the work you're doing!! . . . I know it's been a long time but I was excited to see what you're up to. Great job! ☺ GCCS4life lol."

"GCCS" stands for Grace Community Christian School, which is where we went to kindergarten. I hadn't seen this guy or heard from him since high school, about twenty-five years ago. He reached out to say hello because he saw my reports. We exchanged DMs over the next several days catching up, talking about our families. He sent me a picture of our fourth-grade class photo and we reminisced about all the people in the picture. He asked me about my perspective on the election and I told him I thought it was stolen and I hoped our elected officials would investigate.

He responded, "I truly hope people step up."

I responded. "Same. This week is a big one."

"So, what did you mean by that?" The prosecutor asked me in a serious tone.

Shocked at the stupidity of all of this and the devastating impact it was having on my life, I said, "I meant that this was a very contentious election and I wanted to see what was going to happen."

"Oh. Okay," he said. He proceeded to ask me about people who were fighting about my reports on Twitter—people I didn't know having conversations I wasn't involved in.

"I don't know these people and have nothing to do with this conversation. These are public posts. They started this thread themselves after reading my report," I pointed out.

"Oh okay," he said again. That was it.

I was so angry. These "prosecutors" didn't know anything about me, the case, or (apparently) election law! They had full access to my Twitter account and online communications and the most incriminating piece of evidence they could find was my fourth-grade class photo.

When Tom followed up over a month later to ask if they'd dismiss me, they told him no, because I hadn't given them any useful information. In other words, the truth didn't fit their narrative, so they were going to see how far they could take their lies. They decided to force me to continue to fight for my freedom, despite the fact that they were now painfully aware they had no evidence of my involvement. It was an exercise in futility.

Anti-SLAPP

Before I'd know whether they'd dismiss me, the new judge, Sam Myers, ruled on the first half of our Anti-SLAPP motion.

On January 30, 2025, he ruled that the defendants (me & co.) had met our burden to demonstrate that this case was brought in order to infringe on our constitutional rights (for political purposes). Now, the burden was on the State of Arizona to prove that it was not. In order to meet their burden, the State would have to prove that this is not a novel case, but that it's routinely prosecuted. And that the use of the criminal statute is not a creative reading but is actually a plain interpretation of the law. In reality, this was the first time a case like this had been prosecuted in Arizona, and to bring it under a forgery claim was, to say the least, "creative." The hearing was set for a few months later.

On the day the Attorney General's office was supposed to file their brief supporting their position in the Anti-SLAPP motion, they instead filed a motion to stay the entire case at the Arizona Court of Appeals. Rather than trying to prove their case, they simply asked the Appeals Court to pause the entire thing. The Court of Appeals granted the stay, meaning the defendants (including me) were left without a final ruling. It also allowed the State to delay their argument—an argument they have no evidence to support. That was in March 2025.

Two months later, the Arizona Court of Appeals still had not even ruled on whether they would take jurisdiction of the prima facie finding. Normally, appeals courts only take jurisdiction over final rulings, and this was not a final ruling, but they decided to stay our case anyway—for months. Clearly, the prosecutors are doing everything they can to delay and stall the case, probably because they can't meet their burden of proof.

Court Finds Due Process Violation

The motion to remand my case back to the grand jury (Rule 12.9 motion) was argued on April 17, 2025 (it was specifically exempt from the stay). On May 16, 2025, the court granted my motion and the motion of the other defendants who filed a 12.9. The judge specifically stated, "The court finds that the defendants were denied a substantial procedural right as guaranteed by Arizona law." Basically, the indictment was unlawful.

The prosecutors failed to instruct the grand jury about the Electoral Count Act, which the electors were trying to comply with when they signed the alternate slate of electors. Rather than explaining the requirements of the ECA, the prosecutors instead led the grand jury to believe the only possible explanation for creating the alternate slate of electors was deception. So the case has been remanded. It has not been completely thrown out (yet), but if the Arizona Attorney General wants to continue to prosecute us, she needs to re-empanel a new grand jury to start over. It remains to be seen what she decides to do. My co-defendants and I remain under prosecution while we wait.

So Now What?

As it stands, the defendants have won both the anti-SLAPP motion (at least the first half) and now the motion to remand (12.9). Yet well over a year after we were first unlawfully indicted, my co-defendants and I continue to languish at the mercy of prosecutors on a mission to ruin our lives.

Until the courts decide to truly give us justice, we are stuck being accused felons, with all the devastating ramifications that entails. Our lives are clouded by nine felony indictments. We're tethered to Arizona, still racking up legal fees, unable to move forward. The prosecutors are still trying to throw us in jail for decades for crimes we didn't commit. For crimes that *nobody* committed. For crimes that never occurred.

CHAPTER 29

Sued for $1.6 Billion

$1.6 billion is a lot of money. It's also the amount of money Dominion Voting was demanding from me personally in the defamation lawsuit they filed against me and several other conservative voices surrounding the 2020 election.

Of all the cases against me between 2021 and 2024, this lawsuit by Dominion was the most concerning to me. First of all, the financial threat was overwhelming. Secondly, the case was venued in Washington, DC, meaning the jury (and possibly the judge) would *hate* me simply because of my political beliefs and association with Donald Trump. And third, this was the one case where I had, in fact, made a mistake. Nothing illegal. But I did make a mistake, as I discuss below.

The pressure of $1.6 billion hanging over my head was crushing, and I didn't know how to escape it. Any hope that insurance would save me was dashed when I learned there was no insurance to cover damages, only the cost of defense. So, my legal fees were covered, but any award against me would come out of my own pocket. Also, if I was found liable for intentionally lying to cause harm (defamation), even if the jury didn't award Dominion *any* money, I would most likely lose my law license and therefore my career.

Meanwhile, the liberal media had worked hard to destroy my reputation as a reporter. One of their pieces of "proof" that I was unreliable was the fact that Dominion had sued me for $1.6 billion. The message was simple—I'm a liar and not to be trusted.

Once President Trump won the 2024 election, everyone in his campaign was transitioning to new employment—most went into the Administration. I wanted to return to media in some capacity, but that door was slammed shut with the defamation case and criminal charges pending. I spoke with multiple agents who all told me I was persona non grata until my litigation was over. The Dominion case, together with the Arizona indictment, had scuttled my ability to meaningfully work with my colleagues at the RNC, on the campaign, and in many ways post-election. The election was over, and I was out of work and unemployable. There had to be a way out.

Dominion and The 2020 Election

The Dominion case was directly linked to the 2020 election. In the wake of the 2020 election, conservatives started looking for answers to explain the voting oddities readily apparent which seemed to allow Joe Biden to beat Donald Trump while never leaving his basement. Donald Trump had huge, massive crowds at his rallies, often multiple rallies in a day, and he lost to a guy who barely campaigned. The prevailing belief among conservatives was that the election was rigged. But how?

One accusation of election fraud that several people found compelling was the idea that the Dominion Voting machines were rigged with special algorithms to flip votes, and ultimately the election, to Joe Biden. Several people came forward claiming to specialize in algorithms and computers explaining how the machines rigged the election.

Spreadsheets, graphs, charts, and any number of presentations were floating around social media and the news "explaining" the tabulation errors "caused" by machines. Dominion fever caught fire and several attorneys discussed Dominion machines, stating findings that the machines rigged the election.[1] Democrats dismissed conservatives' accusations as conspiracy theories and claimed there was no evidence that machines changed the outcome of the election. Republicans accused Democrats of participating in the fraud.

My Role in the Dominion Story

At the time of the 2020 election, I was a reporter working for One America News, and I covered the 2020 election extensively. Beginning on November 4, 2020 (the day after the election), I started reporting on abnormalities that concerned me, all detailed in my book—*Stealing Your Vote: The Inside Story of the 2020 Election and What It Means for 2024*. I did not focus my reporting on the machines, but focused on the elected officials running the election, the procedures they followed (or didn't follow), and mail-in ballots.

Neither my reporting nor my book covered the machines for the very simple fact that I did not understand the technical allegations and could not independently verify the accusations of fraud by machine. I'm not trained in computer science, engineering, or any technical skill needed to independently confirm the allegations about the machines.

The Lawsuit

The case had been going on for more than three years when Bill Haggerty, my third lawyer in the matter, took over my defense, and I was hopeful we could get this sorted out. Bill Haggerty is an amazing lawyer and graciously kind person. He has a great demeanor and handles stress extremely well. He's also not the US Senator from Tennessee (that's a different Bill Hagerty).

Bill walked me through the three pieces of defamation Dominion claimed they had against me. The first two were interviews I conducted when I'd simply asked questions of (1) Rudy Giuliani and (2) a random guy on social media. The alleged defamatory statements in those interviews were not made by me.

Dominion's third accusation of defamation was a statement I made criticizing Maricopa County, Arizona, for their lack of control over the election. Dominion interpreted my criticism of the county as defamatory toward Dominion. That was never my intent, but either way, I could prove the statement was true based on a letter the county sent to the Arizona Senate.[2] Those were the three allegations against me personally in the complaint—statements made by other people, and a statement that I could prove was true.

Elsewhere in the complaint, not in the specific claim against me, Dominion mentioned a short clip of me (about three minutes) that had been posted to OAN's YouTube channel but never aired on television, summarizing the accusations against Dominion. The statements I made in that clip summarizing the circulating reports about Dominion turned out to be incorrect. When I checked the original source of the reporting, my sources had backed off those claims. That means I could no longer prove the statements were true, which means, for the purposes of the lawsuit, they were not true. Once made aware of the video and the original sources changing positions, I asked Bill to coordinate with OAN's counsel for the video to be removed.

In order to be liable for defamation, I would have had to make an untrue statement that I knew was untrue with malicious intent to harm Dominion that actually did cause harm. I did not. When I originally recorded that video, I believed my sources were accurate. Only later did I learn they were not—something that happens with unfortunate regularity in the media. But journalists are usually protected in this kind of situation—mistakes without obvious negligence or malicious intent do not meet the legal definition of defamation. Dominion disagreed with my assessment of the facts and wanted $1.6 billion in damages for my mistake. I hoped once they looked closer at my case, they'd change their mind.

Dominion's lawyers are extraordinarily well-credentialed. Two of the lead attorneys had been named "Titans of the Plaintiff's Bar," among other awards. These were the same Dominion attorneys who negotiated a $787.5 million settlement with Fox News in their defamation case.[3] After negotiating three quarters of a billion dollars for massive claims, what did they want with *me*? I hoped I was such a small part of the case that they just hadn't looked closely at me. Maybe, upon closer inspection, they'd come to the same conclusion Bill and I had—my minor involvement wasn't worth litigating.

Hopefully these Titans of the Plaintiff's Bar didn't like wasting time or resources and were not out on some petty quest. I hoped they were as good as they looked on paper.

Buried Under the Weight

It was February 2025, and I still had nine felonies and $1.6 billion hanging over my head. Since 2021, over the span of about three and a half years, I'd been dragged through eight different legal matters against me. I'd been sued, investigated, interrogated, subpoenaed, deposed, or indicted every couple of months, and each case just piled on top of the other.

(1) January 6th Committee Subpoena for testimony and documents, (2) Mar-a-Lago document criminal investigation against me and the grand jury subpoena, (3) Jack Smith's J6 investigation, (4) Smartmatic subpoenaed documents, (5) Dominion's $1.6 billion lawsuit, (6) a subpoena connected to a lawsuit involving Rudy Giuliani, (7) the Capitol police officers suing Donald Trump subpoenaed me, and (8) the California bar investigated me. That doesn't count the threat of a lawsuit that OAN's attorneys fabricated so they could drop me as a client.

And, just for good measure, the Biden Administration cancelled my TSA pre-check.

Each matter meant teams of attorneys, friend and foe, going through all my personal emails, every thought I'd shared with someone, every text message I sent, my call logs, and anything else they could get their hands on. When I wasn't fighting legal battles, I was receiving death threats, even needing to call the local police to my home on multiple occasions due to some specific sense of danger. Text messages, social media DMs, letters to my home, unordered pizza deliveries, the threats came in many ways. Thank God for local police. (I could do without the FBI.)

Perhaps subconsciously, the last three and a half years had convinced me that everyone opposing me hated me because of my political associations and wanted to destroy me in every conceivable way. That actually was what was happening—most of the time.

The fact that DOJ didn't indict me and the California bar found no misconduct was not, in my mind, a reflection of kindness on their part. They simply could not find any evidence of wrongdoing that they could use to indict or disbar me. *There was no wrongdoing.* Going through those investigations, my lawyers and I believed that if I had so much as sneezed wrong, the other side would have pounced on the opportunity to destroy me. I held my breath and waited as they scoured every aspect of my life. They came up with nothing.

Dominion was different. I had made a mistake. I didn't believe I defamed anyone, but my failed sources gave Dominion a reason to disagree. Could I be confident that a DC jury would see things my way? No. If Dominion wanted to destroy me because of my political beliefs, they could. All I could do was hope that wasn't their goal and then wait and see what they did.

A Paradigm Shift

Finally, my phone rang. It was Bill.

"Dominion agreed to dismiss you from the case," Bill said matter-of-factly.

"What! Really?" I was shocked, excited, and scared to hope. Bill had navigated the impossible and I was thrilled. "No settlement? No mandatory agreements? Just a straight dismissal?"

"Yup," Bill said. "No settlement. They're just outright dismissing you."

Silence hung for a moment as I took it in. Bill is a miracle worker. This is amazing news. This Dominion case and the Arizona criminal case had really hurt my career and reputation.

The fact that this case gave the media an opportunity to paint me as dishonest was a particularly low blow. I pride myself on my honesty and integrity. Truthfully, it has been my honesty that got me through every single accusation raised against me. I was honest with everyone, even those trying to ruin my life. Despite my ardent adherence to the truth, I was painted as untrustworthy due to this case.

Dominion dismissing the case against me would be a chance to get my life back on track. Believing that every Democrat was determined to destroy me is a terrible, crushing way to live life. I didn't want it to be true. For the first time in years, circumstances provided an opportunity to see that maybe that wasn't always the case.

By the end of February 2025, it was over. Dominion officially dismissed their charges against me and filed the necessary paperwork with the DC courts. I was immensely grateful to the Dominion attorneys and the plaintiffs for not continuing to drag me through the litigation when they could have. But I was also overwhelmingly saddened. I felt like my house had been burned to the ground and now people were asking me if I was happy the fire was out. Yes. I was happy. And devastated. Could I rebuild my reputation? At least Donald Trump was President again. That definitely makes things better for my future and the future of our nation.

The Final Warning

President Trump is back in the White House. The cases against him have been dismissed. The J6ers have been pardoned. The cases against the electors from 2020 continue to push forward trying to jail conservatives, but no one's really paying attention anymore. Those whose lives were unfairly upended are no longer in the crosshairs (for the most part). Is that justice? Do we just forget and move forward? Leave the little guys to fend for themselves?

Maybe those who deserve justice for the wrongs done by Democrats the last four years won't have loud enough voices to be heard and will simply fall away into oblivion. Maybe we will decide it's time to mend fences and heal wounds, rather than continue to fight.

Having been through four years of lawfare hell myself, I want nothing more than to leave this horrible period of American history behind us. After enduring seven subpoenas, an indictment for nine felonies, a billion-dollar lawsuit, numerous law enforcement interrogations; grand jury testimony, courtrooms, and congressional testimonies; thousands of hours of attorneys' fees, depositions, discovery, and court pleadings . . . I am sorely tempted to slam the door on the past and move on. But we can't pretend it's over until it's *actually* over.

A Stain on Our History

The recent horrors of injustice committed at the hands of elected officials and their appointees are unparalleled in our history. Never before have we seen the very institutions designed to protect our freedoms and our rights be used to punish and silence political opposition at this level. The lawfare waged against Donald Trump was not designed to enforce the laws or uphold the Constitution; it had only one objective: DOJ wanted to make Donald Trump a criminal to undermine his 2024 campaign for the presidency. Consider the charges against him in the Mar-a-Lago case:

> Counts 1–32: Willful retention of classified materials
> Count 33: Conspiracy to obstruct justice
> Count 34: Withholding document or record
> Count 35: Corruptly concealing a document or record
> Count 36: Concealing a document in a federal investigation
> Count 37: Scheme to conceal
> Count 38–39: False statement and representations (39 against Walt Nauta only)
> Count 40: Altering, Destroying, Mutilating, or Concealing an Object
> Count 41: Corruptly Altering, Destroying, Mutilating or Concealing a Document, Record, or Other Object
> Count 42: False Statements and Representations (against Carlos de Oliveira only) *Carlos de Oliveira is the only other alleged co-conspirator with Walt Nauta and Donald Trump in the documents case. He did nothing to deserve the hell DOJ put him through.

In all of these charges, how were they protecting the American people? In every count, they're only alleging that Donald Trump interfered with their unlawful investigation. Even that's not true. He told them to their faces he'd cooperate, and they didn't want to believe him.

There's no charge that he sold classified materials, allowed foreign adversaries access to materials, or anything else that would jeopardize national security, certainly nothing more than Joe Biden did when leaving records in his garage next to his car. None of these criminal allegations arose *before* DOJ opened their investigation. It's all about how Donald Trump and his staff interacted with DOJ once they forced their way into Mar-a-Lago. In other words, if Jack Smith had never opened an investigation, there would be no crimes to allege. DOJ manufactured the crimes.

Our criminal justice system is designed primarily to *deter* criminal conduct and *punish* conduct once committed. This fake documents case does neither. For anyone arguing that the country was better off by prosecuting Donald Trump, I take issue. What did we gain from it? Are we safer? No. Are presidents going to change the way they pack up and move out of the White House? No. Did Donald Trump do anything to harm America? No. This case neither deters future conduct nor does it punish actual criminal conduct. It only serves to punish political opposition.

What good came from this investigation? The Jack Smith investigation did significant harm to our nation and worked to divide the American people politically for years. Good patriotic Americans were scared for their lives and threatened unfairly. Prosecutors intimidated everyone close to President Trump to see if they could scare someone into saying he's a criminal. Junior staff in their twenties who had nothing to do with anything were scared by FBI agents showing up to their house, going through their phones, and seizing their laptops. The FBI didn't "target" the criminals, as they're supposed to. They targeted everyone hoping someone would buckle.

Prosecutions like this have a chilling effect on constitutionally protected political activity. We gained nothing. We paid a very high price only to hurt ourselves. Everyone lost.

The Attacks Continue

While the cases against President Trump have been dropped, the Left has not retreated from their battle stations. Before the ink was dry on President Trump's executive order to uphold US immigration laws, several Democrat governors and mayors promised to defy them. Twenty attorneys general conspired to thwart his administrative changes to executive agencies.[1] The Bureau of Alcohol, Tobacco, Firearms and Explosives appeared to subvert the order to put DEI teams on paid leave by changing the title of Chief Diversity Officer Lisa Boykin. US judges are coming out against pardons made by President Donald Trump and making it difficult for those pardoned to have their cases dismissed. Democrats in New York have announced intentions to file state charges against J6 defendants pardoned by the President. And twenty-two states have filed suit against President Trump's Executive Order on birthright citizenship, while a federal judge has blocked action on the Order.

In less than ninety days, liberals sued the Trump Administration 162 times.[2] The cases range from the FBI employees that were fired suing to get their jobs back; NGOs suing to prevent documentary proof of citizenship on voter registration forms; law firms suing to get their security clearances back (President Trump cancelled many clearances); and lawsuits against Elon Musk's DOGE for lack of transparency (oh, the irony).[3]

Conservative attorneys are facing threats of disbarment at an alarming rate. Rudy Giuliani, John Eastman (the Constitutional scholar who help President Trump in 2020), Jeff Clark (DOJ Official supporting President Trump in 2020), and nearly every conservative attorney who has supported Donald Trump in some way has had their law license challenged, suspended, or worse. At the same time, liberal attorneys seem to be able to do whatever they want without consequence.

The unstated goal of challenging conservative attorneys is to ensure that Americans have no one to oppose the radical leftist agenda. In just a few short years, it's possible the only attorneys left to challenge the radical liberals will be unwilling to fight. I've spoken with several attorneys who don't like what they're seeing but they don't want to get involved, because they don't want to lose their law license. They have a family, a business, and personal interests that they can't afford to lose. The unstated goal of the liberal agenda is to eradicate political opposition.

Thus, it is time to choose. If we turn a blind eye to the corruption and abuse of power that has plagued our country for so long, it will ultimately destroy us. If we fail to properly secure our justice system, from DOJ, the FBI, and federal agencies all the way to state and local prosecutors and even courts, we will never have the opportunity to do so again. These radicals will simply wait it out until they get another chance at power—and once they get it, they will inflict so much pain on us that we can't recover. They will finish the job they started. We win our freedoms back now, or we lose them forever.

Dealer's Choice

So how aggressive should Americans be in our efforts to recalibrate the scales of justice? Certainly, we don't want to use more force than necessary, risking the same evils perpetrated against us for years. The level of pressure Americans, and the Trump Administration, need to use to defeat the radical fascists who've been persecuting their political opponents depends on those that started this mess in the first place. It's dealer's choice.

In President Trump's first term, Trump supporters loved the idea of charging Hillary Clinton for her email scandal. "Lock her up!" they chanted. Shortly after winning the 2016 election, President Trump announced that he would not be investigating Clinton because he wanted to allow her "to heal."[4] He showed her mercy.

He did the noble thing. The peaceful thing. He tried to heal our nation. Did our nation heal? No. The radicals just waited him out. They used every available weapon they had to eliminate him, impeaching him twice, defaming him in the press, suing everyone close to him to deprive him of resources, and anything else they could think of. Once they got their power back, they used that very authority to prosecute him for ninety-one felonies, humiliate him, take him off the campaign trail, and try to destroy him.[5] He paid a heavy price for not abolishing the radical weaponization of justice and abuse of power in his first term. He's not going to make that mistake again—and neither can we, the American public.

In order for the Trump Administration, and the American people, to save our country, the *threat of future abuse* must be eliminated. There are two ways to eliminate the misuse of our justice system: (1) those currently abusing the system can acknowledge their error and agree to stop, or (2) they can be stopped through force—by prosecuting them to the fullest extent of the law. It's their choice.

Most Americans, myself included, would prefer the first option, but the radicals have shown no remorse, repentance, or desire to "lay down their arms." No one from the political establishment is saying that DOJ officials were wrong and the unfair prosecutions of Donald Trump were wrong. They still seem committed to this battle and are simply hoping we don't fight it. Democrats are screaming about how President Trump wants to weaponize the Justice Department,[6] hoping their hypocrisy will go unnoticed. These radicals want to pressure Donald Trump to forgive and forget those who unfairly waged war against him.

There are many conservatives who also believe it's best for our country to avoid punishing the Left for their weaponization of justice—to show mercy to our political foes, rather than extracting retribution. I believe there can be a strong argument for mercy. Mercy is how we ensure that we don't burn our nation to the ground. It allows us to place more value on the future of this nation than on the past sins of our political opponents. However, mercy can only be given where there is true repentance and no threat of future harm. Without an admission of guilt from the perpetrators of injustice and a desire to change course, the threat that they will repeat those actions still exists.

The Emperor Has No Clothes

Even after the American people gave President Trump a clear mandate, the Left has refused to recant or reform. How, then, do we put a stake in the heart of this lawfare?

Someone needs to go to jail.

It's the only way to stop the onslaught against American freedoms. Prosecutors who have abused their authority to try to silence political opposition should be investigated and prosecuted. The CIA, FBI, and other government officials who have been violating the law in order to undermine President Trump should be prosecuted. Government employees leaking information to protect terrorists from deportation must be prosecuted.

Judges need to be impeached. Many conservatives have pushed back on this idea saying that impeachment is too extreme a remedy. Chief Justice John Roberts weighed in saying, "For more than two centuries, it has been established that impeachment is not an appropriate response to disagreement concerning a judicial decision. The normal appellate review process exists for that purpose."[7] Respectfully, the Chief Justice failed to identify the issue.

The rulings, orders, and actions coming from courtrooms today are not "judicial decisions." They are partisan efforts to cripple the political opposition, and they need to be defined as such. They must be stopped.

As someone who has had a judge unfairly subject me to criminal prosecution solely because his preferred political party wanted to score political points, I can tell you that the "normal" appeals process is not the answer. Spending time and money waiting for an appeal of a radical political ruling is not justice. "The normal . . . process" is the punishment and is used as a weapon, not for justice, but for oppression. We can and must do better. We must stop the radical rulings at the trial court level.

When my judge delayed ruling on the anti-SLAPP motion (which alleged this was a political prosecution) past the election, the delay itself was political. The delay served to paint Trump supporters as criminals through the 2024 election cycle. It was not based on the merits of the case; it was intended to further punish the defendants, postponing our day in court, keeping our lives in limbo, all while forcing us to rack up even higher legal bills. It also fueled leftist talking points going into the November 2024 presidential election. Chief Justice Roberts would call the delay a "judicial decision." It is not. It's political activism. A "judicial decision" is an honest interpretation of the law without any political considerations.

The legislature is playing Pollyanna, pretending there's nothing they can do about these rogue judges. In reality, they are abdicating their constitutional role in preventing this abuse by refusing to act. Impeach a judge. If Congress successfully impeached just one judge, the rest would get in line.

The problem lies in the fact that it would take sixty-six votes in the Senate to convict a judge and successfully remove him or her from the bench. Democrats would never impeach the judges doing their dirty work. While impeachment would certainly get the judges in line, it isn't likely to happen. So what can Congress do? Legislate. Pass legislation that will rein in the reach of these district court judges and stop the ridiculous onslaught of political activism from the bench.

Congress—and all Americans—must call these maneuvers by prosecutors, investigators, and judges what they are: naked political activism. The emperor has no clothes. If we continue to pretend that these actions are anything other than an abuse of authority for the purpose of eliminating political opposition, *we* will be the ones who end up in prison. For those hesitant to believe we need to impeach judges and prosecute the prosecutors, I can tell you from experience, they have no hesitation in prosecuting you. As this book goes to print, I'm still facing nine felony charges that could send me to prison for decades because I'm "closely associated with Rudy Giuliani." *That* is the reality of what our nation faces. I may have been on the front lines, but they're coming for you.

Policy vs. Power

Our country has become painfully divided over a host of policy issues—from gay rights to gun rights, from green cards to the Green New Deal. We are constantly fighting with our neighbors, our family members, our community.

That's exactly what the Establishment politicians want. Politicians from both parties have been gaslighting Americans through media, social media, and influencers about a variety of policy issues, all while they focus on the real fight: the fight for power.

Policy is important, and I encourage every American to find an issue you care about and get involved. But policy is secondary where power is consolidated in the hands of the few political elite. Once that happens, American citizens will no longer have the power to affect policy.

Judges are abusing the power of the bench to prevent the President from implementing the policy the people elected him to enforce. Instead of reining in this abuse, Congress is too busy consolidating its own power. Legislators *from both parties* "collaborate" with special interest groups like Big Tech, unions, Big Pharma, etc., who in turn fund their campaigns—which keeps them in power.

Congress is currently controlled by Republicans. So, it should be easy to check the power of rogue judges opposing the President, right? If the Republican Congress (House and Senate) fails to check the balance of power with the judiciary this cycle, every single Republican in Congress should be primaried and replaced in the next election cycle. I'm not exaggerating, because the abuse of power in this nation has reached critical levels.

Our Founders understood that the only way to protect the rights of every individual is for government's power ultimately to be in the hands of the people. We need to ensure that citizens are free to speak out against the government without fear of prosecution. We need to focus less on the policy issues dividing us and focus more on returning the power of government back to the American people.

How to Get Involved

While the Trump Administration battles in court against abuses of the system, Americans need to do our part to protect against the ever-encroaching creep of injustice. Here are the most important things you can do:

1. **Stay informed**. It's hard today to have a good understanding of what's happening. Take the time to find a few different sources of information that you trust, and regularly check in on them. An informed electorate is harder to deceive. Know who your state representative, state senator, county clerk (or recorder),

county supervisor (or commissioner), local judges, and election board members are. Know the names of your Congressional Representatives and US Senators. Know how they all vote and vote them out if they don't represent you well.

2. **Vote**. Especially in small local elections. Local elections have tremendous spillover into national issues. Know the issues, learn about the candidates, vote, and tell others to vote too.

3. **Get involved**. If you have availability, volunteer in your community or with a local grassroots organization that supports an issue important to you. If you don't have time to get involved, donate resources to organizations that support your values. If you don't have money or resources to donate, use your voice. Everyone has a sphere of influence. Use your influence to impact your community on issues that matter to you. Always be friendly and cordial, but we can't afford to be a "silent majority" anymore.

4. **Run for office**. If you're interested in running for office—do it. Be a part of the solution. Get connected with your local party office (Republican or Democrat) and learn what offices are coming up for election and see if any are a good fit for you. You don't have to start by running for Congress. A local school board position, county supervisor, or city position may be available and fit your goals.

5. **Contact your elected officials**. Make sure your representatives, on a state and federal level, know how you want them to vote on legislation. You may feel like "Why would they care about my opinion?" but I'm telling you—they do. Especially when a lot of people contact them on an issue, they pay attention. It's your responsibility to contact your state and federal representatives when legislation is being passed to ensure they vote the way you want them to.

America's Fighting Spirit

Everyone loves a champion. The underdog who beats the odds, fights like hell, and emerges from a challenge victorious. That's largely the draw to Donald Trump. The man taking on the political establishment. Americans love that fighting spirit. Thanks to President Trump, we're finding it again and reviving it.

The overly polished façade of American politicians has been replaced with MAGA trucker hats, American flag T-shirts, and the unvarnished truth. We must continue that momentum, regardless of political preference. The Republican leaders who have failed to fight need to be replaced—and there are a lot of them. The emerging group of Republican officials who are taking on the established political class and fighting for Americans need to be supported.

Left and Right both need to continue the drive toward authenticity, even if the authentic is objectively flawed. Flaws can be fixed but should not be covered. Too much of American politics has been hidden from the American people, leaving the problems to rot and fester.

One of the most remarkable characteristics of the United States of America is that we are a self-governed nation. If we want to remain self-governed, we need to be involved in the process. We can lose our ability to self-govern in multiple ways—either by abusive leadership or voluntary surrender. Do not surrender your right to be a part of the civil process. Get engaged in government however you can and help ensure that the elected officials really work for us, not the other way around.

Whether it's speaking out about the abuses of the justice system or any other issue, this amazing country is designed for citizen participation. It won't work as well without you. Stay informed and get involved how you can. Don't believe everything you hear—do your own research. When the government oversteps its proper authority, don't duck your head and hope someone else will speak up. Be DEFIANT.

Jeremiah 12:5 NKJV

If you've run against men and they've wearied you, how do you ever expect to compete with horses? And if in the land of peace they've wearied you, how will you do in the floodplains of the Jordan?

Do not grow weary.

Endnote

Once President Trump won the 2024 election, I (and every other RNC and campaign staff member) needed to figure out my own transition. I had spent four years going through hell, but I wasn't done fighting. At that time, the $1.6 billion lawsuit was still active and I still faced criminal charges in Arizona. My legal circumstances made my transition difficult, especially the criminal case. Options that otherwise would have been open to me were closed.

I have always been a huge fan of the work Judicial Watch does and reached out to the leadership team there to apply for employment. Thankfully, the senior leadership team, Tom Fitton, Paul Orfanedes, and Chris Farrell were aware of my situation and incredibly understanding. They were willing to consider my application—felony charges and all—and hired me to join their litigation team.

Judicial Watch has been involved in fighting to expose government corruption longer than I have. Every step of the way, whether it was the Mar-a-Lago documents case, J6, Jack Smith investigations, or Congressional inquiries, Judicial Watch was right there working to expose government abuses. I didn't realize it as I ran parallel paths with them through the lawfare, but it only made sense for me to join their litigation team.

I am so grateful to Judicial Watch for bringing me onto the team and allowing me to tell my story. They have already sued DOJ for my FBI records and TSA for their records documenting the decision to pull my pre-check. My own caseload includes lawsuits against the CIA, DOJ, and DHS. I'm excited to see what the future holds for me next.

Acknowledgments

Thank you, President Trump, for letting me tell this story and supporting me in this process. You are the greatest President of our generation, and possibly ever. Thank you for enduring the lies, trials, lawfare, false accusations, and barrage of attacks to help Americans regain control of our nation.

Thank you, Susie Wiles, for supporting me throughout the fight and in writing this book. America is better because of your efforts.

Thank you, Skyhorse Publishing, for your willingness to publish this story. Tony Lyons, it's publishers like you that give us a fighting chance. Without your courage, we would have lost our voice a long time ago. Thank you for your bravery to publish.

Thank you, Marji Ross. You are the greatest editor and agent I could have ever dreamed of. I gave you the ashes of my life and you made something beautiful. Julie Stewart, thank you for your help and insights into this story. Your ideas and perspectives made it better. I'm so glad I met you on this project and hope there are more to come.

Thank you to my family. Mom and Dad, no matter what happened, I always knew I had you as a backstop. Thank you for enduring the sleepless nights and waking nightmares. I'm sorry. And, I'm grateful. Carrie, you are my best friend. I don't know how we do it, but together we always seem to land "jelly-side up." Matt, thank you for taking care of my sister and being the best husband, father, and brother-in-law possible. I'm so grateful for you.

Thank you to the generous family who donated to help my defense. You saved my life.

Thank you to my lawyers. I'm beyond grateful.

Rodney Lord, Jack and Terri Brown, Timmerle Kelly, Beth Moore, and Hal and Cheryl Sacks: Luke 22:28. Thank you for your endurance and persistent prayer. Your prayers moved mountains. Thank you to everyone who prayed with me along the way. I've lost count how many prayers were prayed, but I'm grateful for every single one of them.

Dan Fleuette—You're one hell of a photographer. Thank you for the amazing cover photo.

Notes

Chapter 4: The Raid

1   Matthew Galka, "FBI was authorized for 'deadly force' in Mar-a-Lago Raid," KFOXTV, May 22, 2024, https://kfoxtv.com/news/nation-world/fbi-was -authorized-for-deadly-force-in-mar-a-lago-raid-trump-truth-social-response -majorie-taylor-greene-paul-gosar-doj-statement-federal-classified-documents -suspended-indefinitely.

2   Zoë Richards, "Merrick Garland calls Trump's claims about Mar-a-Lago search 'false' and 'extremely dangerous'," NBC News, May 23, 2024, https://www .nbcnews.com/politics/justice-department/merrick-garland-blasts-trump -claims-fbis-mar-lago-search-rcna153817.

Chapter 9: In the FBI's Crosshairs

1   Devlin Barrett and Carol D. Leonnig, "Material on foreign nation's nuclear capabilities seized at Trump's Mar-a-Lago," *Washington Post*, September 6, 2022, https://www.washingtonpost.com/national-security/2022/09/06/trump -nuclear-documents/.

2   Katherine Fung, "Did Biden Know About FBI Search at Trump's Mar-a-Lago? What We Know," *Newsweek*, August 9, 2022, https://www.newsweek.com/did -biden-know-about-fbi-search-trumps-mar-lago-what-we-know-1732190.

3   Ibid.

4   Ibid.

5   "Attorney General Merrick Garland Delivers Remarks Announcing Motion to Unseal Search Warrant," August 11, 2022, *Archives U.S. Department of Justice*, last modified February 5, 2025, https://www.justice.gov/archives/opa/video /attorney-general-merrick-garland-delivers-remarks-announcing-motion -unseal-search-warrant.

Chapter 10: Time to Get a Lawyer

1   Brad Polumbo, "Here's the List of Billions in Military Equipment the US Left Behind for the Taliban," Foundation for Economic Education, August 30, 2021,

https://fee.org/articles/here-s-the-list-of-billions-in-military-equipment-the-us
-left-behind-for-the-taliban/.
2   Ibid.

Chapter 12: What We Know to Be True
1   Rebecca Beitsch, "Purges at FBI, DOJ trigger 'battle' for career staff," *The Hill*, February 4, 2025, https://thehill.com/homenews/administration/5124328 -trump-administration-purge-fbi/.

Chapter 13: The Backlash
1   Marc Caputo, "Trump lawyer Christina Bobb speaks to federal investigators in Mar-a-Lago case," NBC News, October 10, 2022, https://www.nbcnews.com /politics/donald-trump/trump-lawyer-christina-bobb-speaks-federal-investigators -mar-lago-case-rcna51459.
2   Ibid.

Chapter 14: Presidents and Their Documents
1   Renato Mariotti, "Biden's Documents Case Isn't Similar to Trump's. It's Really Like Hillary's," Politico, January 14, 2023, https://www.politico.com/news /magazine/2023/01/14/biden-documents-trump-hillary-00077923.
2   Philip Bump, "The GOP effort to equate Biden and Trump on classified documents is working," *The Washington Post*, January 30, 2023, https://www.washington post.com/politics/2023/01/30/biden-trump-classified-documents-republicans/.
3   Nathaniel Rakich, Kaleigh Rogers, and Amelia Thomson-DeVeaux, "Is It Fair to Compare Biden's and Trump's Classified Documents Scandals?," Five Thirty Eight, January 24, 2024, https://fivethirtyeight.com/features/is-it-fair-to-compare -bidens-and-trumps-classified-documents-scandals/.
4   Dustin Jones, "Who is Robert Hur, the special counsel testifying in the Biden documents probe?," NPR, March 12, 2024, https://www.npr.org/2023/01/13 /1148934429/robert-hur-doj-special-counsel-biden-classified-documents.
5   Donald J. Trump, Truth Social post, January 24, 2023, 1:31 p.m., https: //truthsocial.com/@realDonaldTrump/posts/109745609909293294.

Chapter 16: Squeezing Team Trump
1   All of the information and quotes in this section come from the Woodward letter and court filing. "Attachment A: Written Materials on the Misconduct Allegations Related to Stanley Woodward," United States District Court for the District of Columbia, Case No. 23-gj-10, Entered on FLSD Docket August 11, 2023, (beginning on page 64), https://www.justsecurity.org/wp-content /uploads/2024/04/JustSecurityNY2016ElectionInterferenceCaseClearingho use%E2%80%94Exhibits-Gov-report-Nauta-counsel-Woodward-allegation -improper-statements-by-Jay-BrattAug.112023unsealedApril-222024.pdf.
2   "Report in Response to the Court's Sealed Order on August 7, 2023," *United States of America, Plaintiff, v. Donald J. Trump, Waltine Nauta, and Carlos*

de Oliveira, Defendants., United States District Court, Southern District of Florida, West Palm Beach Division, Case No. 23-80101-CR-CANNON(s), Filed August 11, 2023, https://www.documentcloud.org/documents/24602063-115 /?responsive=1&title=1.

3   Ibid.
4   Ibid.

Chapter 19: America's Mayor Under Attack

1   "Grothman Plays Video Of Biden Bragging About Getting Ukrainian Prosecutor Fired In Oversight Cmte," House Oversight Committee hearing, Washington, DC, March 20, 2024, posted by Forbes Breaking News, YouTube, 5 min., 49 sec., https://www.youtube.com/watch?v=M-yrD2WMKiA.
2   "New Information Shows CIA Contractors Colluded with the Biden Campaign to Discredit Hunter Biden Laptop Story," June 25, 2024, Press Release, House Permanent Select Committee on Intelligence, https://intelligence.house.gov /news/documentsingle.aspx?DocumentID=1432.
3   "Comer on Fox News: Biden Crime Family Pardons Serve as a Confession of Their Corruption," January 25, 2025, House Committee on Oversight and Government Reform, https://oversight.house.gov/blog/comer-on-fox-news-biden -crime-family-pardons-serve-as-a-confession-of-their-corruption/.

Chapter 20: Unleashing the Hounds

1   Devan Cole and Paula Reid, "Hunter Biden sues Rudy Giuliani and his former attorney, alleging they tried to hack his devices," CNN, September 26, 2023, https://www.cnn.com/2023/09/26/politics/hunter-biden-rudy-giuliani -lawsuit/index.html.
2   Kara Scannell, "Feds end Ukraine-related foreign lobbying investigation into Rudy Giuliani without filing charges," CNN, November 14, 2022, https: //www.cnn.com/2022/11/14/politics/rudy-giuliani-investigation-ends.
3   Alison Durkee, "Judge Lets January 6 Lawsuits Against Trump Move Forward—But Dismisses Case Against Giuliani and Don Jr.," *Forbes*, February 18, 2022, https://www.forbes.com/sites/alisondurkee/2022/02/18/judge-lets -january-6-lawsuits-against-trump-move-forward-but-dismisses-case-against -giuliani-and-don-jr/.

Chapter 21: January 6th—The Federal Government Targets Americans

1   "Trump Pardoned Violent Insurrectionists That Brutally Attacked Police Officers—And Tried to Defund Law Enforcement," War Room, Democratic National Committee, March 4, 2025, https://democrats.org/news/trump -pardoned-violent-insurrectionists-that-brutally-attacked-police-officers-and -tried-to-defund-law-enforcement/. Charlie Savage, "How the Crime of Seditious Conspiracy Is Different From Insurrection and Treason," *New York Times*, May 25, 2023, https://www.nytimes.com/2023/05/25/us/what-is-seditious-conspiracy -insurrection-treason.html.

2   Roger Parloff, "The High-Water Mark of the Jan. 6 Prosecutions," Lawfare, January 6, 2025, https://www.lawfaremedia.org/article/the-high-water-mark-of -the-jan.-6-prosecutions.

3   Ibid.

4   Dianne Derby, "'J6 Praying Grandma' from Falcon denies President Trump's pardon," KOAA News5, January 22, 2025, https://www.koaa.com/news/politics /j6-praying-grandma-from-falcon-denies-president-trumps-pardon.

5   Ibid.

6   Alanna Durkin Richer and Michael Kunzelman, "'J6 praying grandma' avoids prison time and gets 6 months home confinement in Capitol riot case," Associated Press, August 12, 2024, https://apnews.com/article/capitol-riot-praying-grandma -jan-6-7e404e0e228d6e5c8f63688cc2a61f3f.

7   "Arizona Man Sentenced to 41 Months in Prison On Felony Charge in Jan. 6 Capitol Breach," November 17, 2021, Press Release, United States Attorney's Office District of Columbia, https://www.justice.gov/usao-dc/pr /arizona-man-sentenced-41-months-prison-felony-charge-jan-6-capitol-breach.

8   Ibid.

9   Ibid.

10   Kyle Cheney, "Prosecutors say newly aired Chansley footage paints misleading portrait of his Jan. 6 conduct," Politico, March 12, 2023, https://www.politico .com/news/2023/03/12/qanon-shaman-jacob-chansley-footage-00086703.

11   Alex Swoyer and Kerry Picket, "QAnon Shaman's lawyer calls for sanctions against DOJ, prosecutors after his client's early release," *Washington Times*, March 30, 2023, https://www.washingtontimes.com/news/2023/mar/30/jacob -chansley-lawyer-calls-sanctions-against-doj-/.

12   Ibid.

13   Ibid.

14   "Wikipedia: Oath Keepers," Wikimedia Foundation, last modified May 11, 2025, 05:57 (UTC). Accessed on May 20, 2025, https://en.wikipedia.org/wiki /Oath_Keepers#:~:text=Oath%20Keepers%20is%20an%20American,by%20 the%20United%20States%20constitution.

15   Steve Baker, "Analysis: Did Pelosi's security chief perjure himself in Oath keepers trial?," Blaze Media, October 4, 2023, https://www.theblaze.com/columns /analysis/analysis-did-pelosis-security-chief-perjure-himself-in-oath-keepers -trial.

16   "Court Sentences Two Oath Keepers Leaders on Seditious Conspiracy and Other Charges Related to U.S. Capitol Breach," May 25, 2023, Press Release, Archives U.S. Department of Justice, last modified February 6, 2025, https: //www.justice.gov/archives/opa/pr/court-sentences-two-oath-keepers-leaders -seditious-conspiracy-and-other-charges-related-us#:~:text=Rhodes%20 was%20sentenced%20to%2018,and%20the%20U.S.%20Capitol%20 Building.

17   Ibid.

18   Ibid.

19 Meghan Conroy and Jon Lewis, "The Proud Boys and Oath Keepers Are Domestic Terrorists, It's Past Time to Call Them What They Are," Just Security, March 7, 2023, https://www.justsecurity.org/85385/the-proud-boys-and-oath-keepers-are-domestic-terrorists-its-past-time-to-call-them-what-they-are/.

20 Steve Baker, "Analysis: Did Pelosi's security chief perjure himself in Oath Keepers trial?," Blaze Media, October 4, 2023, https://www.theblaze.com/columns/analysis/analysis-did-pelosis-security-chief-perjure-himself-in-oath-keepers-trial.

21 Ibid.

22 Ibid.

23 Ibid.

24 Ibid.

25 Ibid.

26 Michael Kunzelman, "Writer pleads guilty to Capitol riot charges," Associated Press, November 12, 2024, https://apnews.com/article/steve-baker-capitol-riot-blaze-news-writer-2db0b3855c6b5aa88d9d16c189a93959.

27 Chip Rowe, "Update: Jan. 6 Arrests," *The Highlands Current*, November 10, 2023, https://highlandscurrent.org/2023/11/10/update-jan-6-arrests-4/.

28 "Durbin: January 6 Insurrectionists Should Have Never Been Pardoned By President Trump," March 4, 2025, Press Release, Dick Durban, U.S. Senator for Illinois, https://www.durbin.senate.gov/newsroom/press-releases/durbin-january-6-insurrectionists-should-have-never-been-pardoned-by-president-trump; Marshall Cohen, "They assaulted cops and tried to overturn an election. What to know about Trump's mass pardons for January 6 rioters," CNN, January 21, 2025, https://www.cnn.com/2025/01/21/politics/what-to-know-pardons-january-6-trump/index.html.

Chapter 22: Keeping Donald Trump off the Ballot

1 David Propper, "NY man who's spent 4 years in jail on Capitol riot charges gets trial delay as he angles for Trump pardon," *New York Post*, November 21, 2024, https://nypost.com/2024/11/21/us-news/jake-lang-gets-trial-delay-in-hopes-of-trump-pardon-on-jan-6-charges/.

2 Brian Naylor, "Read Trump's Jan. 6 Speech, A Key Part Of Impeachment Trial," *NPR*, February 10, 2021, https://www.npr.org/2021/02/10/966396848/read-trumps-jan-6-speech-a-key-part-of-impeachment-trial.

3 "Select January 6th Committee Final Report and Supporting Materials Collection," December 22, 2022, GovInfo, https://www.govinfo.gov/collection/january-6th-committee-final-report?path=/GPO/January%206th%20Committee%20Final%20Report%20and%20Supporting%20Materials%20Collection.

4 Olivia Beavers and Heather Caygle, "McCarthy makes his 5 GOP picks for Jan. 6 select committee," Politico, July 19, 2021, https://www.politico.com/news/2021/07/19/mccarthy-zeroes-in-on-five-gop-members-for-jan-6-select-committee-500201.

5   William Arkin, "Underestimating the Threat, DC Mayor Muriel Bowser Ordered Up Unarmed Guards," *Newsweek*, December 31, 2021, https://www .newsweek.com/dc-mayor-muriel-bowser-thought-she-needed-just-few-hundred -national-guard-unarmed-1661320.

6   "Christopher Miller says Trump wanted troops to protect supporters on Jan. 6," May 12, 2021, posted by Reuters, YouTube, 0 min., 51 sec., https://youtu.be /dNuYYHOvmd4?si=9PQ630f7EXUX1dWx.

7   "Chairman Loudermilk Publishes Never-Before Released Anthony Ornato Transcribed Interview," March 8, 2024, Committee on House Administration, https://cha.house.gov/2024/3/chairman-loudermilk-publishes-never-before -released-anthony-ornato-transcribed-interview.

8   Ibid.

9   Alan Suderman and Juliet Linderman, "Kash Patel is pushing conspiracies and his brand. He's poised to help lead a Trump administration," Associated Press, July 9, 2024, https://www.ap.org/news-highlights/spotlights/2024/kash-patel-is -pushing-conspiracies-and-his-brand-hes-poised-to-help-lead-a-trump-administration/.

10 "Chairman Loudermilk Publishes Never-Before Released Anthony Ornato Transcribed Interview," March 8, 2024, Committee on House Administration, https://cha.house.gov/2024/3/chairman-loudermilk-publishes-never-before -released-anthony-ornato-transcribed-interview.

11 Ibid.

12 Ibid.

13 Ibid.

14 Ibid.

15 "Final Report," December 22, 2022, Select Committee to Investigate the January 6th Attack on the United States Capitol, 117th Congress Second Session, House Report 117-663, https://www.govinfo.gov/content/pkg/GPO-J6-REPORT /pdf/GPO-J6-REPORT.pdf.

16 "Donald Trump tells supporters to 'go home' after they storm Capitol," January 6, 2021, posted by *The Telegraph*, YouTube, 1 min., 04 sec., https://youtu.be /ZB8kjR4nYzk?si=14BQUBQQVAtDFUs7.

17 "Initial Findings Report on the Failures and Politicization of the January 6th Select Committee and the Activities on and Leading up to January 6, 2021," March 11, 2024, House Administration Subcommittee on Oversight, First Session of the 118th Congress, https://cha.house.gov/_cache/files/d/9/d96ba6ce -03fb-4fc8-a4a7-5b5daf19d064/4F510144C1F427873D3298D955C8E19F .initial-findings-report.pdf.

18 Ibid.

19 Ibid.

20 "Order Granting Motion to Dismiss Superseding Indictment Based on Appointments Clause Violation," *United States of America, Plaintiff, v. Donald J. Trump, Waltine Nauta, and Carlos de Oliveira, Defendants,* United States District Court, Southern District of Florida, West Palm Beach Division, Case No. 23-80101-CR-CANNON, Entered on FLSD Docket July 15, 2024,

https://storage.courtlistener.com/recap/gov.uscourts.flsd.648653/gov.uscourts
.flsd.648653.672.0_4.pdf.

21 Sean O'Driscoll, "Jack Smith Spent Over $50M Prosecuting Trump Before
Cases Collapsed," *Newsweek*, November 12, 2024, https://www.newsweek.com
/jack-smith-donald-trump-indictments-election-fraud-classified-documents
-inauguration-january-1982754.

22 "Superseding Indictment," *United States of America v. Donald J. Trump,
Defendant*, United States District Court for the District of Columbia, Criminal
No. 23-cr-257 (TSC), Filed August 27, 2024, https://storage.courtlistener.
com/recap/gov.uscourts.dcd.258148/gov.uscourts.dcd.258148.226.0.pdf
. "Indictment," *United States of America v. Donald J. Trump, Defendant*, United
States District Court for the District of Columbia, Criminal No., Grand
Jury Original, Filed August 1, 2023, https://www.justice.gov/storage/US_v
_Trump_23_cr_257.pdf (note: criminal number not listed in document).

23 Rex Bossert, "Efforts to Keep Trump Off 2024 Ballot Move Through State
Courts," *State Court Report*, December 5, 2023 (updated December 19, 2023),
https://statecourtreport.org/our-work/analysis-opinion/efforts-keep-trump
-2024-ballot-move-through-state-courts.

Chapter 24: The Indictment

1 "DNC Statement on New RNC In-House Conspiracy Theorist and Senior
Counsel Christina Bobb," War Room, Democratic National Committee,
March 13, 2024, https://democrats.org/news/dnc-statement-on-new-rnc-in
-house-conspiracy-theorist-and-senior-counsel-christina-bobb/.

2 Michael Scherer, Josh Dawsey, and Marianne LeVine, "Trump takes control
of the RNC with mass layoffs, restructuring," *Washington Post*, March 12,
2024, https://www.washingtonpost.com/politics/2024/03/12/rnc-trump-firings
-takeover/.

3 Alex Kaplan, "Trump attorney Christina Bobb goes on QAnon show tour to
promote her book while pushing election fraud claims," Media Matters for
America, February 2, 2023, (updated February 8, 2023), https://www.media
matters.org/qanon-conspiracy-theory/trump-attorney-christina-bobb-goes-qanon
-show-tour-promote-her-book-while.

4 Kristen Holmes, Daniel Strauss, and Marshall Cohen, "RNC to add new lawyers focusing on claims of election fraud—including one key figure from 2020
challenges," CNN, March 12, 2024, https://www.cnn.com/2024/03/12/politics
/rnc-trump-takeover-lawyers-election/index.html.

5 "RNC hires election integrity lawyer who claims 2020 election was stolen,"
MSNBC Morning Joe, March 13, 2024, https://www.msnbc.com/morning-joe
/watch/rnc-hires-election-integrity-lawyer-who-claims-2020-election-was
-stolen-206421061789.

6 Michael Scherer, Josh Dawsey, and Marianne LeVine, "Trump takes control
of the RNC with mass layoffs, restructuring," Washington Post, March 12,
2024, https://www.washingtonpost.com/politics/2024/03/12/rnc-trump-firings
-takeover/.

7   Chris Cameron, "New R.N.C. Chair Declares 'a United Front' With Trump
     After Sweeping Changes," *New York Times*, March 14, 2024, https://www
     .nytimes.com/2024/03/14/us/politics/rnc-chair-trump.html.
8   Isabella Murray and Hannah Demissie, "New RNC zeroes in on 'election
     integrity,' hires Trump ally who denied 2020 results," *ABC News*, March 15, 2024,
     https://abcnews.go.com/Politics/new-rnc-zeroes-election-integrity-hires
     -trump-ally/story?id=108116724.
9   Ethan Cohen, Eric Bradner, and Melissa Holzberg DePalo, "Recount confirms
     Democrat Kris Mayes won Arizona attorney general race," CNN, December
     29, 2022, https://www.cnn.com/2022/12/29/politics/arizona-mayes-hamadeh
     -recount-attorney-general/index.html.
10   Caitlin Doornbos, "Arizona's final election results delayed after printer
     problems cause ballot difficulty," *New York Post*, November 8, 2022, https:
     //nypost.com/2022/11/08/arizonas-final-election-results-delayed-after
     -printer-problems-cause-ballot-difficulty; Bill Chappell, "Arizona's Maricopa
     County says it's identified a solution for voting equipment issues," NPR,
     November 8, 2022, https://www.npr.org/2022/11/08/1135179319/maricopa
     -county-polling-places-voting-machine-issues.
11   Ibid.
12   "Verified Petition for Writ of Quo Warranto & Writ of Mandamus Civil,"
     Abraham Hamadeh, as an individual legally entitled to the office of Attorney General,
     Petitioner, v. Kris Mayes, Attorney General of Arizona, Respondent, Adrian Fontes,
     in his official capacity as Secretary of State of Arizona, Katie Hobbs, in her official
     capacity as Governor of Arizona, Bill Gates, Clint Hickman, Jack Sellers, Thomas
     Galvin, and Steve Gallardo in their official capacities as members of the Maricopa
     County Board of Supervisors; the Maricopa County Board of Supervisors, and
     Stephen Richer, in his official capacity as Maricopa County Recorder, Defendants,
     Superior Court for the State of Arizona in and for the county of Maricopa, Case
     No. CV2023-054988, Filed December 28, 2023, https://www.clerkofcourt
     .maricopa.gov/home/showpublisheddocument/6153/638398713147981125.
13   Ibid.
14   Ibid.
15   Cohen, Bradner, and DePalo, "Recount confirms Democrat Kris Mayes won
     Arizona attorney general race." CNN, December 29, 2022, https://www.cnn
     .com/2022/12/29/politics/arizona-mayes-hamadeh-recount-attorney-general
     /index.html.
16   Jessica Huseman, "Arizona recount uncovers several ballot-counting errors in
     Pinal County," *AZ Mirror*, December 30, 2022, https://azmirror.com/2022/12
     /30/arizona-recount-uncovers-several-ballot-counting-errors-in-pinal-county/.
17   Caitlin Sievers, "Appeals court rejects Abe Hamadeh's third challenge to his
     2022 AG loss," *AZ Mirror*, April 11, 2024, https://azmirror.com/2024/04/11
     /appeals-court-rejects-abe-hamadehs-third-challenge-to-his-2022-ag-loss/.
18   Ibid.

19 Matthew Impelli, "Trump Lawyer Could Spend Rest of Her Life in Prison," *Newsweek*, April 29, 2024, https://www.newsweek.com/donald-trump -lawyer-christina-bobb-could-spend-life-prison-1895309.

Chapter 26: Judicial Corruption Run Amok

1 "Strategic actions against public participation; motion to dismiss or quash; definitions," Arizona Statute 12-751, Arizona State Legislature, accessed May 20, 2025, https://www.azleg.gov/ars/12/00751.htm#:~:text=12%2D751%20 %2D%20Strategic%20actions%20against,party%20to%20file%20a%20 response.

2 "Attorney General Raúl Torrez Releases Investigative Findings and Recommendations For Amending the Election Code to Prevent Fake Presidential Electors," January 5, 2024, Press Release, New Mexico Department of Justice, https://nmdoj.gov/press-release/attorney-general-raul-torrez-releases -investigative-findings-and-recommendations-for-amending-the-election -code-to-prevent-fake-presidential-electors/#:~:text=Although%20prosecutors %20determined%20that%20New,clear%20legal%20authority%20for%20 prosecuting.

3 "Arizona Judge in 2020 Electors Case Demanded Judges Defend Kamala Harris," *Arizona Daily Independent*, November 7, 2024, https://arizonadaily independent.com/2024/11/07/arizona-judge-in-2020-electors-case-demanded -judges-defend-kamala-harris/.

4 Ibid.

5 Fred Lucas, "Exclusive: Nonprofit Laid Out Road Map for Prosecuting Trump Supporters, and Arizona's AG Seems to Have Followed It," The Daily Signal, November 21, 2024, https://www.dailysignal.com/2024/11/21/arizona -indictments-trump-supporters-mirror-nonprofits-suggestions/. "States United Democracy Center," Influence Watch, accessed May 20, 2025, https://www .influencewatch.org/non-profit/states-united-democracy-center/.

6 Ibid.

7 Ibid.

8 Stacey Barchenger, "Who influences Arizona's leaders? This nonprofit has a direct line to 3 top Democrats," *AZ Central*, January 6, 2025, https://www .azcentral.com/story/news/politics/arizona/2025/01/06/states-united-democracy -center-has-influence-with-azs-top-democrats/77093149007/.

9 "States United Democracy Center Inc, Form 990 for 2023," ProPublica, Nonprofit Explorer, accessed May 20, 2025, https://projects.propublica.org /nonprofits/organizations/861704152/202433179349301953/full.

10 "Elias Law Group is a mission-driven firm committed to helping Democrats win, citizens vote, and progressives make change," Elias Law Group, accessed May 20, 2025, https://elias.law/.

11 "States United Democracy Center Inc, Form 990 for 2023," ProPublica, Nonprofit Explorer, accessed May 20, 2025, https://projects.propublica.org /nonprofits/organizations/861704152/202433179349301953/full.

12 "Wikipedia: Institute for Strategic Dialogue," Wikimedia Foundation, last modified April 7, 2025, 07:42 (UTC), accessed on May 20, 2025, https://en.wikipedia.org/wiki/Institute_for_Strategic_Dialogue.

13 Barchenger, "Who influences Arizona's leaders? This nonprofit has a direct line to 3 top Democrats." *AZ Central*, January 6, 2025, https://www.azcentral.com/story/news/politics/arizona/2025/01/06/states-united-democracy-center-has-influence-with-azs-top-democrats/77093149007/.

14 Ibid.

Chapter 27: The Cancer Spreads

1   Joey Cappelletti, "Michigan Republican charged in false elector plot agrees to cooperation deal," Associated Press, October 19, 2023, https://apnews.com/article/fake-elector-michigan-trump-fdfe984cfbefb4bc374ca844b80ed825.

2   "Indictment," *The State of Georgia v. Donald John Trump, Rudolph William Louis Giuliani, John Charles Eastman, Mark Randall Meadows, Kenneth John Chesebro, Jeffrey Bossert Clark, Jenna Lynn Ellis, Ray Stallings Smith, III, Robert David Cheeley, Michael A. Roman, David James Shafer, Shawn Micah Tresher Still, Stephen Cliffgard Lee, Harrison William Prescott Floyd, Trevian C. Kutti, Sidney Katherine Powell, Cathleen Alston Latham, Scott Graham Hall, Misty Hampton AKA Emily Misty Hayes.,* Fulton Superior Court, Clerk No. 23SC188947, Filed August 14, 2023, https://d3i6fh83elv35t.cloudfront.net/static/2023/08/CRIMINAL-INDICTMENT-Trump-Fulton-County-GA.pdf.

3   "Trump co-defendant claims Fulton County DA had 'improper' relationship with prosecutor," Fox 5 Atlanta, January 9, 2024, https://www.fox5atlanta.com/news/fulton-county-da-fani-willis-relationship-filing-mike-roman-indictment.

4   "User Clip: fani admits taking cash from campaign," C-SPAN, February 15, 2024, https://www.c-span.org/clip/public-affairs-event/user-clip-fani-admits-taking-cash-from-campaign/5106803.

5   Marshall Cohen et al, "Takeaways from DA Fani Willis' stunning testimony in Georgia," 6ABC Action News, February 16, 2024, https://6abc.com/fani-willis-on-stand-case-nathan-wde/14431946/.

6   Kelsi Karruli, "Did Fani Willis, 53, wear her dress BACKWARDS on the stand? Beleaguered DA is mercilessly mocked by eagle-eyed social media users for sporting zipper at the FRONT of her pink frock," *Daily Mail*, February 16, 2024, https://www.dailymail.co.uk/femail/article-13092639/fani-willis-dress-backwards-georgia-misconduct-hearing.html.

7   Andrew Stanton, "Fani Willis Allowed to Continue RICO Case Embroiled in Controversy," *Newsweek*, August 9, 2024, https://www.newsweek.com/fani-willis-young-thug-mistrial-chaos-case-1937021.

8   Dan Gooding, "Fani Willis Forced to Pay Trump Co-Defendant's Lawyer After Ruling," *Newsweek*, October 22, 2024, https://www.newsweek.com/fani-willis-fulton-county-michael-roman-open-records-ruling-1973269.

9   Elizabeth Elkind, "Nathan Wade admitted to multiple White House meetings during Trump Georgia probe, transcript suggests," Fox News, October 21, 2024, https://www.foxnews.com/politics/nathan-wade-admitted-multiple-white-house -meetings-during-trump-georgia-probe-transcript-suggests.

10 Olivia Rubin, "Fani Willis rebuffs GOP lawmaker's request for documents, says Trump election case is 'ongoing,'" ABC News, December 13, 2024, https://abcnews.go.com/US/fani-willis-rebuffs-gop-lawmakers-request-documents -trump/story?id=116781910. Travis Maurer, "Fulton County judge rejects DA Willis' Bid to quash Senate committee subpoenas," Fox 5 Atlanta, February 26, 2025, https://www.fox5atlanta.com/news/fulton-county-judge -rejects-da-willis-bid-quash-senate-committee-subpoenas.

11 Kate Brumback, "Read the full decision by state appeals court removing Fani Willis from Georgia election case," PBS News, December 19, 2024, https: //www.pbs.org/newshour/politics/read-the-full-decision-by-state-appeals -court-removing-fani-willis-from-georgia-election-case.

12 Rio Yamat, "Nevada attorney general revives 2020 fake electors case," Associated Press, December 12, 2024, https://apnews.com/article/nevada-fake-electors -trump-michael-mcdonald-2b7b1e9862058bf8e66cd1272e03d59e.

13 Ibid.

14 Brie Sparkman, "Charges against Michigan fake electors provide blueprint for accountability," Citizens for Responsibility and Ethics in Washington, August 4, 2023, https://www.citizensforethics.org/reports-investigations/crew-reports /charges-against-michigan-fake-electors-provide-blueprint-for-accountability/.

15 Scott Bauer, "Wisconsin Elections Commission rejects complaint against Trump fake electors for a second time," PBS Wisconsin, December 20, 2023, https://pbswisconsin.org/news-item/wisconsin-elections-commission-rejects -complaint-against-trump-fake-electors-for-a-second-time/.

16 Ibid.

17 Ibid.

18 Scott Bauer, "Trump lawyers and aide hit with 10 more felony charges in Wisconsin over 2020 fake electors scheme," PBS Wisconsin, December 10, 2024, https://pbswisconsin.org/news-item/trump-lawyers-and-aide-hit-with-10 -more-felony-charges-in-wisconsin-over-2020-fake-electors-scheme/.

19 Laura Schulte, "Charges in Wisconsin fake elector case advance after first court hearing," Milwaukee Journal Sentinel, December 12, 2024, https://www .jsonline.com/story/news/politics/elections/2024/12/12/charges-in-wisconsin -fake-elector-case-advance-after-court-hearing/76455018007/.

20 "Tina Peters," Truth & Liberty Foundation, accessed on May 20, 2025, https: //www.truthandliberty.net/bios/tina-peters.

21 Ibid.

22 Sharon Sullivan, "Tina Peters, former Mesa County clerk, sentenced to 9 years in prison over voting systems breach," Colorado Newsline, October 3, 2024, https://coloradonewsline.com/2024/10/03/tina-peters-former-mesa-county -clerk-sentenced-to-9-years-in-prison-over-voting-systems-breach/.

23   "Tina Peters," Truth & Liberty Foundation, accessed on May 20, 2025, https:
      //www.truthandliberty.net/bios/tina-peters.

Chapter 28: The Attorney General Doubles Down

1   Alexandra Marquez, "Arizona attorney general says she has 'no intention' of
      dropping fake electors case," NBC News, November 10, 2024, https://www
      .nbcnews.com/politics/2020-election/arizona-attorney-general-says-no-intention
      -dropping-fake-electors-case-rcna179505.
2   Not his real name

Chapter 29: Sued for $1.6 Billion

1   David Folkenflik, "The 'wackadoodle' foundation of Fox News' election-
      fraud claims," NPR, February 20, 2023, https://www.npr.org/2023/02/20
      /1158223099/fox-news-dominion-wackadoodle-election-fraud-claim.
2   "Response to your May 12, 2021 letter to Chairman Sellers," Maricopa County
      Board of Supervisors, May 17, 2021, https://www.maricopa.gov/Document
      Center/View/68972/20210517-Response-Letter-to-Senate-President-Fann
      ---FINAL.
3   "Stephen Shackelford Partner," Susman Godfrey Attorneys, accessed May 20,
      2025, https://www.susmangodfrey.com/attorneys/stephen-shackelford/.

Conclusion: The Final Warning

1   Zach Schonfeld, "20 Dem AGs sue over Trump efforts to fire probationary
      employees," *The Hill*, March 7, 2025, https://thehill.com/regulation/court
      -battles/5182126-trump-federal-workers-firing-lawsuit/.
2   "Litigation Tracker: Legal Challenges to Trump Administration Actions," Just
      Security, May 19, 2025, https://www.justsecurity.org/107087/tracker-litigation
      -legal-challenges-trump-administration/.
3   Ibid.
4   "Trump team won't pursue charges against Hillary Clinton," BBC News,
      November 22, 2016, https://www.bbc.com/news/world-us-canada-38069585.
5   Tonya Mosley and Alan Feuer, "How Trump's trials for 91 felony charges in 4
      states could take over his campaign," *Fresh Air* transcript, NPR, February 22,
      2024, https://www.npr.org/2024/02/22/1233132273/how-trumps-trials-for-91
      -felony-charges-in-4-states-could-take-over-his-campaign.
6   "Watch: Sen. Schiff Warns of Trump Administration's Weaponization of
      Justice Department," March 13, 2025, Press Release, Adam Schiff, US Senator
      for California, accessed on May 20, 2025, https://www.schiff.senate.gov/news
      /press-releases/watch-sen-schiff-warns-of-trump-administrations-weaponization
      -of-justice-department/.
7   Chris Megerian, Lindsay Whitehurst, and Mark Sherman, "Roberts rejects
      Trump's call for impeaching judge who ruled against his deportation plans,"
      Associated Press, March 18, 2025, https://apnews.com/article/donald-trump
      -federal-judges-impeachment-29da1153a9f82106748098a6606fec39.

Index

A

Armstrong, Kelley, 191

B

Baker, Steve, 185–187

Banks, Jim, 191

Bannon, Steve, 76–77

Biden, Hunter, 166, 169–171, 173–174, 178–179

Biden, Joe, 74–75, 78, 89–90, 118, 121–126, 166, 168–169, 171, 173, 195, 201, 246, 269

Bill and Melinda Gates Foundation, 235

Blinken, Antony, 169

Bowser, Muriel, 191

Boykin, Lisa, 270

Bratt, Jay, 22–23, 25–26, 105

Burisma, 166–167, 170

Bush, George H. W., 121

Bush, George W., 121

C

Cannon, Aileen, 193

Carlson, Tucker, 184

Central Intelligence Agency (CIA), 169

Chansley, Jacob, 183–184

Cheney, Liz, 191–192

Chesboro, Ken, 248

CIA. *See* Central Intelligence Agency (CIA)

Clark, Jeff, 270

Clinton, Bill, 121, 123–124

Clinton, Hillary, 122, 124, 271–272

Cohen, Bruce, 227, 229, 232–233

Cologne, Steve, 159

Corcoran, Evan, 8–15, 17–21, 23–24, 26–31, 36, 43, 57–61, 66, 69, 97, 101, 103–104, 107–111, 133, 137–138, 140–141, 143

D

Davis, Rodney, 191

de Oliveira, Carlos, 268

DePerno, Matt, 247

Devine, Miranda, 171

DOJ. *See* Justice Department (DOJ)

Dominion Voting Systems, 117, 178, 259–265

Droz, John, Jr., 177

E

Eastman, John, 159, 216, 243, 270

ECA. *See* Electoral Count Act (ECA)

Eisen, Norm, 235

election

  1960, 202–203

  2020, 7, 149, 152, 154, 160–161, 166–
    167, 169, 171–172, 201–208, 210–
    239, 241–243, 246–249, 260–265

  2024, 194–196, 237, 243–246, 281

Electoral Count Act (ECA), 256

Elias, Mark, 235

Epshteyn, Boris, 7, 9, 17, 28, 97–98, 100

F

FARA. *See* Foreign Agents Registration
    Act (FARA)

Farrell, Chris, 281

FBI. *See* Federal Bureau of Investigation
    (FBI)

Federal Bureau of Investigation (FBI),
    8, 12, 15–16, 18–26, 28, 32–40, 51,
    54–55, 59, 62, 66, 71–80, 82, 86–88,
    92–94, 102, 105, 111, 136–137, 269

Fitton, Tom, 281

Foreign Agents Registration Act
    (FARA), 167

Fox News, 263

G

Garland, Merrick, 38, 74, 77–79, 118,
    126, 193

Gass, David, 215

Giuliani, Rudy, 7, 119, 160–161, 165–170,
    172–179, 207, 216, 222, 224, 243, 270

Gottlieb, Michael, 178

Graham, Lindsey, 170

H

Haggerty, Bill, 261–262, 264–265

Halligan, Lindsey, 3, 55–57

Hamadeh, Abe, 213–214

Harris, Kamala, 232

Hegseth, Pete, 1

Henry, Ed, 72

Herring, Robert, 150, 152

Herschmann, Eric, 224

Hobbs, Katie, 238

Hur, Robert, 126

I

Institute for Strategic Dialogue (ISD),
    235

Internal Revenue Service (IRS), 118

inventory list, 63–69

IRS. *See* Internal Revenue Service (IRS)

ISD. *See* Institute for Strategic Dialogue
    (ISD)

J

Jackson, Amy Berman, 123

Jacobs, Tom, 221–223, 225–227, 230–
    231, 252–253

January 6, 34, 113–114, 118–119, 163–164,
    181–190, 196, 270

January 6 Select Committee, 34, 117–
    119, 163, 178, 184, 190–196, 208

Jean-Pierre, Karine, 75
Jordan, Jim, 191
Judicial Watch, 77, 92, 123–124, 281–282
Justice Department (DOJ), 8, 10–11, 13–15, 19–26, 37, 39–40, 45–47, 51–59, 62–66, 71, 73–79, 82, 84, 92–93, 98–99, 127, 129–132, 144, 146, 164, 269

K

Kaul, Josh, 248–249
Kennedy, John F., 202–203
Kerik, Bernie, 119, 177
Kern, Anthony, 216
Kinzinger, Adam, 191
Kise, Chris, 80, 83–86
Klingerman, Nicholas, 200

L

Lang, Jake, 187–188
Lauro, John, 83–87, 91, 93–94, 108, 111, 113–114, 129, 135–136, 155, 157–159
Lavrenz, Rebecca, 182–183
Lewandowski, Corey, 177

M

Martin, Daniel, 226
Mayes, Kris, 213–215, 241–242
McCarthy, Kevin, 191
Meadows, Mark, 191–192, 216, 243
media, 73–76, 79, 114–116, 124–125, 170–171, 207, 210
Merchant, Ashleigh, 243–244
Meyer, Kate, 164

Miller, Chris, 191–192
Musk, Elon, 270
Myers, Sam, 238–239

N

Napolitano, Janet, 239
NARA. *See* National Archives and Records Administration (NARA)
National Archives and Records Administration (NARA), 108, 122
Nauta, Walt, 144–146
Nehls, Troy, 191
Neiman, Jeff, 161–163, 196, 205, 211
Nessel, Dana, 246–247
Nixon, Richard, 202–203

O

OAN. *See* One America News (OAN)
Oath Keepers, 184–186
Obama, Barack, 121, 126
One America News (OAN), 150, 152, 155–156, 261–262
Open Society Foundation, 235
Orfanedes, Paul, 281

P

pardon
  Biden's, 195
  of January 6ers, 188, 270
Pelosi, Nancy, 191–192
Pence, Mike, 126–127, 183
Peters, Tina, 249–250
Pfingst, Paul, 159–161
Poroshenko, Petro, 166

PRA. *See* Presidential Records Act (PRA)

Presidential Records Act (PRA), 121–124

Prince, Erik, 167

R

raid, 29–38

Real America's Voice, 72

Reinhart, Bruce, 36–37, 43, 80

Rhodes, Elmer Stewart, 184–185

Roberts, John, 273–274

Roman, Mike, 204, 216, 243–244, 248

Russia, 169

S

Secret Service, 22, 25–26, 31, 33, 38, 55–56, 107

Shokin, Viktor, 170

Smith, Jack, 119, 126–127, 161–164, 184, 193–194, 251, 263, 269, 281

Solomon, John, 170

Soros, George, 151, 156, 235

States United Democracy Center, 235–239

Stone, Roger, 63–64

storage room, 24–28, 104

T

target letter, 85–86

theft, 79–80

Troupis, Jim, 248

Trump, Donald, 1–5, 7–8, 16, 19–20, 23, 27, 66–67, 75–76, 106, 115, 124–125, 143, 188, 191–195, 268–269

Trump, Donald, Jr., 119

Trump Organization, 43, 51, 53, 55

Turk, Karyn, 72

U

Ukraine, 166–167

V

Vance, J. D., 2–3, 5

W

Wade, Nathan, 244–245

Ward, Kelli, 204, 216, 224, 237

warrant, 30, 33, 35–37, 39–40, 43–44, 48, 61–62, 73

Watters, Jesse, 121–122

Wiles, Susie, 31, 34–36, 46–48, 59, 66, 68, 153

Willis, Fani, 154–156, 194, 243–245

Woodward, Stanley, 145–147

Wray, Christopher, 74

Z

Zuckerberg, Mark, 168–169